Democratisation in the Himalayas

Democratisation is a formidable task in the Himalayan region owing to its immense cultural heterogeneity. The process of democratisation has accentuated ethnic competition, assertion of identity, and demand for ethnic homelands to protect, safeguard, and promote political and development interests of various groups.

This volume discusses competing interests, identity politics that permeates political formations, the transformations in the traditional forms of governance and their adaption to democratic institutions, the genesis and periodic eruptions of ethnic assertions, and attempts to resolve ethnic conflict. It shows how recent efforts at deepening democratic values and implementing social justice have been resisted and contested. The book argues that the play of ethnicity, the creation of political parties and interest groups, the emergence of social movements, and the voice of protest and opposition do not indicate a crisis in democracy but comprise the instruments by which the state is pushed towards reform, welfare, and inclusive politics, and is obliged to listen to the people.

Rich in ethnographic research, this volume will be useful to scholars and researchers of social and political anthropology, political studies, South Asian studies, Nepal and Himalayan studies, sociology, and development studies.

Vibha Arora is Associate Professor of Sociology and Social Anthropology at the Department of Humanities and Social Sciences, Indian Institute of Technology Delhi, India.

N. Jayaram is Visiting Professor at National Law School of India University, Bengaluru, India.

Nepal and Himalayan Studies

This series will bring the larger Nepal and the Himalayan region to the centre stage of academic analysis and explore critical questions that confront the region, ranging from society, culture and politics to economy and ecology. The books in the series will examine key themes concerning religion, ethnicity, language, identity, history, tradition, community, polity, democracy, as well as emerging issues regarding environment and development of this unique region.

For a full list of titles in this series, please visit www.routledge.com/Nepal-and-Himalayan-Studies/book-series/NHS

Nepali Diaspora in a Globalised Era
Edited by Tanka B. Subba and A. C. Sinha

Goddesses of Kathmandu Valley
Grace, rage, knowledge
Arun Gupto

The Himalayas and India–China Relations
Devendra Nath Panigrahi

Democratisation in the Himalayas
Interests, Conflicts, and Negotiations
Edited by Vibha Arora and N. Jayaram

Democratisation in the Himalayas
Interests, Conflicts, and Negotiations

Edited by Vibha Arora and N. Jayaram

LONDON AND NEW YORK

First published 2017
by Routledge
2 Park Square, Milton Park, Abingdon, Oxon OX14 4RN

and by Routledge
711 Third Avenue, New York, NY 10017

Routledge is an imprint of the Taylor & Francis Group, an informa business

© 2017 selection and editorial matter, Vibha Arora and N. Jayaram; individual chapters, the contributors

The right of Vibha Arora and N. Jayaram to be identified as the authors of the editorial material, and of the authors for their individual chapters, has been asserted in accordance with sections 77 and 78 of the Copyright, Designs and Patents Act 1988.

All rights reserved. No part of this book may be reprinted or reproduced or utilised in any form or by any electronic, mechanical, or other means, now known or hereafter invented, including photocopying and recording, or in any information storage or retrieval system, without permission in writing from the publishers.

Trademark notice: Product or corporate names may be trademarks or registered trademarks, and are used only for identification and explanation without intent to infringe.

British Library Cataloguing-in-Publication Data
A catalogue record for this book is available from the British Library

Library of Congress Cataloging-in-Publication Data
A catalog record has been requested for this book

ISBN: 978-1-138-24428-3 (hbk)
ISBN: 978-1-315-27698-4 (ebk)

Typeset in Galliard
by Apex CoVantage, LLC

To
Our respective families.

Contents

List of illustrations   ix
Notes on contributors   x
Preface   xi

Introduction: steering democratisation and
negotiating identity in the Himalayas   1
VIBHA ARORA AND N. JAYARAM

PART I
Shifting selves and competing identities   25

1 Seeking identities on the margins of democracy:
   Jad Bhotiyas of Uttarkashi   27
   SUBHADRA MITRA CHANNA

2 The politics of census: fear of numbers and
   competing claims for representation in Naga society   54
   DEBOJYOTI DAS

3 The making of the subaltern Lepcha and
   the Kalimpong stimulus   79
   VIBHA ARORA

PART II
Negotiating democracy   115

4 Monks, elections, and foreign travels: democracy and
   the monastic order in western Arunachal Pradesh,
   North-East India   117
   SWARGAJYOTI GOHAIN

5	'Pure democracy' in 'new Nepal': conceptions, practices, and anxieties AMANDA SNELLINGER	135

PART III
Territorial conflict and after 159

6	Demand for Kukiland and Kuki ethnic nationalism VIBHA ARORA AND NGAMJAHAO KIPGEN	161
7	Displacement from Kashmir: gendered responses CHARU SAWHNEY AND NILIKA MEHROTRA	186

Index   203

Illustrations

Figures

3.1	Sonam Tshering Lepcha offering prayers at Mt Tendong, 2002	93
3.2	P. T. Lepcha, 2002	93
3.3	Group that went to Mt Tendong to offer prayers and construct a shrine, 2002	96
3.4	River Teesta flowing through Sikkim	102
4.1	Late Tsona Gontse Rinpoche giving blessings in his chamber at Dirang, 2008	121
4.2	Monastery under construction in Dirang, 2013	125
6.1	Kuki National Front (KNF) armed cadres	173
6.2	Map of Kukiland	180

Tables

2.1	Population of Nagaland, 1901–2001	67
2.2	Projected population of Nagaland	68
6.1	Landholding pattern of Nagas and Kukis in Manipur's hill districts	175
6.2	List of major Naga and Kuki massacres reported in Manipur	176

Contributors

Vibha Arora is Associate Professor of Sociology and Social Anthropology at the Department of Humanities and Social Sciences, Indian Institute of Technology Delhi, India.

Subhadra Mitra Channa is Professor of Social Anthropology at the University of Delhi, India.

Debojyoti Das is Global Studies Associate at the Global Studies Centre, University of Sussex, United Kingdom.

Swargajyoti Gohain teaches Sociology and Anthropology in the Department of Humanities and Social Sciences at the Indian Institute of Technology Kanpur, India.

Ngamjahao Kipgen is Assistant Professor of Sociology at the Department of Humanities and Social Sciences, Indian Institute of Technology Guwahati, India.

Nilika Mehrotra is Professor of Social Anthropology at the Centre for the Study of Social Systems, Jawaharlal Nehru University, India.

Charu Sawhney is Research Associate in the Department of Sociology, University of Delhi, India.

Amanda Snellinger is an anthropologist with a focus on activism, youth, politics, and legal change in South Asia.

Preface

The young democratic regimes located in the fragile topography of the Himalayas show how challenging it is to sustain and foster democratisation. Democracies have to be constantly sustained, nurtured, and invigorated as a legitimate form of governance. The governments – elected, contested, dissolved, or toppled – in this region highlight the dynamics of democratic evolution. The encounter between procedural aspects of democracy and development aspiration emphasises the difficulties in fostering common ground and the different trajectories democracies can take. Predictably the deep connection between ecology, polity, and a socially heterogeneous population has taken a regional form, as is evident in the different case studies comprising this volume. The topographic fragility of the region and different natural hazards and disasters – earthquakes, forest fires, cloudbursts, and flash floods – that this region has suffered in the recent past have constantly tested the young democracies there.

Our first volume *Routeing Democracy in the Himalayas: Experiments and Experiences* (Routledge 2013) encouraged us to plan this second volume to fill gaps in existing literature and also showcase how young scholars are documenting the political encounters in the Himalayan amphitheatre. If the first volume was a beginning of our experimental journey into understanding how local conceptions are interacting with national and global waves of democratisation, this second volume both consolidates the legitimacy and enhances the seductive appeal of this undertaking. As co-editors we have benefitted from this critical engagement and scholarly exchange. We hope to have deepened and enriched the debate and kindled further academic interest in this region.

Compiling an acknowledgement list is always a daunting task; several people have helped us in manifold ways. First and foremost, we thank our contributors for their patience, as the volume took a little more time than we had anticipated due to unforeseen reasons. We thank the Indian Sociological Society for allowing us to republish two essays that were published in its official journal: '"Pure Democracy" in "New Nepal": Conceptions, Practices, and Anxieties' by Amanda Snellinger (which earlier appeared as 'Democratic Form: Conceptions and Practices in the Making of "New Nepal"'), *Sociological Bulletin*, 58(1), January–April 2009, pp. 43–70, and 'Displacement from Kashmir: Gendered Responses' by Charu Sawhney and Nilika Mehrotra, *Sociological Bulletin*, 62(1), January–April 2013, pp. 83–99.

Our thanks are also due to the librarians and staff of the British Library, London; Indian Institute of Advanced Study, Shimla; Indian Institute of Technology Delhi; Institute for Social and Economic Change, Bengaluru; Namgyal Institute of Tibetology, Gangtok; and Tata Institute of Social Sciences, Mumbai. We would particularly like to thank our friends for their unstinted encouragement, stimulating conversations, and sage advice. We are grateful to our colleagues at the Indian Institute of Technology Delhi and Tata Institute of Social Sciences, Mumbai, for their advice and support. We thank Shoma Choudhury at Routledge for encouraging and sustaining us through the life of this project. Our respective families have been the bedrock on which this book project rests; we dedicate this book to them as a token of our gratitude.

Introduction
Steering democratisation and negotiating identity in the Himalayas

Vibha Arora and N. Jayaram

Democracy is undeniably a political framework of legitimate governance and the framing question of post-colonial era. It describes a particular set of relationships between the state and society, as it marks the shift in power to civil society. The actors making up the state also have their interests. The state has the necessary wherewithal of coercion and violence. Hence, democratisation requires the building of a democratic state (institutional change, representative politics, and transforming of functions) based on legitimate power, persuasion, and accountability to citizens (Grugel 2002: 68–70). It is an ideology founded on egalitarianism and, above all, a contractual promise positing the inclusion of the hitherto marginalised sections of society.

For D. Beetham, the core meaning of democracy is to be 'a mode of decision-making about collectively-binding rules and policies over which the people exercise control' (1992: 40). Herein citizens have the right to run for public office; suffrage is inclusive; free and fair elections are held regularly; public has the right to information; and people have the right and possibilities of forming associations, interest groups, and political parties. This minimal definition of democracy highlights the singular importance of having elections for forming the government and exercise of choice by members of society; it does not, however, give much importance to civil society. The government has a responsibility and accountability to those in whose name the political leaders and representatives exercise power and authority. For some political scientists, the crafting of democracy requires institutional transformation and bringing structural changes in the executive, judiciary, legislatures, enlarging the scope of political parties and interest groups, and the electoral system (Przeworski 1995, cited in Grugel 2002: 71).

An extended understanding of democracy emphasises the ready availability of a rights-based framework for citizens and communities, who, in turn, should be able to access resources earmarked for their welfare and development. People should have the capacity to politicise basic interests and mobilise support and represent them. Democracy is characterised by the qualities of 'participation, authorised, representation, accountability, transparency, responsiveness and solidarity' (Beetham 1999, cited in Tornquist 2004: 201). The subordinated social groups should have access to decision-making processes of the state and be represented (Rueschemeyer, Stephens and Stephens 1992) in an extended public sphere (Tornquist 2004: 202). The state must not merely reflect or safeguard dominant interests in a democracy. Social struggles facilitate democratic consolidation (Tilly 1997). This understanding highlights the expansive path and process of democratisation generally and, to an extent, in the Himalayan region that specifically concerns us. In our previous volume, *Routeing Democracy in the Himalayas: Experiments and Experiences* (Arora and Jayaram 2013), and the present volume, we underscore the strong influence of geography and regional topography in influencing local engagements with democratisation. Ideas and political processes have traversed national boundaries and shaped the ethnic-national imaginations of various communities, even though they may formally be part of large nation-states such as India or smaller ones such as Nepal and Bhutan.

The spread of democracy in the Himalayan region has been neither uniform nor even. Civil society is widely perceived to be the bedrock of any democracy, having the power to transform the state itself (see Jayaram 2005). A weak civil society is reflective of a weak democracy. The development of a robust civil society is perceived to be a strong indicator of the deepening of democracy. The play of ethnicity, the formation of political parties and interest groups, the emergence of social movements, and the voice of protest and opposition do not indicate crisis of democracy, or the painful transition to democratic politics, but comprise the instruments by which the state is pushed towards reform, welfare, and inclusive politics, and is obliged to listen to the people. The various chapters of this volume indicate these struggles and contentious voices of democracy and how governments need to be responsive to social forces. The deepening of democracy is rooted in the idea of justice, which enables the articulation of subaltern voices, and transformative politics of an assertive tribal subjectivity (Arora, in this volume). It is not the emerging noise of protests but the unheard silent wail of the oppressed that undermines the democratic fabric.

In *Routeing Democracy in the Himalayas* (Arora and Jayaram 2013), we have highlighted how this geopolitical region parades a spectrum of young democracies and how democratisation was unfolding, being negotiated, and working in various specific contexts within India and in other Himalayan nations. Certain political geographies were represented in that volume, and this second volume seeks to focus on other critical encounters and experiments furthering democratisation. This volume continues that regional analytical focus, further mapping and documenting people's experiences and bringing new ethnographic case studies to deepen focus and further comparative discussion. We highlight the competing interests, the identity politics permeating political formations influencing governance, the transformations in the traditional forms of governance and their adaption to democratic institutions, the withering and failure of political experiments, the genesis and periodic eruptions of ethnic assertions, and attempts to resolve ethnic conflict.

The Himalayan region parades what R. Dahl (1989: 221) defines as 'polyarchy', resting on a combination of elected government and civil liberties, which ensures access of different groups to the political system. Good examples of this are available in the polities of Nepal, Bhutan, and Northeast India. More than two-thirds of the population of Nepal, including the indigenous nationalities, dalits, and *madhesi*s (plains people), are excluded from governance. Mahendra Lawoti in the opening paragraph of his edited volume *Contentious Politics and Democratisation in Nepal* reflects: 'Can the fundamental right to dissent, mobilise, and protest work against new democracies?' (2007: 17). The restoration of democracy in Nepal in 1990 provided the space for the mobilisation of the marginalised and ethnically dominated groups. Contentious politics can contribute towards democratisation if the state had been responsive and not centralised and captured by the elite. Has the Maoist movement fostered inclusion, ensured accountability of public officials, and deepened democracy in Nepal? The collective mobilisation of various groups resulted in political coercion, violence, breakdown of law and order, and generally disorder that hampered development and political stabilisation of a new Nepal.

Democratisation needs to be steered and constantly monitored. Who is steering democracy? Who will take this responsibility? What role models are available for adoption? We may be asked these leading questions. Nonetheless, based on what we find germinating on the ground, we note not merely the difficult trajectory and possibility of steering democracy in a particular direction but also the differing responses to top-down measures or bottom-up aspirations. The steering should have gently glided the institutions of the state, the political parties, the members of civil society, and other interest groups towards resource redistribution and social justice. This second volume may provide partial answers to some of these questions while raising many others in our mind. This is explicitly our intention to further a critical lens.

Democracies need to be consolidated, and states have to earnestly protect rights and translate citizen preferences into effective development policies. Theorising from a developing-country perspective, Rajani Kothari

(2005) continually emphasised the normative linkage between democracy and justice, the empowerment of the weak, and extension of development to those who need it the most. Struggles over democracy have been guided by a strong belief that citizens have a right to liberty, dignity, and development. The test of democracy lies in ensuring redistribution of power, enforcing programmes of inclusive development, furthering participation, and ameliorating the conditions of those who are located at the margins of society, and the nation-state.

Democratisation must ensure the meaningfulness of democracy (Harriss, Stokke and Tornquist 2004: 6; Tornquist 2004), the exercise of rights by those who were traditionally excluded from polity such as women, the poor, tribal people, dalits, and the ethnic and other minorities (see Grugel 2002). To be sustained peacefully and consolidated, democracy requires continual effective participation of alert citizens, the organisation of a critical civil society, and the accountability of the elite. 'Consolidation implies both the deepening and stabilisation of democracy' (ibid.: 36). Socioeconomic and political inequalities should decline, and there should be movement towards equitable distribution. Authoritarian practices of the state should be opposed and resisted by a vibrant civil society, and democratisation facilitates legitimisation of such struggles. Tragically, power has become an instrument of patronage and profit. Disgruntled groups have taken up arms, formed militia, submerged the landscape in ethnic violence, and caused untold misery by perpetrating destruction of life and property and disrupting everyday civic life.

The Himalayan region, with its immense cultural heterogeneity and political experiments over the past few decades, has demonstrated that democracy is not a mere choice in a menu of options; it is a political necessity and contextually close to indigenous forms of governance in some regions where leaders had greater accountability and wide welfare commitments. Democratisation is a formidable task; it comprises several options and pathways, and real-world experiments reveal the ambiguity and partiality of its roots. The literature on social movements and ethnic mobilisation provides a picture of a sharply contested democratic space and elitist tendencies of a centralised state. This volume is thus a sequel to *Routeing Democracy in the Himalayas: Experiments and Experiences* (Arora and Jayaram 2013), which underlines varied experiences and on-going experiments of citizen engagement with the state and efforts of civil society to maximise development gain. We have collated empirical case studies from various parts of the Himalayan region in these two volumes and endeavoured to further critical engagement while reflecting on substantive questions.

We have emphasised the necessity of going beyond procedural democracy and fostering conditions that will operationalise the principles of substantive democracy, and our contributors have engaged with the meaning of both democracy and development in particular areas. The local context requires immediate interventions in socio-economic sectors (health infrastructure, generation of local employment, educational access, disaster management, and environmental risk), and citizens are now demanding greater attention from the national governments using the historic lament of locational marginalisation and extensive extraction there. Our attempt is to sharpen critical attention on the Himalayan region, capture the aspirations of people, and document their emergent voices. Our contributors demonstrate the building and operation of democracies and incorporate the impact of globalisation on these processes.

The global political economy demands a transition to a hegemonic model of liberal formal democracy. For instance, the World Bank reports insist on 'good governance' as an essential complement to economic development (see Harriss, Stokes and Tornquist 2002: 7). We have not reached the stage of what Peter P. Houtzager terms 'radical polycentrism' that can solve the problem of development: 'A loosely bounded set of ideas and beliefs that the uncoordinated and highly decentralised actions of civil society entities, market actors and local agents are engaged in a mutually reinforcing movement to produce all good things for all people' (cited in ibid.: 8–9).

As far as the Himalayan region is concerned, the state continues to be the locus of politics and a key actor in consolidating democracy. State-sponsored development has been critiqued by emerging social movements (of women, tribal people, dalits, and the poor) although development continues to be regarded the duty of the state. Development discourses may suppress local cultures, identities, and histories; nonetheless, development alternatives have not been crystallised (Escobar 1995). Many scholars declare India to be an example of deviant democratisation and, even if we ignore the Emergency period of 1975–77, regional disturbances have often led to suspension of democracy and restrictions on political liberties (McMillan 2008).

The seven chapters in this volume analytically focus on different aspects of democratisation: first, the state as an arena (actor and outcome); second, civil society as the space where associations demand accountability from the state, identity politics is played out, and marginalised voices get articulated; and third, the global context of democratic transitions (Grugel 2002). The divisiveness of movements and political activism based on issues, interests, and identities have led to 'pro-democratic fragmentation' (Harriss, Stokke and Tornquist 2004: 14–15, 19) and 'the political deficit in substantial democratisation' (Tornquist 2004: 201–25). Democratisation has resulted in an enlarged political elite who are capturing power and impeding substantial democratisation in Northeast India and in Nepal. Democracy is far from being transformative, and we must critically examine conditions that check effective citizenship (Stokke and Tornquist 2013). Considerable politics is embedded in democratisation, and this itself needs to be debated and reflected upon in a critical manner. There have to be generation of knowledge, learning of strategies, and sharing of experiences in the region. Interventions for building capacities of individuals and communities have to be designed and engendered accordingly. Inclusive development and democracy require enhancement of social protection measures by the government. Otherwise, a deficit will continue to shape the form and practice of democracy.

The smoking guns of militants, counter-insurgency operations, and muscular responses of the government will only undermine the base of any democratic formation. The sections caught in the crossfire of terrorism, militancy, and civil unrest, such as women, children, the internally displaced families, and the impoverished, indicate the crises and challenges of consolidating democratisation (Sawhney and Mehrotra, in this volume). In some cases, women have taken the lead in demanding the restoration of rights, peace, and law and order, and offered resistance to state repression – the Naga Mothers Association in Northeast India (Banerjee 2008; Sammadar 2005), the Meira Paibis of Manipur (Chakravarti 2010), the Association of Persons of Disappeared Persons in Kashmir (Qutab 2012), and so on. The sacrifice of charismatic individuals like Irom Sharmila against the Armed Forces Special Powers Act (AFSPA) should not go waste. The act allows democracy to be suspended; it subjects people to continual surveillance in areas officially declared by the central government to be 'disturbed'. The 'disturbed' condition is not open to judicial review, hence cannot be challenged, and militancy has thrived under it. This act has created a continuous state of exception in some parts of the Himalayas for more than fifty years (McDuie-Ra 2009) and, unless the law is repealed, it is impossible to even imagine the possibility of peace here. How can justice even take root if AFSPA persists and negates democratic rights?

Democratisation and politicisation of identity

Identity is not a singular construction; it is always shaped and negotiated with an 'other'. In the Himalayan region, fluid boundaries between groups aligned and functioning cohesively in the past have increasingly become compact, impermeable, and fixed. The necessary conditions for identity assertion (feeling of relative deprivation, socio-economic marginalisation, cultural heritage, subsistence livelihood patterns, and educational backwardness) may exist per se, but only after these are/were supplemented by other sufficient conditions (emergence of strong leadership, acute political competition over resources, government policies and programmes, bureaucratic corruption, geographical location, and information flows) that identities are evoked, asserted, and mobilised to demand access, control, and assert as a matter of right.

The quest for cultural and political identity is simultaneously a quest for development (Chaube 1999). Democratic politics and formal state recognition of marginalised collectivities have unduly politicised ethnic identities and redefined ethnic relations. Identity politics has become a catalyst for accessing and obtaining a proportional share of development resources released by the national government in the entire Himalayan region. Here boundaries are being fostered based on cultural differences and livelihood between settled agriculturists and nomads, and between the plains and the hills, and here ethnic histories are being cited or fabricated from oral and written traditions (Arora 2007; Bhan 2009; Channa, in this volume; Toffin 2009). Democratic recognition of unique identity and grant of associated privileges to communities have fostered the need to maintain stronger boundaries and vocalise distinctiveness – regional, ethnic, or tribal. Identity politics has enlarged and broadened the political elite, but it has not changed the living conditions of the disadvantaged in any significant way (Arora 2013).

Identities are increasingly getting consolidated as part of local democratic institutions and representative politics that requires all collective entities be named and identified; they have generated a multiplier effect. Census enumeration was used as a grand design to establish the colonial gaze over the colonised people. The census continues to play a critical part in classification and ethnic differentiation in post-colonial India. This explains the obsession with numbers, ethnic affiliation, and internal politics (merger, separation, partition). Being recognised as scheduled tribe and enumerating ethnic demography in the census in the past few decades have prompted groups to proclaim and produce documentary evidence and anthropological studies to historically establish uniqueness of their identity. The Limbu and the Tamang were recognised as Scheduled Tribes in 2002 in Sikkim, but they are still fighting for their entitlements in the state legislative assembly, bureaucracy, and educational institutions (Arora 2007). It is only in the 2011 Census that demographic data pertaining to them has been separately collected. The 2001 Census operations of Nagaland show how certain sub-tribes influenced data collection and over-represented themselves, thereby skewing decadal growth rate (see Das, in this volume). Pitched within the census politics were the electoral gain and loss and the development benefits that Naga civil society organisations felt were compromised through enumeration results. This has brought in competition between sub-tribes and assertion of sub-tribal identities. The census in Manipur shows how certain groups historically located in the Kuki category have progressively shifted their identity and proclaimed themselves as Nagas (Arora and Kipgen 2012).

Electoral politics and demarcation of constituencies has further crystallised vote banks, and potential representatives compete with each other to consolidate their voter base (invoking primordial loyalties of tribe, caste, region, religion, and not merely socio-economic parameters) and promise they will work for welfare of their members. Constituencies are often reserved for special categories (women, Scheduled Castes, Scheduled Tribes, other backward classes) and specific ethnic groups, so procedural democracy has buttressed divisive identity politics. The historically marginalised neither are united in their efforts against the hegemonic groups nor able to forge alliances among themselves to demand or foster greater participation in decision-making processes. In many parts of the Himalayan region, the marginal and ethnic minorities are too busy fighting among themselves to make their governments accountable. Self-governance may not necessarily and substantively deliver either. Some democratic experiments have failed, while others have succeeded in the Himalayan theatre. Generation of political consensus is desirable, but it is a very difficult task in highly differentiated regional contexts. Amanda Snellinger's chapter on student politics in Nepal in this volume highlights the rhetoric use of democratic principles and the performance of electoral politics.

Identity politics has fostered a vicious cycle: as the Government of India recognises a tribe, new ones constantly emerge, with no tribe willing to cast away or admit its forward condition as a dominant group in the region. In Northeast India, regardless of migration history, politico-economic conditions, and cultural similarities, tribal identity movements have reached epidemic levels, tracing this politicisation to their historic resistance to colonial rule and its administrative policies. Tribal entitlements have led to inter-tribal and intra-tribal rivalry and conflict in many parts of Northeast India (Arora 2007; Arora and Kipgen 2012; Das, in this volume; Xaxa 2005). The furtherance of collective interests has promoted an instrumentalist orientation and divisive competitiveness such that tribal siblings are becoming hostile, cooperation is being replaced by rivalry, peaceful co-existence is being supplanted by ethnic clashes, and territorial divisiveness overrides accountable governance.

Democratic institutions, processes framed to empower, and resources granted to reduce inequalities and foster development are being sorely mismanaged. The Nagas and the Kukis of the Northeast are a prime example of tribal fusion and fission. The Naga and Kuki-Chin groups are today found in nearly all the north-eastern states (except Arunachal Pradesh and Sikkim) and live across the international border in neighbouring Myanmar.

Colonial discourse had differentiated and categorised various groups under the Naga and Kuki (old and new) groups for administrative utility (Sanajaoba 1995: 24) despite the fact that these groups functioned independent of such aggregations. The militant Nagas are definitely a case of strong tribal identity forged under colonial rule and furthered by policies of the post-independent Government of India aiming at pacifying, appeasing, and negotiating with the Nagas. Secessionist aspirations of the insurgent Nagas have been countered partly by playing the Kuki card and splintering tribal groups with a divide and rule policy. Within larger ethnic categories such as the Kukis and the Nagas, ethnic competition over preferential allocation of development resources for backward groups has promoted fissiparous subtribal assertion. Presently there are thirty-three recognised Scheduled Tribes in Manipur, and tribalism has promoted a convention of self-naming and shifts in political alignment. The Hmar have declared their independence of both Naga and Kuki-Chin groups, while the Anal and the Monsang have aligned themselves with the politically dominant Nagas in Manipur (Arora and Kipgen 2012: 438–42). Access to funds, jobs, and development resources is being shaped by identity politics, and one finds tremendous intra-tribal competition.

Ethnic affiliations oscillate over time with the emergence of self-consciousness, and identity assertion is shaped by the political aspirations of the elite that negotiate with the government on behalf of and in the name of representing their constituencies. The marginalised are rising, shaping their own future, and, under the guidance of visionary leaders, becoming an assertive subaltern in democratic spaces (Arora, in this volume). The political elite may represent ethnic associations, insurgent militant outfits, and select historical geographies (Arora and Kipgen 2012; Arora and Kipgen, in this volume; Bhan 2013; Channa, in this volume; Ghosh 2003; Mawdsley 1999; van Beek 1997). Democratisation of polity and secularisation of politics have not undermined or displaced the power that religious functionaries and institutions (temples, monasteries, churches, and madrasas) play in shaping who gets elected, the prioritisation of socio-economic issues, and the implementation of development programmes (Arora 2006). This is peculiarly true of ethnic nationalities living in the perilous Himalayan region.

The transition of traditional chiefs, tribal leaders, and priests (shamans, *lama*s, Hindu priests) who negotiated with and organised communities in the past to post-colonial democratic politics has varied between groups, but invariably their capability to mobilise and help in selection of ethnic leaders has not decimated into insignificance in democratic secular India. The traditional elites have adapted to modern politics quite successfully and, in particular ethnic contexts, become brokers, kingmakers, and sometimes reformers encouraging re-tribalisation (Arora 2006, 2007; Channa, in this volume; Gohain, in this volume). In other contexts, youth are getting politicised and emerging as leaders. Many regional movements have been led by disgruntled youth, while it is the youth who have demanded and fostered a stronger engagement with electoral politics, as in Nepal (Snellinger, in this volume). The Tibetan independence movement is being strongly sustained by the youth, while the Tibetan government in exile experiments with democratic governance in a deterritorialised nation (McConnell 2013).

It is fifty-seven years since the flight of the Dalai Lama and his followers from Tibet, following the Chinese invasion of Tibet in March 1959. The life of Tibetan Buddhists in exile has attracted substantial scholarship. According to Sudeep Basu (2012), it would be erroneous to ascribe a homogenous orientation to Tibetans' enforced existence outside Tibet or Tibetan-ness. With the hope that they would be able to return to Tibet remaining just that, the Tibetans have had to face squarely the prospect of a protracted exile that necessitated, among other things, 'a reformulation of their strategy in exile centred on the idea of "return" and the preservation of the "rich cultural heritage of Tibet"' (ibid.: 233). Basu highlights the plurality of practices and ideas of Tibet and the Tibetan diaspora that are continually being constructed by Tibetans and non-Tibetans alike.

In her review of 'Tibetan democracy-in-exile', included in our earlier volume, Fiona McConnell (2013) explained the uniqueness and limitations of democratic procedures in a territory-less polity. The political geography of Tibet is sharply contested, and exilic Tibetan polity is challenged to frame it for its citizens and pronounce it internationally, and in opposition to the Chinese one (Basu 2012). The Dalia Lama's government in exile has a formal democratic structure, but routinisation and internalisation – democratic consolidation – is a slow process and far from being a linear one. The exile context constrains the government's capacity for political reform and *mangtso* (democracy) (Frechette 2007). Younger Tibetans demonstrate greater support for democratic form and general awareness of the nature of political accountability and have requested international assistance to take democracy back to the Tibetan people in Tibet. Freedom and independence have distinct meaning for the young Tibetans living in exile. The idea that democracy can function as a form of empowerment and not merely as a gift from above of the Dalai Lama is increasingly becoming prominent.

Regional identities are historic formations. 'We are Nagas by birth and Indians by accident' is a proclamation often heard and documented by scholars (Hussain 2008). It has been observed that Northeast Indians often refer to mainland as being India, distancing themselves and affirming their distinct identity: 'They do not truly belong to that state [India]' (de Maaker and Joshi 2007: 381). The Northeast Indian is quite exclusive and not inclusive of large numbers of people residing in Northeast India. The colonial hand shaped the ethnic map of this region; the colonial legacy of an inner line has shaped the identity of the Northeast region. Depending on the need of the political economy and imperial political design, a large number of labourers were invited and settled in Sikkim, Darjeeling Hills, Assam, and other parts of the Northeast. The demography of the region underwent radical change in many localities with the settlement of tea-tribes, the Nepali labourers, and Marwari merchants who came here during the colonial period.

India's Northeast is home for a large population that migrated from Nepal more than a century ago. Broadly clustered and defined as Nepali, these Indian citizens are not welcome members of the Northeast. They constitute an ethnic Nepali group, which is culturally and religiously heterogeneous. If one interviews Punjabis, Marwaris, Nepalis, Bengalis, and so on residing in Shillong, Gangtok, Dispur, or Guwahati, and many of them have been minimally settled here for two generations, they continually lament the use of 'you Indians' by residents who iterate their outsider status. The Indians are being perceived as exploiters in Nepal, Bhutan, and in the Northeast. Conveniently, people ignore and gloss over how many hydropower projects are located on River Ganga to emphasise the exploitation and appropriation of River Teesta or Barak River or the Brahmaputra River. In the context of development projects, many indigenous groups of the region protesting against the appropriation of their lands and forests often declare 'the British may have left India, but the legacy of exploitation continues under the Indian masters'. The citizens of India are welcome here as tourists, as migrants offering skills, as educators, and as investors of capital, but the natives are reluctant to allow them to settle and buy their land.[1] Sikkim's administrative inclusion into India's Northeast in 2002 may not have been vocally opposed or resisted, but its belongingness has not been facilitated either. Sikkim is rarely included in the Northeast identifier unless done so administratively, and the Sikkimese people equally emphasise their historic identity as a protectorate of India, but being an independent nation until 1975.

Tripura, Sikkim, Bhutan, and Nagaland had historically functioned as independent entities, and the incorporation of Sikkim and Nagaland into India was guided by both regional and geopolitical considerations. The ethnic politics and upheavals in Bangladesh and ethnic clashes in Tripura do influence each other. The boundaries between India and Myanmar have divided historic territories inhabited by the Naga and Kuki-Chin groups. The migration histories of many groups have become a vibrant area of research and documentation as ethnic groups seek to demarcate ancestral domains and establish their indigeneity. Many groups have trans-border identities and cross-border connections. The Maoist insurgency in Nepal, and the violence unleashed as part of the Gorkhaland movement in India, has profoundly impacted the ethnic politics of Sikkim, Bhutan, and Northeast India. The Bhutanese government was concerned about the loyalty of the Lhotshampa (Nepali-speaking people who historically migrated to Bhutan and were settled by the British) and, in its desire to fabricate a homogenous nation (single language, single ethnic composition, and religious identity), precipitated their exodus in the 1990s (Evans 2010). The exodus of Lhotshampa from Bhutan impacts and has made the Nepali diaspora insecure and ethnically politicised. If demand for Gorkhaland is conceded in India, this may incite other groups such as migrants from Bangladesh settled in India to agitate for concessions.

Democratisation has furthered ethnic competition; assertion of identity; and demand for ethnic homelands to protect, safeguard, and promote political and development interests of groups in the Himalayan region. Undoubtedly, there are regions within regions, and ethnic aspirations for territorial autonomy and internal political autonomy have taken varied forms. Popular perceptions of regionalism, tribal homelands, and ethnic homelands have been long accepted under Indian federalism, and this legitimised the emergence of seven sisters of the Northeast from colonial Assam in post-colonial India. Subrata K. Mitra (2013) emphasises how India's asymmetric but cooperative federalism has enabled regions to become sites of governance following the transformation of regional movements into political parties. In many regions, political coalitions with rebellious groups have transformed them into stakeholders. While Mitra provides us with an optimistic picture of political capital in India, others are quite critical of its transformative politics. S. Baruah (2005) declares that the redrawing of the political map of Northeast India was a hurried exercise in political engineering to manage radical political mobilisation and defuse secessionist tendencies of the Nagas and the Mizos.

New states were produced in the post-colonial period by cartographic surgery (Khongreiwot 2009: 438–40) – combining or demarcating territories of various tribes (with or without their consent). For instance, Meghalaya was formed into an autonomous administrative unit by combining territories of the Garos, the Khasis, and the Jaintias from the colonial state of Assam in 1969 and was given statehood in 1971. Mizoram State was founded in 1986 after the Lushai Hills were severed from Assam and upgraded into a union territory in 1971. Many of these states were carved to extinguish secessionist tendencies and divide dominant tribes (such as Nagas) and their political elite. The recognition of Manipur State in 1971, after its incorporation into India in 1949, has fragmented Naga territories and withered the ancestral domain already divided between India and Burma.

However, these administrative responses failed and have been challenged by continued political insurgency there. The absolute numbers of resistance movements, ethnic militia, and revolutionary groups that have emerged have eventually submerged the region into a state of durable disorder (Baruah 2005). At the time of finalising this volume, the ambush in Manipur in June 2015 conducted by the Naga insurgents (Khaplang faction based in neighbouring Myanmar) that claimed the lives of eighteen soldiers and injured many others and a retaliatory surgical commando operation of the Indian Army on militant camps in Myanmar proclaimed the end of the ceasefire agreement between the Government of India and the Naga insurgents (Bhaumik 2015).

Ethnic ties do not neatly coincide with state boundaries in the Northeast, and the region's ties – historic, cultural, social, and economic – do not stop at the international boundaries either. The challenge or difficulties of negotiating with trans-national militant outfits should compel greater cooperation between neighbours to uproot militancy. The cartographic surgery of Northeast India did not take into account the pre-colonial political boundaries of various ethnic groups (Khongreiwot 2009: 440–51) while creating frontiers and transforming international boundaries into thirsty battlefields. The post-colonial state has not realised the core cause of 'durable disorder' either and reinforced colonial policies. Khongreiwot suggests that the present states of Northeast India will have to be de-organised and then re-organised on the basis of pre-colonial lines. It does not matter how many small states will be created, but what is important is their ability to co-exist separately and have mutual respect for each other (ibid.: 443).

Ethnic homelands tend to overlap, thus escalating further conflict and the formation of militia. They have become a costly mirage (Bhaumik 2009). The historic Naga–Kuki conflict is guided by the impossibility of carving contiguous ethnically homogenous territories. Ethnic cleansing seeks to create a majority where there is none. Ethnic cleansing has led to realignment and internal displacement of tribal members as political elite aspire to create ethnically homogenous contiguous areas, undermine development, deny entitlements, and violate human rights of their neighbours and tribal siblings (Arora and Kipgen, in this volume). Militant factions negotiating with the Government of India are guilty of unleashing considerable violence and engaging in ethnic cleansing to exert pressure, and muscular responses of the Indian Army have furthered alienation. This scenario is explicit in Manipur, Nagaland, and Tripura; it is equally true of other parts of India.

What we find here are a range of regional demands and ethnic configurations. While Ladakh is part of Jammu and Kashmir, Ladakhi-ness is above all an expression of socio-political marginalisation and consolidates regional (and religious) differences. Mostly Buddhists, the Ladakhis are against the communal identities of Kashmir (Muslim) and Jammu (Hindu). The Ladakh Buddhist Association has played a critical role in furthering the Buddhist representation of Ladakh, although Kargil has a significant Shia Muslim population. To counter political marginalisation, regional movements were organised in the 1980s that culminated in the national government granting scheduled tribe status to eight distinct tribes in 1989 (more than 80 per cent population), the formation of Autonomous Hill Development Councils in Leh in 1995 and Kargil in 2003. Currently, Ladakh is demanding union territory status (Bhan 2013; van Beek 1997). The numerous local and Hindu shrines, the *math*s (monasteries), and the *paharia* (culture of hill communities) culture have informed the decision to carve out Uttarakhand from the state of Uttar Pradesh. The demand for focused regional development rallied the inhabitants together to press for a separate state, and demand for sustainable regional development forged common ground among groups who were historically competing (Garwhal and Kumaon) into a regional entity.

The central and state governments have always kept the door open for negotiations with agitating activists, or insurgents, to counter political militancy while keeping geopolitical interests in mind. This explains the decision to establish autonomous hill councils in Ladakh, Darjeeling, Assam, and Meghalaya; establish tribal development boards for uplifting the indigenous; and create new hill states such as Himachal Pradesh in 1971 and Uttarakhand in 2002 (Arora, in this volume; Bhan 2013; Mawdsley 1999; van Beek 1997; Vandekerschove 2009), which are based on the constituentification of historic geographies (van Beek and Bertelsen 1997). B. Karlsson (2003) contends there is no blueprint for indigenous sovereignty, and separate ethnic homelands are not a viable political solution for India's Northeast. The Bodo case demonstrates how 'as regions develop within regions, they both mimic and subvert the latter by challenging the hegemony of dominant groups in the reorganised state' (Das 2011: 254).

Do democratic institutions and their functioning at the local level improve in delivery and effectiveness with political autonomy? The experience of various tribal development councils does require careful assessment and a critical one, and the ground-level experience of Meghalaya and Ladakh may not be even comparable given the ethnic-national context of their functioning and relationship with other states and nations. Democratisation and development are not necessarily interlinked in practice, despite the common theoretical perception and assumptions. Both are necessary conditions for creating a framework for enforcing the rights-based approach to entitlements and creating conditions for inclusive politics and enhancing capabilities, but are not sufficient for cultivating social democracy and ensuring the inclusion of the historically marginalised. Procedural democracy is located in multiple sites, variedly exhibited in institutional contexts, and contested in locales having different levels of civil society assertions, such that political change (reformist or radical) gets transmitted across the region. This regional aspiration and interpenetration influences the possibility of its extension and deepening in the Himalayas.

Organisation of the volume

The seven contributions in this volume are organised under three parts: the first deals with competing identities and identity politics focusing on the Jad Bhotiyas, the Nagas, and the Lepchas; the second explores negotiation of democracy in western Arunachal Pradesh and Nepal; and the third discusses the consequences of ethnic conflict in the Northeast and in Kashmir. This organisation, to be sure, is influenced by analytical considerations. Substantively, the contributors to the volume touch upon many intersecting themes across these three parts, as dictated by their areas of ethnographic engagement and thematic concerns.

The three chapters in Part I elucidate the dynamics of identity formation, articulation, and expression in the context of democratisation of polities in the Himalayan region. Subhadra Mitra Channa explores the formation and negotiation of identity by the Jad Bhotiyas of Uttarkashi. Officially, the Jad Bhotiyas have been listed as Scheduled Tribes since the mid-1960s. As a consequence, their identity has gradually become objectified and accepted as 'real'. Through her anthropological exploration in Uttarkashi, Channa highlights the disjunction between the 'administrative imagination' of the Jad Bhotiyas as Scheduled Tribes and the ethnographic reality of their lived experience. This so-called tribe, she finds, is 'a fairly heterogeneous mix of people from different locations on the Himalayan border, speaking and possessing a variety of languages and myths of origin'. Their identity, she observes, is primarily based on a sharing of resources in a unique ecological terrain.

Trying to find out 'who is a Bhotiya', Channa reviews the scholarship on the Himalayan region, covering the works of N. J. Allen, Vibha Arora, C. W. Brown, Christoph von Fürer-Haimendorf, M. P. Joshi, and Charles Ramble, among others. The dynamics of Jad Bhotiya identity is explained in terms of their displacement from their upper Himalayan habitation near the Neilang Pass and relocation in Bhagori village in Harsil village following the China–India border conflict in 1962. This displacement and relocation weakened their association with Tibet and brought them closer to the local *pahari* Hindus, especially Garhwal Rajputs.

Channa also discusses the nature of the social organisation of Jad Bhotiyas, the impact of development programmes on their everyday life, and the role of gender in politics, especially in the context of democratic institutions. She shows how the institution of elections has been a divisive force for the Jad Bhotiyas. The resulting flux in their identity makes her conclude, 'The term "identities", rather than "identity", better describes the on-going social and political processes.'

The bearing of democratisation, especially electoral politics, on identity formation and negotiation is delineated by Debojyoti Das with reference to the Nagas. Das, however, takes a different vantage point for his analysis, namely the objectification of identity through census enumeration. Numbers play an important role in a democracy as regards both electoral representation and the benefits of development programmes. In Nagaland, census enumeration has resulted in contested claims in terms of tribes and sub-tribes. The fact that some of the sub-tribes have been recognised as 'backward tribes' in Nagaland for protective discrimination has resulted in the intensification of the political rhetoric, struggle for political representation, and demand for a share in state-directed development programmes by other sub-tribes (who are territorialised by their ethnic boundaries).

Substantively, Das analyses the Naga ethnicity in historical context, the emergence of 'forward' and 'backward' categorisation among the Nagas, and identity (re)construction resulting from the debate about the census enumeration. He delineates the consequences of the politicisation of census enumeration for village-level politics and in the functioning of village councils and village development boards. His analysis reveals,

> Reservations and demarcation of new territories to appease the newly recognised 'backward tribes' has created its new set of problems in the Naga society polarising along tribal identities that have been rearticulated through emergent discourses of and categories of 'backwardness' and 'underdevelopment'.

While the state policies and democratic politics, no doubt, play a significant role in the formation and expression of identities by groups, one cannot ignore the importance of the stimulus that the groups themselves generate in this regard. This is the thrust of Vibha Arora's chapter, which elucidates the making of the subaltern Lepcha, and she locates her contribution within the discourse of subaltern studies and draws inspiration from that body of substantive scholarship. The rise of the subaltern Lepcha (emphasising the construction and its distance from a vanquished or disappearing group), Arora observes, 'signals the consolidation of democratic institutions, the emergence of political space for representing marginalised groups, and furthering inclusive politics'. It 'signals the deepening roots of a participatory democracy in the eastern Himalayas'.

After a brief socio-historical introduction to the Lepchas, Arora discusses the trope of a threatened and vanishing community used to describe them. She then distinguishes between the Lepchas of Sikkim and those of the Darjeeling Hills and delineates the differential impact of history on their respective political consciousness and struggles. Based on data collected from archives and extended multi-sited ethnographic fieldwork in the region, Arora thereafter discusses, what she terms, 'the Kalimpong stimulus' and the role of 'organic intellectuals' in shaping and asserting their uniqueness, declaring their indigeneity, and proclaiming their prior rights over resources in specific locales that get transformed into 'sacred' landscapes. Finally, she contrasts the aspirations of the Lepcha political elite to carve out political space in two democratic contexts – Sikkim and Darjeeling Hills.

How do societies which are new to democracy negotiate it? The two chapters in Part II address this question in two different contexts, namely western Arunachal Pradesh and Nepal. Swargajyoti Gohain explores the central role played by Buddhist monks in electoral politics in Tawang and West Kameng, two districts, located in western Arunachal Pradesh, inhabited by the Monpas, a Tibetan Buddhist ethnic minority. While it would be tempted to see this as reflecting an increasing democratisation of monasteries, she argues that 'monk's participation in electoral processes is linked to livelihood and authority issues in a system where traditional means of sustenance have been substantially reduced and the leadership role of monks in society has been diluted'.

Apparently, the institution of participatory democracy, with its emphasis on governance by and for the people, is at odds with the Buddhist conception of authority, 'which was traditionally based on an elite leadership with a strong monastic composition, and was sustained by a system of manorial estates and taxation (*khre*)'. Based on her ethnographic research, Gohain shows how monks in Tawang and West Kameng utilise 'the formal procedures of electoral democracy in order to retain their authority in non-monastic spheres'. The monks' engagement with electoral institution, she argues, 'is not to change but to preserve the monastic authority structure'.

Substantively, her analysis covers politics as social work among the Buddhists of Arunachal Pradesh, the legislative assembly elections in Dirang (a small town in West Kameng district) in October 2009, and the monastic interest in materialistic values. Her analysis reveals, 'A critical public discourse on monkhood, circulated as gossip, circumscribes monk's abilities to cross monastic bounds, and reduces the effect of elections as a channel for restoring monastic authority.'

In Nepal, the experiment with democracy is on-going; the political stalemate there is part of a political trend in Nepal's socialisation as a democratic republic. In this process of socialisation democratic principles take on various forms depending on the historical context. Starting from this vantage point, Amanda Snellinger examines ethnographic case studies of Nepali student organisations' internal political processes. Based on her anthropological research on the transactions at the campus, district, and national conventions of these student organisations, she elucidates the different political attitudes towards electoral process in Nepal.

Snellinger's focus on student organisations is heuristic. After all, the student organisations in Nepal are 'subsidiary' or 'sister' organisations of the mainstream political parties. It is in student organisations that individuals receive their 'initial training and indoctrination' into Nepali party politics. Hence, 'analysis of the student organisations' processes and political attitudes demonstrates the more pervasive conceptions of democracy'. Based on her study of six national conventions and numerous campus and district conventions of the student organisations (during 2006–7), Snellinger analyses the different conceptions of the democratic practice in Nepal, focusing on such topics as 'deliberation', the distinction between 'arranging things' and 'full consensus', the idea of 'safe landing' and 'pure consensus', and 'direct elections' and establishing a mandate.

Notwithstanding the mechanisms that are institutionalised for containing dissensions and controlling conflicts that arise in a democracy, the breakout of conflict, often violent, cannot be ruled out. In a multicultural polity like India, such dissensions and conflicts often relate to ethnicity and identity. They result in displacement of people from their homeland. The two chapters in Part III deal with this theme: one discusses ethnic nationalism and the demand for a 'homeland' and the other analyses gendered responses to displacement from homeland.

Vibha Arora and Ngamjahao Kipgen explain the rise of Kuki ethnic nationalism in the Northeast, particularly in Manipur, and the demand for a Kuki homeland. Tracing the history of this ethnic nationalism and focusing on the ethnic violence of the 1990s, they highlight the role of Kuki chiefs and political elite and the Kuki organisations in mobilising support for their cause. Analytically, they cover such issues as the role of identity politics in shaping the nationalistic aspirations of ethnic groups, the territorial aspirations and ethnic competition over resources in Manipur, the correlation between ethnicity and nationalism among the Kukis and the Nagas, and the rise of militancy and the escalation of ethnic violence among the Kukis. Arora and Kipgen highlight the complexity of the Kuki–Naga ethnic imbroglio.

Interrogating the main theories of ethnic nationalism in the context of the Kukis in Manipur, and similar cases elsewhere in the Northeast, Arora and Kipgen argue that 'it is not merely history and ideologies, but instrumental orientation and aspirations of controlling territory and gaining access to political power and material benefits that are fuelling ethnic conflict in contemporary Manipur'. They conclude that as long as the political demands live in the imagination of Kuki elites, Manipur will continue to witness violence and ethnic hatred.

The concluding chapter by Charu Sawhney and Nilika Mehrotra focuses on the Kashmiri Hindus displaced from Kashmir due to the escalation of political turmoil in the Kashmir Valley in the 1990s. Based on an ethnographic study of two locations – Jammu camps and Noida apartments – where a significant proportion of the displaced Kashmiri persons are resettled, Sawhney and Mehrotra show how their prolonged living in new locations has resulted in social and cultural changes and how they are redefining their traditional socio-cultural practices in the new locations.

Sawhney and Mehrotra find that the responses of Kashmiri Hindus to displacement and relocation are gendered. Through individualised personal narratives linked to displacement, they analyse 'the meaning of violence suffered by the survivors and the redefinition of men's and women's roles'. Substantively, they focus on the use of women as scapegoats, the changes in status identities, gender relations and changing conjugality, and changes in inter-generational relations. Sawhney and Mehrotra find the experience of resettlement – coping with the constraints and making use of the opportunities – varies in terms of not only gender but also the possession or otherwise social and cultural capital.

Conclusion

Collectively, the chapters in this volume attest to the complexity of the on-going process of democratisation and negotiation of identity in the Himalayas. They document the formation, articulation, and expression of identity, especially by the marginalised communities – the Jad Bhotiyas of Uttarkashi, the Nagas of the Northeast, the Lepchas of Darjeeling Hills and Sikkim, and Kukis of Manipur. They explore the nature of engagement with democratic institutions of elections and representation – especially Buddhist monks in Arunachal Pradesh and student organisations in Nepal. They discuss what it means to be displaced and relocated – the Kashmiri Hindus in refugee camps.

This volume is, in a way, a continuation of the analyses presented in our earlier volume *Routeing Democracy in the Himalayas: Experiments and Experiences* (Arora and Jayaram 2013). Reading through these volumes together, it will be clear that the Himalayan region, far from being idyllic, as one may wish to imagine it to be, is characterised by complex crosscurrents of social and political processes. Some of the complexities and challenges arise from the fragile landscape that has shaped the socio-cultural life here, and embedded politics strongly in the local while being connected to regional, national, and international processes. During the period of compiling and the finalisation of this volume, three major natural disasters (the 2011 Sikkim or Great Himalayan earthquake, the June 2013 cloudburst at Kedarnath, and the April 2015 Nepal earthquake) exposed the precarious roots of unplanned development in this geologically fragile region. Nature's fury has reclaimed the landscape and caused immense destruction, set back human development by decades, and exposed the rocky foundations of reckless growth. These disasters, we hope, will be addressed in a focused volume of their own in the near-future.

Despite efforts to elicit and cover Himalayan regions of Pakistan, Afghanistan, and Bhutan, we were unable to get suitable chapters on these areas. This volume continues to be India-centric ethnographically, while being regionally comparative and highlighting historical similarities. These two volumes have touched upon some of the salient processes and forces at work. More work, to be sure, is needed before one can attempt to theorise on democracy in the Himalayas. We hope that we will be able to garner greater focus and give impetus to scholarship on the region. We also hope that democratisation in the recently shaken Himalayas can propel debates on ecologically sensitive development, responsible governance, and political accountability.

Note

1 This explains why there are restrictions being imposed on inter-ethnic marriages and tribal laws are being enforced to retain land (productive resources) and women (reproductive capacities) within the community. The leaders of many ethnic groups are taking strong steps to prevent the dilution of their ethnic identity (e.g. among the Khasi, Naga, Kuki, Lepcha, and Mizo), and ethnic associations have sprung up in urban areas such as New Delhi, Mumbai, Bangalore and Hyderabad that have a sizeable student and working population of Northeast Indians.

References

Arora, V. 2006. 'The Roots and the Route of Secularism in Sikkim', *Economic and Political Weekly*, 41 (38): 4063–71.

———. 2007. 'Assertive Identities, Indigeneity and the Politics of Recognition as a Tribe: The Bhutias, the Lepchas and the Limbus of Sikkim', *Sociological Bulletin*, 56 (2): 195–220.

———. 2013. 'The Paradox of Democracy in the Northeast and the Eastern Himalayas', in V. Arora and N. Jayaram (eds.), *Routeing Democracy in the Himalayas: Experiments and Experiences,* pp. 101–32. New Delhi: Routledge.

Arora, V. and N. Jayaram (eds.). 2013. *Routeing Democracy in the Himalayas: Experiments and Experiences.* New Delhi: Routledge.

Arora, V. and N. Kipgen. 2012. 'The Politics of Identifying and Distancing from Kuki Identity', *Sociological Bulletin*, 61 (3): 401–22.
Banerjee, P. (ed.). 2008. *Women in Peace Politics*. New Delhi: Sage Publications.
Baruah, S. 2005. *Durable Disorder: Understanding the Politics of Northeast India*. New Delhi: Oxford University Press.
Basu, S. 2012. 'Interrogating Tibetan Exilic Culture: Issues and Concerns', *Sociological Bulletin*, 61 (2): 232–54.
Beetham, D. 1992. 'Liberal Democracy and Limits to Democratisation', *Political Studies*, 40 (1): 40–53.
Bhan, M. 2009. 'Refiguring Rights, Redefining Culture: Hill Councils in Kargil, Jammu and Kashmir', *Sociological Bulletin*, 56 (1): 71–93.
———. 2013. *Counterinsurgency, Democracy, and the Politics of Identity: From Warfare to Welfare*. New Delhi: Routledge.
Bhaumik, S. 2009. *Troubled Periphery: Crises of India's Northeast*. New Delhi: Sage Publications.
———. 2015. 'Army's Trans-border Raid in Myanmar: Interrogating the Claims', *Economic and Political Weekly*, 50 (25): 15–17.
Chakravarti, P. 2010. 'Reading Women's Protest in Manipur: A Different Voice', *Journal of Peace-building and Development*, 5 (3): 47–60.
Chaube, S. K. 1999. *Hill Politics in Northeast India*. Hyderabad: Orient Longman.
Dahl, R. 1989. *Democracy and Its Critics*. London: Yale University Press.
Das, S. K. 2011. 'Regions within but Democracy Without: A Study of India's Northeast', in A. Kumar (ed.), *Rethinking State Politics in India: Regions within Regions*, pp. 246–74. New Delhi: Routledge.
de Maaker, E. and V. Joshi. 2007. 'Introduction: The Northeast and Beyond: Region and Culture', *South Asia*, 30 (3): 381–90.
Escobar, A. 1995. *Encountering Development: The Making and Unmaking of the Third World*. Princeton, NJ: Princeton University Press.
Evans, R. 2010. 'The Perils of Being a Borderland People: On the Lhotshampas of Bhutan', *Contemporary South Asia*, 18 (1): 25–42.
Frechette, A. 2007. 'Democracy and Democratisation among Tibetans in Exile', *The Journal of Asian Studies*, 66 (1): 97–127.
Ghosh, B. 2003. 'Ethnicity and Insurgency in Tripura', *Sociological Bulletin*, 52 (2): 221–43.
Grugel, J. 2002. *Democratisation: A Critical Introduction*. London: Palgrave Macmillan.
Harriss, J., K. Stokke and O. Tornquist (eds.). 2004. 'Introduction: The New Local Politics of Democratisation', in J. Harriss, K. Stokke and O. Tornquist (eds.), *Politicizing Democracy: The New Local Politics of Democratisation*, pp. 1–28. London: Palgrave Macmillan.
Hussain, W. 2008. 'The Naga Dream and the Politics of Peace', *Asia Europe Journal*, 6 (3–4): 547–60.
Jayaram, N. 2005. 'Civil Society: An Introduction to the Discourse', in N. Jayaram (ed.), *On Civil Society: Issues and Perspectives*, pp. 15–42. New Delhi: Sage Publications.

Karlsson, B. 2003. 'Anthropology and the Indigenous Slot: Claims to and Debates about Indigenous Peoples Status in India', *Critique of Anthropology*, 23 (4): 403–23.

Khongreiwot, R. 2009. 'Understanding the Histories of Peoples on the Margins: A Critique of "Northeast India's Durable Disorder"', *Alternatives: Global, Local, Political*, 34 (4): 437–54.

Kothari, R. 2005. *Rethinking Democracy*. London: Zed Books.

Lawoti, M. 2007. 'Contentious Politics in Democratizing Nepal', in M. Lawoti (ed.), *Contentious Politics and Democratisation in Nepal*, pp. 17–47. New Delhi: Sage Publications.

Mawdsley, E. 1999. 'A New Himalayan State in India: Popular Perception of Regionalism, Politics, and Development', *Mountain Research and Development*, 19 (2): 101–12.

McConnell, F. 2013. 'Tibetan Democracy-in-exile: The "Uniqueness" and Limitations of Democratic Procedures in a Territory-less Polity', in V. Arora and N. Jayaram (eds.), *Routeing Democracy in the Himalayas: Experiments and Experiences*, pp. 204–31. New Delhi: Routledge.

McDuie-Ra, D. 2009. 'Fifty-Year Disturbance: The Armed Forces Special Powers Act and the Exceptionalism in a South Asian Periphery', *Contemporary South Asia*, 17 (3): 255–70.

McMillan, A. 2008. 'Deviant Democratisation in India', *Democratisation*, 15 (4): 733–49.

Mitra, S. K. 2013. 'How Exceptional Is India's Democracy? Path Dependence, Political Capital, and Context in South Asia', *India Review*, 12 (4): 227–44.

Qutab, S. 2012. 'Women Victims of Armed Conflict: Half-widows in Jammu and Kashmir', *Sociological Bulletin*, 61 (2): 255–78.

Rueschemeyer, D., E. Stephens and J. Stephens. 1992. *Capitalist Development and Democracy*. Cambridge: Cambridge University Press.

Sammadar, R. (ed.). 2005. *The Politics of Autonomy: Indian Experiences*. New Delhi: Sage Publications.

Sanajaoba, N. 1995. 'The Roots', in N. Sanajaoba (ed.), *Manipur – Past and Present: The Ordeals and Heritage of a Civilization* (Vol. III: Nagas and Kuki-Chins), pp. 1–17. New Delhi: Mittal Publications.

Stokke, K. and O. Tornquist (eds.). 2013. *Democratization in the Global South: The Importance of Transformative Politics*. New York: Palgrave Macmillan.

Tilly, C. 1997. 'The Top-down and Bottom-up Construction of Democracy', in E. Etzioni-Halevy (ed.), *Classes and Elites in Democracy and Democratisation*, pp. 275–84. New York: Garland Publishers.

Toffin, G. 2009. 'The Janjati/Adivasi Movement in Nepal: Myths and Realities of Indigeneity', *Sociological Bulletin*, 58 (1): 25–42.

Tornquist, O. 2004. 'The Political Deficit of Substantial Democratisation', in J. Harriss, K. Stokke and O. Tornquist (eds.), *Politicizing Democracy: The New Local Politics of Democratisation*, pp. 201–25. London: Palgrave Macmillan.

van Beek, M. 1997. 'Contested Classifications of People in Ladakh: An Analysis of the Census of Jammu and Kashmir', in H. Krasser, M. T. Much,

E. Steinkellner and H. Tauscher (eds.), *Proceedings of the 7th Seminar of the International Association for Tibetan Studies* (Vol. 1), pp. 1873–941.

van Beek, M. and K. B. Bertelsen. 1997. 'No Present without Past: The 1989 Agitation in Ladakh', in T. Dodin and H. Rather (eds.), *Recent Research on Ladakh VII*, pp. 43–65. Proceedings of the Seventh Seminar of the International Association for Ladakh Studies, Bonn, 1995.

Vandekerschove, N. 2009. 'We Are Sons of This Soil', *Critical Asian Studies*, 41 (4): 523–48.

Xaxa, V. 2005. 'Politics of Language, Religion, and Identity: Tribes in India', *Economic and Political Weekly*, 40 (3): 1363–70.

Part I
Shifting selves and competing identities

1 Seeking identities on the margins of democracy
Jad Bhotiyas of Uttarkashi

Subhadra Mitra Channa

The Indian democracy, unlike some others, for example, the French, has built itself upon the recognition of multiculturalism as well as protectionism towards those it considers marginal and weak. Terms such as scheduled castes and scheduled tribes were used in the Constitution of India to identify such groups of people who were viewed as only marginally integrated into the mainstream of Indian nation, and positive discrimination policies have been directed towards achieving the goal of fuller integration or ironing out of differences. Various mechanisms such as those of education and of communication like the media, mostly television and radio, have been extensively used for this purpose. Preceding such administrative action was the important assumption that there were entities that could be identified and labelled and then classified (put into a schedule). Such assumptions informing administrative action are to be found in most of the emerging nations as well as the colonial metropolis preceding them. As Ian Angus puts it, 'Modern nation states have been built upon an assumption that the normal basis for a society is a shared ethno-cultural tradition, and the assumption has silently entered into the large part of modern social and political thought' (1997: 163). Thus, whether like classical anthropology (mostly colonial) that defined a 'tribe' as a bounded and static given unit or contemporary social thinkers who have variously carried out a discourse on 'ethnies' (Smith 1986) or ethnic groups (Barth 1969) or some such entity, 'which they impute with a primordial authenticity' (Silverstein 2002: 123), the existence of 'a people', 'group', or 'tribe' has rarely been questioned.

Democracy as a process of nation-building has somehow attempted to 'recognise' such units, classify them, and then create a sense of symbolic unity that has been identified by most students of the nation-state as 'constructed' or 'imagined'. But, again, as Silverstein (ibid.) points out, the constituent units such as tribes or ethnic groups or linguistic categories have rarely been understood as constructed, as if their 'reality' was beyond question. Thus, while it is well recognised that the nation is a generalised and diffuse entity, mostly imagined and less concrete, the segments that are its constituents are almost always taken for granted as real and concrete. Thus, while one may 'imagine' a nation, one need not imagine a tribe. The latter has an objective existence, conveniently converted into ethnographies by anthropologists and documented in gazettes by administrators (see Atkinson 1980; Dalton 1872; Francis 1908; Hutchinson 1909).

In this chapter I take up one such case, that of the Bhotiyas, who, according to the Gazetteer of Uttar Pradesh (Rizvi 1979), have been identified as one of the 'tribal' groups in the state and classified as 'scheduled tribe'. B. S. Bisht mentions that 'in Uttar Pradesh only five tribal communities, that is, Bhotiyas, Buxas, Tharus, Rajis and Jaunsaries [were] declared as Scheduled Tribes in 1967' (1994: 15). From the same source we find that the Bhotiyas have been declared as geographically distributed in the districts of Almora, Chamoli, Pitthoragarh, and Uttarkashi. All government programmes under the policy of positive discrimination have been provided to a category of people so identified. The administration has no doubts about their existence, their identity, and, of course, their structure; thus, the Bhotiya identity has gradually become objectified and accepted as real.

At the same time, the gazettes and secondary literature (Bagchi 1977: 365–66; Brown 1990: 159; Levine 1987: 3) do acknowledge that all groups put under the category of Bhotiya are not really the same.

> For a long time Bhotiyas of Uttaranchal[1] have been inhabiting in seven river valleys after which they derive their name, namely, Joharis, Darmisa, Vyansis, Chaudasis (in Kumaon), Marchhas, Tolchhas and Jads (in Garhwal). . . . These Bhotiyas are believed to be of different origins.
>
> (Bisht 1994: 25)

Thus, there remains a disjunction between administrative imagination and the ethnographic reality that I could also discover through empirical investigation using anthropological methods.

After travelling to the district of Uttarkashi and locating myself in a village called Bhagori (a tiny settlement on way to the shrine of Gangotri) in Harsil district, where I did fieldwork during 1997–2001,[2] I was able to find out that what was an administrative reality had little basis in any 'primordial' unity, or in any of the anthropological definitions such as 'endogamy' and 'origin myth'. What really pass off as 'a tribe', namely the Jad Bhotiyas, is, as of now, a fairly heterogeneous mix of people from different locations on the Himalayan border, speaking and possessing a variety of languages and myths of origin. They have an identity that is primarily based on a sharing of resources and what Arturo Escobar (2008: 63–64) has termed 'emplacement', a unity of identity with a place, where place is not merely empty space but reflects an embodied relationship.

Who is a Bhotiya?

The most significant associations of the term 'Bhotiya' are with Tibet and erstwhile cross-border trading involving that part of the Himalayan ranges that lie alongside Tibet. Two popular ways of interpreting this term have been either by linking them to cross-border trade across the Tibet border involving neighbouring countries like India and Nepal or by associating with the 'Bhot' region, meaning the region lying on the Himalayan higher altitudes comprising northern parts of Chamoli and Pithoragarh districts extending into the valleys of the major rivers flowing here. Christopher von Fürer-Haimendorf writes,

> All along the Himalayan main range there are areas of high altitude where small communities subsist by combining agriculture and animal husbandry with vigorous trading activities. The Himalayan mountain dwellers thus acted largely as the middle men between two distinct economic zones, the arid Highlands of Tibet and the more fertile monsoon zones of Nepal's middle ranges and low lands as well as the corresponding zones of India.
>
> (1981: x)

von Fürer-Haimendorf has linked the Bhotiyas with a generic Tibetan-speaking people engaged in barter trade with Tibet from both Nepal and Indian borderlands (1975: 4, 1978: 339).

There are many references to the term 'Bhotiya', or 'Bhot', by scholars of the Himalayan region. N. J. Allen (1997: 314) prefers to link it to Buddhism and to Tibet, while Charles Ramble says, 'Literally a Bhotiya (Bhote) is someone from Bhot. Bhot in turn derives from the Tibetan term Bod, meaning Tibet' (1997: 391). A more recent work by Vibha Arora (2007: 198–99) also mentions the Bhotiyas (Bhutias) of Sikkim as having Tibetan links and a tribal identity. In a detailed account of cross-border trade involving Tibet, M. P. Joshi and C. W. Brown mention that such trade probably existed from at least the 3rd century BCE and involved 'salt and probably horses and dogs were brought from Tibet while *guda* and cloth were imported from the plains' and 'Traill (1851) notes the sale of hawks, musk, *dupees*, frankincense . . . Borax, salt, *punkhees*, ponies, *chowries* (yak tail), roots and herbs' (1986: 59, 61). From the same source we find that borax was an important item of import from Tibet from at least the 6th century CE, and there is evidence of it being used by the goldsmiths of Kumaon.

C. W. Brown (1987, 1990) discusses the manner in which British trade interests fostered and to some extent consolidated the identity 'Bhotiya'.[3] The most interesting point mentioned by Brown (1990) is that the Bhotiyas, at least on the Indian side, were not Buddhists but Hindus and claimed Rajput status, which was not recognised by the surrounding Hindu population because of their assumed descent or kinship with the Tibetans and also because of reasons of trade and their Mitra system (a system of hereditary trade partnership with the Tibetans). They were also sharing food with the Tibetans, who not being Hindus were considered 'untouchable by the upper-caste Rajput and Brahmin Garhwalis' (ibid.: 164).

Thus, the term 'Bhotiya' carries itself across borders of at least three countries or geopolitical entities (as technically Tibet is no longer a country), namely Tibet, India, and Nepal. While in Nepal the Bhotiyas are explicitly associated with the Tibetan language and Buddhism (also in Sikkim as described by Arora [2007]), in India the so-called Bhotiyas in the region of Garhwal were always claiming a Hindu upper-caste identity, as we have seen from the work of Brown quoted earlier. The Bhotiyas were further consolidated as a 'people' who were cross-border traders by British trade interests, who found them very effective carriers across the difficult Himalayan terrain. Thus, the Bhotiyas, for their trade interest, had to jeopardise their Hindu claim. But, by the time I conducted my fieldwork during 1997–2000, the situation had changed enough for them to renegotiate this identity with a vigour that was supported by several factors – economic, political, and historical.

The Jad Bhotiyas' claim to recognition as an entity is based more on situational than on historical or primordial associations. Their incorporation within the Indian nation and their performance within the Indian democracy are necessarily incumbent on the fact that they self-recognise and operationalise this identity. For ethnographic and descriptive purposes, this situational identity has been used but with apologies. One needs to assume that at any point when referring to the Jads I have always foregrounded them as 'as and then' and not as given and fixed.

Displacement and relocation

The Jads have been subjected to displacement and relocation simultaneously – shifted from their upper Himalayan villages near the Neilang Pass and relocated in the slightly lower and pre-existing village at Harsil – following the China–India border conflict of 1962. When I say only slightly lower, about 10 km away, and also pre-existing, it means that this particular village, namely Bhagori, was already existent as a higher-altitude village for the transhuman pastoral group. Thus, prior to 1962, they had three villages in the higher altitudes, which was used as summer villages, and one large village at Uttarkashi, called Dunda, which was used as a winter village, along with a winter camp at Chorpani in the forests near Hrishikesh. But after displacement the three higher-altitude villages were merged into one, although they still retain their pre-existing identities for some purposes at least. Those who originally belonged to the village at Harsil often tease the displaced persons as refugees, calling them *Chongsa Rong-pas* (displaced *Rong-pas*), *Rong-pa* being the name they prefer to use for themselves, in their own Tibeto-Burman language.[4] A colleague from the Himalayan Studies Institute at the Centre National de la Recherche Scientifique, Paris, told me that, in Tibeto-Burman language, *Rong-pa* means those who inhabit a high mountain range. Also earlier, the high-altitude village Neilang, rather than Bhagori, was the focus of their identity, and they were often referred to as the Jads or the people of Neilang (Rizvi 1979). In Neilang they had more land and were able to do agriculture using yaks and a plough, while in Bhagori their primary subsistence crops (namely naked barley) could no longer be grown and only a little horticulture is carried out by the women. Thus, from a self-sufficient people, who grew their own food and obtained the rest through barter trade, they have now been integrated into a cash economy where they have to buy their primary food items like rice and wheat, mostly from state-run ration shops.

The villages were and are still run primarily by the women, who carry on agriculture and processing of wool, and knitting and carpet-weaving; they also sell these items either directly from the village or in the nearby markets. The women keep the proceeds of the sale with them. The men take the sheep for grazing on a typical route, divided into two 4-month blocks called *chaumasa* (four months), so that they spend four summer months on the high-altitude pastures and four months moving downwards through the forests, when they camp near the village and shear the sheep, passing on the wool to the women. At this time, some wool is sold along with some male sheep for cash that the men keep for themselves. Once they reach the lower-altitude pastures, they graze their animals near the forests near Dehradun and Hrishikesh, where they share these pastures with other pastoral groups from near Niti and Mana and Chamoli. Earlier they shared these pastures with the sheepherders of Kinnaur as well, who have also been referred to in literature as similar to the Bhotiyas.[5]

It is customary for the Jads to marry in the groups with whom they share pastures, as a degree of familiarity is formed while sharing common resources. Thus, there were many men and women in the Jad village at Bhagori who had come from other villages of similar sheep-grazing groups, with whom the Jads have a kinship derived from sharing of resources. Anybody married into the Jad village becomes a Jad if he or she shares the same lifestyle as that of the Jads, which requires them to come up to the summer village in the higher altitude and to participate in their rituals and pay allegiance to the village god Me-Parang.[6] Thus, at any time in a Jad village, one would have men and women from other parts of the Himalayas, who are still identified by their origins as Kunnuba (from Kinnaur), Nitali (from Niti), and so on.

Before the borders were closed, the men combined grazing activities with trading, bringing salt, borax, precious stones, yaks, wool, dogs, and so on. The entire village also moved from the high-altitude village to the lower-altitude village in winter, and back again to the higher-altitude village in summer. In addition to their seasonal movements between the high- and low-altitude villages, the women and some men along with children take the horses and goats and other animals like yaks and cows to the forest camp at Chorpani (hidden water) to graze in winter. As I have described elsewhere (see Channa 2002), they kept as much distance as they could from the plains people, with whom they felt no identity. They felt safe only after reaching their own village, Dunda at Uttarkashi, but before that, while coming up from Hrishikesh, they would hide in the night to travel and avoid interaction as much as possible.

Trade with the plains people was and is still mostly carried on at Chorpani, where they remain hidden in the deep forests and have minimal interaction with the local traders, who now come to them to buy wool, carpets, puppies (of the Bhotiya dogs), and knitted items. Previously, while they were still trading with Tibet, the main attractions were borax, salt, and precious stones along with yaks and mountain horses. From the plains they would carry primarily rice, tea, sugar, and utensils. Currently, they sell for cash woollen items that they make themselves and other items such as jungle herbs and mushrooms. I often saw young men and women go deep into the forest looking for specialties like mushrooms and herbs, which they later sold for high prices. The distrust of the plains is still very much a part of their cognitive world, as is the safety and purity of the high-altitude places that they inhabit.

The Jads consider their high-altitude village to be the focus of their social life and identity, a place where they are 'their own selves'. Most old people express a desire to die at their high-altitude village and ascend to heaven on a pyre of deodar wood. In their own words the higher altitudes are *sangma*, meaning pure and unsullied. They are explicit that there were no gods in the plains, '*The gods live on the high mountains where everything is Sangma.*'

The Jads, in moving away from the border and from cross-border trade with Tibet, redefined to some extent their marginal status as *junglee* (wild, but with polysemic meanings) with their local Garhwali neighbours. But this term is still being used for them by the people from the plains. The teachers in the local government–run school, where I had stayed during one of my fieldworks, found it strange that I, an apparently well-educated woman, would like to voluntarily go and mix with the *junglee* people. Their classification as a tribe also reinforces such a worldview. As Sumiut Guha puts it, *junglee* refers to the 'definitive others against whom the civilised folk measured themselves' (1999: 17). Stereotypical notions – such as they get drunk in the evening, their women have loose morals, they are not like 'us' – were some of the deterrents used to prevent my going and working there. Even while I was leaving for the field some senior teachers warned me that 'it was no place for a woman to go and do fieldwork and certainly not to spend nights and evenings'. Veena Das and Deborah Poole (2004: 9) have identified three concepts of margins, and one of them is that the margins are containers for people who are 'unruly' or 'natural' subjects of the state (meaning uncivilised).

Their earlier dress and language as well as their celebration of some Tibetan festivals, such as the Tibetan New Year, Losar, which they still celebrate with gusto, and their belief in the magical powers of the *lama*s have also led the Jads to be designated as 'Tibetan' and Buddhists. Their villages are marked by the fluttering of Buddhist flags from the rooftops, which they put up on the instructions from the *lama*s who play an important ritual role in their lives. Yet the fact that they consider the *lama*s to be powerful religious functionaries does not take away from their self-identification as Rajputs, a fact in which the Jads and other Bhotiyas on the Indian side (including the Kinnauries of Himachal) have always believed in. This identity had historically been reluctantly compromised in view of their profitable trade with their Tibetan (Mitra) partners, and the cessation of this trade was reason enough for them to reaffirm this upper-caste identity. The increase in trade and political relationships with the Indian mainland became an added incentive to the pursuit of an upper-caste identity.

The process of relocation and improved communication with the Indian mainland had a dual function. For the side of the Jads, it provided a rational and practical reason to give up their association with Tibet and assert a greater tie with local Hindus, especially Garhwali Rajputs, in a bid to improve their social standing within the local *pahari* community. The improved communication, the presence of the army and the rising population of the Jads (due to better health care facilities) encouraged the Indian state to engage in 'pedagogy of conversion' (ibid.) to bring these 'marginal' people within the folds of Indian democracy. The paradox lies in an unrecognised tension between being upper caste and a *janjati*, an identity that they simultaneously perceived as an advantage, especially in their relation to the state (see Arora 2007).

The Jads in relation to the Indian state

While the Jads had little idea of the central Indian government or of the abstract identity 'India', they had never been an anarchic people, in the sense of not recognising higher authority. They had been under the influence of the local sovereign, the rajah of Tehri Garhwal, as well as bound by the legalities of Lhasa, representing Tibetan sovereignty, while conducting trade with Tibet. While Tibet lost its sovereignty to China (after 1959), it still owes allegiance to the rajah of Tehri, whose photographs continue to adorn its walls (an additional reason is that the rajah of Tehri is recognised as Bolanda Badri, the living manifestation of Badrinath by the people of Garhwal even today). After coming down from Neilang (and Jadung), they became more aware of the local Garhwali society, and their aspiration as of now is to find a respectable position within the *pahari* society, an ambition that has been fuelled by the formation of the separate state of Uttaranchal in 2000.[7]

The central and state governments, on the other hand, have been wooing the Jads with protective discrimination policies such as reservations in and facilities for education, employment, and so on. Their strategic position on a politically volatile border, their ability to navigate across difficult and inhospitable terrain, and their recognised access to what is now considered as 'enemy' territory had led them to be 'pampered' by the Indian army, who often used them to spy on the border. The Jads maintain a friendly and equalitarian relationship with the lower ranks of the Indian army posted there as well as with the Indo-Tibet Border Police. Liquor is exchanged, and much barter trade with the army goes on while they graze sheep into the deep hinterlands of the forests, to which they are the only civilians to have access. While doing fieldwork, I was often witness to the cricket matches that were enthusiastically arranged by the local army, and Indo-Tibet Border Police, with the local youth on the army helipad, to which the entire village came out to cheer. Special concessions are given to the Jad children in view of their transhumant lifestyle, and a special school, called Neilang-Chorpani school, travels with them, giving primary education to the small children. I met the elderly man, who has been the only teacher of this school in the winter of 1999, when I was visiting their camp at Chorpani near Hrishikesh. He told me that his task had become easier ever since the Jads were relocated in Harsil. Now high schools have been opened near their villages; the Jad children have the facility to study at both the high-altitude school at Harsil and the lower-altitude school at Dunda, without interrupting their studies.

In 1992, the Seventy-Third Amendment of the Constitution made significant changes in their participation in democracy, with the formation of the statutory gram panchayat. The majority of Jads view the process of elections as an intrusion into their community life. As one young man put it, 'The sarkar [government] has pitted brother against brother and sister against sister. We had a harmonious community life before but now factions have been created within us.' This shows how mindless introduction of macro-democratic policies can have a deleterious effect, for the Jads had very little by way of internal stratification. They never had any concept of headman or village council. Their population before they came down to Harsil was very small, barely a couple of hundred people. Women told me how every year, during the rainy season, most children below the age of one would die of stomach-related diseases. The genealogies collected by me showed very small families[8] and high death rate. Apart from high infant mortality, tuberculosis, and accidental deaths (like falling from mountains) are common-enough causes of mortality.

Such a small population was able to maintain a fair degree of internal order believed to be with the help of supernatural beings who laid down 'dos' and 'don'ts' and imposed their will by sanctions mostly in the form of ill health and misfortunes. Every misfortune, such as illness, is believed to have a supernatural causation, and the reason is always the wrath or displeasure of some supernatural being. Whenever someone is ill or has a problem, the first recourse is to divination to find out what mistake has been made, or what rule has been broken by the person concerned. It is obvious that people adhere to rules and norms because of this 'invisible surveillance' that is impossible to bypass.

The only person, about 90 years old, who was identified as a 'group leader' held an office they called *malguzar*. When I interviewed him, he told me that his job was to negotiate on behalf of the Jads with the officials on matters related to payment of taxes and so on. However, he told me with a twinkle in his eyes,

> My more important work was to act as go between for lovers. Since I was good at making speeches, boys would ask me to go to their girlfriends and plead on their behalf. I could make eloquent and poetic propositions and persuade many a girl to meet with her lover.

But, when it came to real authority, the Jads provided a test case for what anthropologists have called acephalous (Evans-Pritchard 1940) societies, that is where most decisions were taken on a community level and with supernatural interventions. Thus, the local authorities invoke no fear or respect in the Jads, who remain mentally at least a 'free' people.

The relative position of men and women is also paradoxical as the women have control over the social life of the village even as the men are considered ritually superior. In this sense, their participation in the democratic process is of a different nature than is expected in a largely patriarchal domain.

Gender and politics

During the period of my fieldwork, a woman was the *pradhan* or statutory head of the panchayat of five villages, of which only one was a Jad-inhabited village. She was an active, vocal, and assertive woman; she went for all meetings and all by herself to the district headquarters at Bhatwari, but had very little authority within the village. I often saw her going out of the village in a Western-style blue woollen coat of which she was very proud, trying to look important, while most others looked at her with suppressed grins and passed snide remarks. In fact, the Jads have no cultural ways to show deference to anybody; they treat everyone equal. Also, being a woman, her taking care of affairs outside of the village was not taken seriously by anyone. It is paradoxical that, while women are regarded as proper caretakers of village affairs, they are not supposed to be going out of their own space to interfere in the men's world. Yet the men too do not feel that politics is their forte, as the locus of the gram panchayat is the village. Earlier they were used to negotiating with outsiders, but the inner realm of the village is not seen as having any particular need to be 'governed', so to say. Whatever is done by the local body within the village is not taken as of any use. If necessary, they go to a religious practitioner to get their problems solved; the concept of a secular caretaker is alien to them. Thus, the incursions of democracy into their lives have stirred up more debates and controversies than brought about any need-felt transformation.

On my very first visit to the village in 1997, I witnessed one of the stormy panchayat meetings, where while the village *pradhan* stood in the centre, a group of vociferous women surrounded her and there was a verbal fight. The visiting officials of the Zila Parishad (District Council) sat around in embarrassed silence and the men of the village stood around amused. Elsewhere (Channa 2010c) I have discussed how in the Jad cosmology the women occupy central position in the social world; it is they who practically run the village. The men, being traditionally shepherds and traders, spend most of their time travelling outside of the settlements. Thus, most of the social life revolved around women and is considered their responsibility. On any day one would find women forming groups to do agricultural work on the fields, sitting in large groups in the centre of the village, knitting, or doing other wool-processing work. They are mostly in charge of conducting ceremonies even though it is men who should be doing them officially. One woman told me,

> The rituals of offering to ancestors and other important rituals such as at Losar are to be properly done by men, but my husband is always out

of the village grazing sheep or gone for some work, so what am I to do? I perform all the rituals on his behalf.

When I asked Kamala, the then *pradhan*, how she felt about her role as a political functionary, she said,

> It is alright but the most difficult part is for me to travel outside of the village. I have to go and stay sometimes overnight at Bhatwari (the district headquarters) and I do feel uncomfortable in the presence of strange men. But it is my responsibility so I have to do it.

Interestingly, Kamala made no mention of how her husband felt or if his opinion was of any consequence. I learnt that this man had very little say in his wife's affairs and preferred to stay out of all her business. I would see him sitting under a tree with his flock of sheep and meditate into space, while his wife made herself busy. Her daughters (six in all), however, were enthusiastic about their mother's position, and at the meeting that I have already described, they were serving tea. If she wanted to discuss something, she would do it with her daughters. Women normally took charge of most activities around the village, and during the celebration of a wedding in the village, a local Border Security Force jawan told me, 'In our village the men do all the work of arranging weddings, but here I see that women are doing everything. This is a place where women do everything.' The men have no legitimate space within the village. So, when they are around, one sees them either in the local shop drinking liquor or playing a local variety of chess sitting under a tree; the younger men play cricket on the army helipad. They are not supposed to be around the house, unless they are too old or very young.

Under such a scenario, where politics is located in the village, men can legitimately engage in it. Paradoxically, they are not taken seriously within their own community. In fact, it is women who take part in political activities; it is women who are taken more seriously. Gender issues form a key line of disagreement and negative stereotyping between the local Garhwalis and the Jads, as the former consider the latter to be inferior precisely because their women seem to have so much freedom and mobility. Jad women move freely, have control over their own money, brew millet beer (local *chang*), make all important household and even village-level decisions, conduct rituals, and, in short, have complete control and agency.

The men are considered ritually sacred, more pure, and more equated with nature. In the Jad cosmology, the village is secular, the seat of everyday existence, and the proper place for women to be, because women are not pure and superior like the men who go into the high-level pastures, from which women are debarred. Men can also traverse the forests and go to faraway places because they are pure and superior to women. In the Western understanding informed by Judeo-Christian theology, humans are superior to nature and are meant to dominate nature (Eliade 1978: 354). Women are closer to nature because they are driven by instinct and men are guided by reason that is cultural. These ideas were further concretised during the scientific era of industrialisation, when greater value was attached to reason and human potential to conquer nature (MacCormack 1980: 6; Ortner 1974). But Jad cosmology deviates distinctly from the Western view. First, there is no clear distinction between nature and culture, and second, the natural, in the sense unsullied by human presence, such as the high mountain tops, considered pure and sacred, is superior. Men by way of their pure bodies can converse with the natural, but the women who are not so *sangma* (pure) must keep away. The very ritual superiority of the men situates them appropriately in the wild, for the forests are sacred and the village is not (Channa 2010a).

Because the nation-state prioritises human habitation, such as the village or town, as the seat of power, we have a dilemma, something that makes the participation in the democratic process somewhat problematic for the people here. They are not used to having any kind of person in authority within the village, man or woman. Second, it is difficult for them to accept men as central focus of village authority. The men are attempting to redefine their position within the village but with little success. I found that young men who study in the plains, in cities, to be particularly reticent in interaction with outsiders. They would be very silent and try to be as invisible as possible; none of them, for example, would speak to me. The integration of the Jads into a primarily patriarchal political system thus remains somewhat shaky.

The divisive effects of elections

The democratic process that requires people to vote and select candidates is bringing to surface all kinds of internal divisions that were suppressed or were not relevant. The people who live in this village draw their name and identity from their occupation of a certain space and not because they have necessarily common origins (Fisher 2001: 35).[9] Locality has pre-eminence in the political domain over ethnic differences. Thus, while the democratic process has been initiated into this village based on the rather misinformed notion that the Jads are a tribe, in reality it is reemphasising all the hidden cracks in their village society that arise from different origins, different clan gods (*kuldevta*), and even the fact that many of them had originally belonged to different villages (Neilang and Jadung) or have come from different regions like Kinnaur, Chamoli, Niti, and Mana passes.

I was told that certain gods (*devta*) are the clan gods only of some people in the village and they only will perform a certain ritual or that even some of the main rituals like Panoh were performed at two different sites within the village, as people originally from Neilang want to have a separate medium than those from Bhagori. Hence, the divisions between 'gods' reflect political differences between groups and express their belonging to their locality; this is also found in other Himalayan societies and Bhutias of Sikkim (Arora 2007).

At a ritual that was initiated by the then village *pradhan* as divination for her ailing daughter, one of the key roles of a *devi* (Draupadi) could not be played by the woman who usually is the medium for this particular deity, as she was the wife of the main political rival of this woman (his sister having fought the election against her and lost). They had to get a woman from another village to act as the shamanic medium.[10] The internal divisions that formal politics has created or furthered are reflected in this instance.

The external imposition of administrative processes was particularly problematic for men. They were required to participate more with other men in the district, not a very comfortable situation for them or for the women either. The men were uncomfortable in their roles as being responsible for the village, while the women mocked them and did not take them seriously. Women in the village were not used to any of the ways of the general patriarchal system of the local Garhwalis. Men, who interacted more with outsiders, did recognise that their position within the village was not commensurate with those of other men they knew, again had no cultural means to deal with it.

Presence of state power and impact of development programmes

The state has made its presence felt for these people in the shape of the erstwhile princely state of Tehri, as like all pastoral people they had to depend on the power of the state to grant them grazing rights on large tracts of land. Unlike Kumaon, which was a part of British India, Tehri had maintained its symbolic independence, as the British ruled through its semi-divine ruler. They say that it is the rajah who granted them grazing rights to the upper-altitude pastures, a right that has been recognised by the Government of India after independence; it still issues special passes to them to cross over to that part of the border that is closed to all other civilians. The Jads recognise a close relationship with the military and police on the border and have stories to tell about how they help them in getting information.

The Indian state's presence is marked by the military, the Indo-Tibet Border Police, and the occasional presence of a minor local politicians or higher state officials who arrive at the helipad to visit the shrine at Gangotri. But rarely do the officials have any direct interaction with the Jads, who remain hidden in their village that is situated such that it is not even visible to the outside world.[11]

The second way in which the Jads recognise the existence of the state is when they have to pay taxes to the *sarkar* for use of the lower-altitude pastures. The men are the main nodes of interaction in these, as it is they who go grazing, pay taxes, and meet other people in the lower altitudes. For the Jads, it is the towns or cities that are wild and dangerous and need to be negotiated carefully and necessarily only by men (see Channa 2010a).

In 1995, this village was selected as an Ambedkar Village under the Ambedkar Gram Vikas Yojana.[12] Through this Yojana funds were channelled into this village, and the first heated discussion that I witnessed in a panchayat meeting was regarding the use of some of this fund to build a road (of no use at all) in the village. The village is built on a mountainside with steep inclines, and roads make no difference to how one walks, because the local people are used to climbing over rocks and find it more comfortable to do so. Vehicular traffic cannot cross the deep gorges to enter the village. Many shops were vacant in the village as they were of no use for the Jads, who do not like shop-keeping. Given the small population and practically no visitors, such shops have no commercial relevance in this out-of-the-way place. The *sarkar* remains a shadowy figure for them, at least for most of them who rarely go to the plains or have visited any town or city.

It is paradoxical that in the Jad village women are supposed to be the centre of authority within the village, yet in dealing with the outside world of the government and its administrative machinery, it is the men who are expected to interact in conformity with the patriarchal norms of Indian society. When such interaction was limited to paying of taxes and tributes for grazing and trading, these were acceptable to the social norms. But the situation is becoming problematic as politics is entering the internal affairs of the village.

The workings of democracy, especially the implementation of the Panchayati Raj institutions, have brought external governance to the village. In the Jad context, women consider it only natural that they should have all the say in the village matters, while the administrative officers coming from other areas find it embarrassing to deal with the vocal and assertive Jad women. For instance, at one panchayat meeting that I witnessed, the officials sat in incredulous silence as they watched the women argue regarding issues while the village men hung around as mute spectators. No doubt, such gender roles are further used to strengthen the notion of *junglee*.

The local *pahari* society

Since most Jads, especially women, find the outside society and *sarkar* ephemeral and unintelligible, it is within the local *pahari* society that they want to relocate themselves as local Rajputs, at par with the Garhwali Rajputs whose names they have borrowed and whose worldview they share and identify with. One way in which they seek this location is by acquiring a village *devta* (deity). Each village in Garhwal, and also adjoining Himachal Pradesh (that is a culturally similar and intermarrying area), has what they call a village *devta*, whose status is that of a ruling deity. The rajah of Tehri Garhwal,[13] the human manifestation of Badrinaryan (Lord Vishnu), is located at the apex of a system in which all the other local village gods and goddesses are viewed as ruling monarchs over their territory.[14] The ruling gods have their treasury and their coterie of functionaries who take care of and manage the god's property. The identities of people and local power hierarchies are inextricably tied to the sovereign and living village gods, and most people identify themselves as the *praja* (subjects) of their presiding village deities, although a variety of other superhuman beings, including clan gods or *kuldevta*, play important roles in the social and political life of the villagers.[15] Most decisions – like when to plant crops, when to harvest them, when to take the sheep on their grazing routes, and even whom to marry – are believed to be controlled by the will of the ruling *devta*. As described by Jean Claude Galey, 'Most village gods associate in common festivals, migrate to visit one another and constitute a local pantheon, having one of their temples for headquarters' (1994: 197).

The movements of the *devta*, which is exactly like that of human beings on social visits or of kings to map out territories or to show the extent of their influence, have been described by other scholars such as Channa (2010b, 2013), Mazumdar (1998), and William Sax (2000, 2002), writing on this cultural area, which is known in anthropological literature as *pahar* (Berreman 1972, 1983). Most of the local gods are bound by kinship relationship with each other, including that of marriage. The female goddesses go to visit their *mait* (mother's place) (Sax 1991) and also to visit their husbands. There is also a recognised as well as contested hierarchy of these gods.

In this context, it is relevant to discuss the acquisition of a village god by the Jads as most people were quite uncertain about the aetiology or origin myth or any kind of ethno-history of this *devta*, who is also not the local form of a higher Hindu deity like Badrinath or Parvati or even a Mahabharatian figure like Hidimba. The *pahar* is also known for its symbolic and ritual association with the Mahabharata and elsewhere (see Channa 2005) I have described the incorporation of the Pandava in their rituals along with their claim to a Kshatriya status. Sax mentions the significant fact that 'Garhwalis associate Mahabharata not only with their region but also with their own bodies. Garhwali Kshatriyas . . . say that they are descended from the Pandavas' (2002: 57). Thus, the Jad's claim to be Kshatriyas in the *pahar* has more significance than a mere claim to high-caste status; it incorporates them within the ritual kinship of the region.

The village deity appears to be an ancient nature god worshipped in the form of bamboo pole with pieces of red cloth tied to it, identified by the Jads as fire and grandfather (*Me* means both and *Parang* is an honorific in the Jad language). He has no kinship or relationship with any other local god and is not yet the part of any local hierarchy. This suggests he may have been a later incorporation as the Jads were struggling to get recognition in the local Garhwali society or in the culture of the *pahar*. Today, the Jads not only possess a *devta*, but they also take him out on ritual processions (*yatra*) as a public demonstration of their claim to a central upper-caste *pahari* identity (Channa 2010b).

Another way in which the Jads are shifting their identity towards the centre of *pahari* society is by distancing themselves from the Tibetan association that has been an integral aspect of their identity as Bhotiyas, but which had also denied them an upper-caste Hindu status, reducing them to being *junglee*. They have entered into a discourse of their ritual and social superiority to the Tibetans by claiming that they consider the latter almost as 'untouchables'; they never marry into them and consider their women to be like inauspicious widows (*raan mool*). I call this a discourse because most of these differences are verbalised for the benefit of outsiders than actually practised.

Marriage had always been out of question, but cultural similarities do prevail, as does their belief in the Buddhist *lama*s, a belief that is shared by the Tibetan refugees in their villages whom they refer to as Khampas. They have a Buddhist monastery and a female religious practitioner, the Chomo, who is regarded highly by all, Jad or Khampa. I have seen them share food and attend funerals and marriages at each other's houses. Yet, when I asked the Jad women about the Khampa, they made faces to tell me that 'they are different from us. These women do not put a bindi or put vermilion (sindoor) in their hair like Hindu women do'. But I never saw a Jad woman with these trappings either. Sometimes for fashion or decoration a young woman would put a *bindi*, but it was never put on religiously like Garhwali Hindu women and never did I see anyone with *sindoor*. It was quite impossible to tell the Jads apart from the Tibetans, both old and young, and I often found myself interviewing a man or a woman who I thought was a Jad but turned out to be a Khampa.

Thus, it is the *denial* rather than the actual dissociation that is important, for it is through denial that a new identity is being negotiated, that of an upper-caste Hindu Rajput and not one associated with the Tibetans (who being non-Hindus are considered untouchable by caste Hindus). However, while the Jads may deny the Tibetan link, they do not deny their association with Buddhism as a matter of faith. It is here that they may verbalise, 'We believe in both Hinduism and Buddhism, for we are in between both these people.' The presence of the monastery in their village and going to the *lama*s for magico-religious practices are never denied. Some young Jads today are even asserting a Buddhist, non-Hindu identity as self-identification to counter what they feel as the Hindu arrogance in denying to them a place in upper-caste Hindu society. In fact, Buddhism as a religion has made an entry into their lives only after H. H. The Dalai Lama came to India with his followers. The *lama*s who came with him spread out mostly into the hilly regions of the north and built many monasteries and also came in face-to-face contact with the local people. Buddhism is thus something that belongs more to their future sense of identity than the past.

As recalled by older people, there were no *lama*s in Neilang prior to the closure of the border with Tibet. What the Jads practised then was a village form of animistic religion similar to that of the border villagers of Tibet, situated far away from the influence of Lhasa. Thus, both Hinduism and Buddhism, at least in their recognisable forms, are more recent acquisitions of these people.

It is mostly the younger men and women who have travelled and interacted with actual upper-caste Hindus, who feel the futility of trying to negotiate a place within Hindu society, especially outside of the *pahar* where they are still stereotyped as 'Tibetan' or *junglee* or, if nothing else, as scheduled tribe and, therefore, not Hindu. What the young and more educated persons among the Jads understand is that there is an inherent contradiction between being classified as a scheduled tribe, a classification that brings them some benefits, and being an upper-caste Hindu. The older people do not see any such contradiction for they are not aware of how the term 'scheduled tribe' is actually assigned. In fact, for them, the significance of such a classification is as ephemeral as the presence of the state.

The two most important areas where state presence is felt in civil society, namely justice and law and order, are maintained here more through the *devta* than through any state mechanism, which hardly makes its presence felt in this remote area. At present, it is through their *devta* that the Jads are negotiating a position in the local *pahari* society. Thus, it was the younger people who seemed more involved with Me-Parang and his significance. It is they who usually described how they went with him to the shrine of Gangotri and how important he was for their village. The elderly seemed much less concerned and, according to some, Me-Parang was someone who has entered the village only in more recent times.

Participation in local politics and emerging identities

Over the years, the Jads have come to realise their importance within the local *pahari* society. In fact, there has been a shift in identity from being closer to the Tibetans and cross-border traders to being Garhwali Rajputs, an identity that was always present (Brown 1990: 164) but which they could not express because of lack of acceptance by others. After their physical shift from the borders, they were made aware of the actual extent and the implications of their marginality. While they were engaged in highly profitable active trade with the Tibetans, they probably were both unaware and did not care about their position vis-à-vis the Garhwali Hindu society. It is only when they became economically dependent and more physically integrated with the Hindu Garhwalis that they realised they were a socially and culturally marginal people, the *junglee* and the social outcastes. But the Jads, like the Thakalis (Fisher 2001: 6)[16] are a very adaptive people. Since they do not have any sense of a primordial identity, they are ready to adapt to any situation and negotiate.

As mentioned, the identity of Jads is closely tied to a sense of 'emplacement', a tie to a place rather than to any specifically kinship-based grouping. Since they had now 'shifted' spatially, they consider it expedient to adapt to the new situation. In fact, shift or movement is something that is intrinsic to their worldview as a transhumant people engaged in grazing and trading (Channa 2013: 12–14). Therefore, shifting into another identity is not considered illegitimate or an out-of-the-ordinary situation.

Angus defines 'social identity' as 'a feeling of belonging to, or identifying with, a socially defined form of human organization' (1997: 11). The Jads have redrawn their boundary of belongingness, from the Indo-Tibet border to a social space situated centrally to the *pahari* society. They are now making efforts to create all the cultural apparatus that they may need to be identified as *pahari* Rajputs. These include having a village *devta* and for the *devta* to negotiate his space in the local social network of *devtas*, to incorporate the Pandava cult identified by some scholars as the 'icon' of *pahari* society (Sax 2000), to take on Garhwali Rajput clan names like Bhandari and Rawat, and even to change their personal names to sound more like Hindu commonplace names such as Ranjita, Babita, and Sanjit.[17]

However, no amount of efforts from the Jad side would have brought any fruits unless the larger Garhwali society too considered at least some of the Jads' claims as legitimate. A considerable degree of such legitimacy, one that now allows them to take their village *devta* in a public procession to the shrine of Gangotri, comes from two sources. The first is the relative economic prosperity of the Jads, who are wealthier than the Garhwali peasant populations, because of the items they produce/trade in, namely animals, carpets, woollen goods, and now apples. Most of the Garhwalis in comparison have to depend on salaried jobs to supplement their meagre income from cultivation in a mountainous region with little cultivable resources.

Second, the Uttaranchal movement has drawn all the *pahari* communities together as against their common enemy, the plains people and to some extent the central and also Uttar Pradesh government. The plains people had been exploiting the resources of the mountains while creating derogatory stereotypes of the mountain people. This exploitation, along with the cultural arrogance of the upper-caste plains Hindus, led to a claim for a separate state for the hill people in the 1990s. After almost a decade of struggle, which drew all who were having or aspiring for a *pahari* identity (like the Jads) together, the new state of Uttaranchal finally came into existence in April 2000.

The Jads' support for this movement and its success has now legitimised their claim for a more significant place and location within the *pahari* society. A prominent member of the *pahari* community in Harsil told me during the peak period of the struggle for a separate state, in 1999, 'We consider the Jads as Rajputs like ourselves. Some *outside people* (bāhar wale) look down upon them but we consider them as our brothers.' The term 'outside people' was an obvious reference to the people from Uttar Pradesh or the plains.

The redrawing of political boundaries has led to a redefinition of belongingness. The Jads, by virtue of being *pahari*, are now a positive reference group. The local *paharis* realise that, if the plains people regard the Jads as *junglee*, they too are not regarded as much better. They feel it is better for the *pahari* people to stand together. To this end they would redefine the boundaries and put the onus of defining *junglee* in its various degrees,[18] on to the plains Hindus. Thus, the feeling of being *pahari* together, to some extent, does make possible an integration of the Jads with the local people. Also with increasing population, the possibility of greater village endogamy makes for the emergence of an actual internally homogeneous Jad population in the future, leading to the phenomenon of having an ethnic identity actualising itself because of 'outside' interpretation and also political need.

The Jads are realising that, as a people or a tribe, they have a political identity that may be beneficial to actualise, especially in view of the benefits that such an identity bestows on them in the form of preferential treatment and concessions from the central government. At present, they are evolving an identity and giving it a concrete shape in the form of the village god and common rituals. But the very democratic process that expects them to be 'a tribe' simultaneously threatens their social unity by exposing the internal fracture lines of this put-together identity. The very process of voting pulls them apart in terms of their past links and associations. There is a contradictory message that is received by them from the *sarkar*.

Thus, the earlier mention in this chapter of Jad being a situational rather than a primordial identity, which is determined by residence at any moment and on a common sharing of resources, is always fragile. As soon as people are expected to compete against each other, a necessary condition of the democratic process, this Jad Bhotiya identity becomes brittle and tends to crack. But it is democracy and the state again that made the existence of such an identity necessary in the first place for, to engage in any kind of interaction with bureaucracy and state administration, the Jads need to identify themselves, and they have been doing that as Jad Bhotiya. Interestingly, the women and those who are not in touch with outside administration are often ignorant of this label.

It is because Jads are not able to make legible all that they receive from the state that interacts with them through the local political and social nodes that they are yet to develop any stable relationship to the 'abstract' Indian nation making its presence felt as the *sarkar*. Suspicion and distrust of outsiders is prevalent, yet there is a movement towards integration. Sometimes, this integration is global, like the young man who had named his two daughters Martina and Monica after the tennis stars Martina Navratilova and Monica Seles. At some levels, like when they are watching a cricket match, a sense of nationhood is also emergent but not completely understood.

The very small size of the community also makes the Jads fairly 'invisible' in political terms and, as far as I know, no major political figure or even local politician or lawmaker has ever visited them, given the inaccessibility of their terrain. The names of the major political parties like the Bharatiya Janata Party and Congress are familiar to some of them, especially the young men and women who have travelled outside to study. The major impact on their community has been in terms of the benefits of positive discrimination by virtue of which several of them have received high professional degrees and employment. Even around 2000, at least one young couple were medical doctors in the All India Institute of Medical Sciences in New Delhi, and several young men were studying in medical and engineering colleges in the plains of Uttar Pradesh.

The making of the separate state of Uttaranchal has not resulted in any specific change in Jads' position in spite of the very process of making of the state having conferred on them a more accepted Garhwali identity. This again creates both a tension and a confusion as most of them would like to be accepted as Garhwali Rajputs of high status, and they have also taken up such names as Negi, Rawat, and Bhandari to effectively make their identity fused with that of the locals. At the same time, the pull of being *janjati*, with its benefits as well as their cultural differences, makes them wary of too much integration. One major hurdle in the process of such integration lies in their substantively different gender cosmologies. As I could assess, their major goal was to be accepted as social equals of the local Rajput Garhwalis but not to merge with them culturally so as to *become them*.

Conclusion

The Jads exhibit the uneasy and problematic relationship that may exist between 'democratic values' and democracy as an institutional set-up, with its hierarchies and administrative mechanisms. Thus, as a people who have always believed in the essential equality of all beings, in spite of the differences, the procedural aspects of a democratic form of governance that involves something like voting make no sense. 'Why do we need to choose between our kin and brethren?' was something most of them could not understand. Anything that was hierarchical was essentially in the realm of the supernatural like the village god and the rajah of Tehri (embodied form of Badrinath). Thus, to them democracy appears as hierarchy rather than equality, a curtailment rather than freedom of choice. The *sarkar* is thus an external entity, visible only in the form of the *sarkari babu*s (government representatives), whose presence in their village is rare and far between. The so-called elected representatives are nothing more than go-betweens with this ephemeral and just-to-be-tolerated *sarkar*. There is no sense of leadership as it is known in other parts of the country. In this way, the movement for a separate state, the most recent and effective political movement of which they were a part, was not something that happened under anyone's guidance but a spontaneous movement of the people of the *pahar* against those of the plains. The word heard most in the context of the movement in these areas is the collective, *hum* (we), rather than the name of any particular leader.

The relative lack of gender hierarchy is also reflected in the Jad tendency to place women at front, when they refer to the collective, as against the brotherhood of men implied in most other places in north India, one point where they mark their difference from the 'others'.

The local panchayat heads are dismissed as essentially some people who are required by the outside system and have no role in the local social set-up. No form of deference or any kind of importance is attached to the present or former panchayat heads. A special problematic is the acceptance of men as village leaders. Gender remains a key issue that prevents them from accepting the external forms of governance that is totally mismatched with their concept of appropriate gender roles; it is women and not men who should be in charge of village affairs!

The democratic process here is thus something that is outside of the local cognitive space. The Jads are having a taste of their preliminary exposure to state and to democracy imposed from outside, and the external democracy is actually antithetical to some of the core democratic values of their society. They are yet to even decide what identity they want for themselves, as the most coveted identity of being an upper-caste Hindu Rajput is at variance with their perceived advantageous identity of being a tribe. But being a tribe has no sense of value for them for, unlike the larger tribes such as those of the northeast or central India, they are a small population enclosed by upper-caste *pahari* Hindus. They share a politically charged *pahari* identity with all Garhwalis that makes more emotional appeal to them as it is part of their experienced world of discrimination. Most of them have felt and still feel alienated from the world below their mountains that appears to them as wild and dangerous (Channa 2010a). There is thus little desire in them to break away from the identity of being Garhwali and Rajput and to establish a proud tribal identity (Arora 2007; Xaxa 1999). An alternative identity to being Hindu and Garhwali is to reinvent the Tibetan and Buddhist connection. Some young people who realise that they are not likely to be accepted as upper-caste Hindus, especially with respect to the world below the mountains, are turning to the Buddhist identity as a way to establish respectability and status. Around 2000–2001, many young women had expressed a desire to become nuns, and by 2013, a visit to the field showed that many of them had indeed done so.

Thus, alternative trends are appearing as one generation had shown the desire to shed the Tibetan identity and become 'Hindus', the next generation is again going back towards the Buddhist connection. The Jads would visualise their own selves as simultaneously Hindu, Rajput, *janjati*, pastoral, and Buddhist. They would also view as different from themselves all who practise agriculture, who live in cities, who are of a different social domain, and so on. Flux rather than any stability seems the order of the day, and conclusive statements would not be realistic to make. The term 'identities', rather than 'identity', better describes the on-going social and political processes.

To draw together all the threads, it is probably pertinent at this point to comment that 'democracy', as imposed by the state, follows a monolithic pattern that refuses to acknowledge differences of cognition and life ways of marginal people such as the ones described. Here, for example, a key difference is that of gender relations. The democratic process will continue to encourage invention of identities where none existed, reinvent and transform, re-create and disturb existing ones (e.g. create hierarchies where none existed), and remain overall and universally problematic, but perhaps necessary. The nation-state as an invention works with invented identities, and in the process of participation in the democratic process, some tend to become real or tend towards self-acceptance, like the Jad Bhotiya. The forces of internal contradictions continue to pull back such assertions, while self-interest and political and economic gains may push forward for acceptance. Various people, even within the group, find themselves on different platforms and all arenas to be dynamic, contested, and reworked over and over. Such is democracy.

Notes

1. The term 'Uttaranchal' refers only to the northern part of the region, and not to the state of Uttarakhand, which was not in existence in 1994.
2. The data presented here was collected by anthropological fieldwork techniques that involved staying in or near the village for about two months at a time and carrying out observations and interviews as well as collection of genealogies. The fieldwork was made possible by a grant from the University Grants Commission. I was helped by my field assistants, Ms Anamika Verma and Mr Bhaskar Singh, and I thank them both.
3. Details of such trade and their political implications can be found in Brown (1990, 1994) and Cammen (1951).
4. The Jads are bilingual: they speak their own language within their community but can communicate in fluent Hindi with outsiders.
5. During a recent visit to Kinnaur, I found that the sharing of pastures has been discontinued because of the political division between the two states of Uttaranchal and Himachal Pradesh. In some way, this may also be seen as an effect of democracy when people began to identify themselves with their local states and preferred to forget historical associations.
6. Me-Parang is the village god who is given offerings at any time. In addition, he is taken in a ritual procession to Gangotri on the occasion of Janmashtami. Also, he appears at any other divination ritual such as Panoh (see Channa 2005, 2010b).
7. The state of Uttaranchal was formed as a separate entity form Uttar Pradesh in 2000 after a prolonged struggle by the people of this area, largely propelled by, among other reasons, the negative image of the *paharis* prevalent in the plains and the view of the plains people as exploitative by those in the hills.
8. In 1997, when I took the first demographic survey of the village, I found that the older generation had on an average only one or two children, although some, like Kaushlya, my friend, had had seven children, out of whom only four survived. There were many instances of only one or two or no surviving children. However, in 2000, when on a revisit, I was told that there has been a baby boom; there were about eleven babies in the village, a record for them.
9. About the Thakali, Fisher writes, 'So many divisions exist, in fact, that it is apparent that what often looked like a coherent upwardly mobile group and was interpreted as such by many outside observers was, in many ways, a heterogeneous population' (2001: 35).
10. All the gods (*devta*) here have their designated medium into who they descend for ritual purposes. Such mediums are fixed and lifelong (see Channa 2005).

11 The Jads say, for safety, a village should be located in a *gurgur* (a depression). For them, it actually means that the village is situated about 18.3 m below the road level, completely hidden from the main road towards Gangotri by trees and surrounded by mountainsides and also separated from the small town of Harsil by deep gorges and flowing streams. Unless specifically guided there, no one can chance upon this village easily.

12 Dr Ambedkar Rural Development Department (Dr Ambedkar Gram Vikas Vibhag) was established on 12 August 1995 for effective implementation of Dr Ambedkar Gram Vikas Yojana. The department has one section with twenty-six posts and a cell with twenty-nine posts. These posts were created vide Government Order No. 01/66-95-48/95 dated 19 September 1995. The Yojana was initially launched by the Government of Uttar Pradesh on 2 January 1991.

13 The state of Uttarakhand is divided into Garhwal and Kumaon divisions. Garhwal comprises the districts of Chamoli, Pauri, Tehri, and Uttarkashi. Kumaon was annexed by the British during the colonial period, but Garhwal remained independent under the king. It is interesting that the Jads do not identify with the Bhotiya tribes of Kumaon, possibly because it is not the territory of their king.

14 The concept of Bolanda Badri is strictly confined to the *pahar*. The Hindus of the plains believe in the shrine of Badrinath and worship him only in his iconic form. The concept of living gods or god in the human form is ridiculed by the plains' Hindus.

15 Sax writes, 'I wish to focus on the fact that these deities all figure as divine kings, with sovereign rights over their respective territories and subjects' (2002: 172).

16 The Thakalis, who, like the Jads, were engaged in salt trade, and after the cessation of this trade, 'purposefully and unilaterally' moved towards Hinduisation (Fisher 2001: 6).

17 It must be noted that most of these names are borrowed from television serials or Hindi films, as they do not have much direct interaction with people from the plains. It is also likely that Garhwali Hindus might also be borrowing these names from the same sources.

18 Even the upper-caste Garhwalis are regarded as 'inferior' by the plains Hindus, who look down upon their drinking and meat-eating habits. At the same time, we can quote from Berreman that 'the high-caste mountain people also look down upon the plains people. They put forward better status of women and a less rigid caste system as evidence of their own superiority' (1983: 252).

References

Allen, N. J. 1997. 'Hinduization: The Experience of the Thulung Rai', in D. Gellner, J. Pfaff-Czarnecka and J. Whelpton (eds.), *Nationalism and Ethnicity in a Hindu Kingdom: The Politics of Culture in Contemporary Nepal*, pp. 303–25. Amsterdam: Harwood Academic Publishers.

Angus, I. 1997. *A Border within: National Identity, Cultural Plurality, and Wilderness*. McGill: Queen's University Press.

Arora, V. 2007. 'Assertive Identities, Indigeneity, and the Politics of Recognition as a Tribe: The Bhutias, the Lepchas and the Limbus of Sikkim', *Sociological Bulletin*, 56 (2): 195–220.
Atkinson, E. F. T. 1980. *Kumaun Hills: Its History, Geography and Anthropology with Reference to Garhwal and Nepal*. New Delhi: Cosmo Publications.
Bagchi, G. 1977. 'Miscellaneous Notes: Some Socio-economic Aspects of Stratification of East Himalayan Society', *Man*, 57 (4): 363–67.
Barth, F. 1969. *Ethnic Groups and Boundaries: The Social Organization of Cultural Difference*. Oslo: Universitetsforlaget.
Berreman, G. 1972. *Hindus of the Himalayas*. Berkeley, CA: University of California Press.
———. 1983. 'The U. P. Himalayas: Culture, Cultures and Regionalism', in O. P. Singh (ed.), *The Himalaya: Nature, Man and Culture*, pp. 227–66. New Delhi: Rajesh Publications.
Bisht, B. S. 1994. *Tribes of India, Nepal, Tibet Borderland: A Study of Cultural Transformation*. New Delhi: Gyan Publications.
Brown, C. W. 1987. 'Ecology, Trade and Former Bhotiya Identity', in M. K. Raha (ed.), *The Himalayan Heritage*, pp. 125–38. New Delhi: Gyan Publishing House.
———. 1990. 'What We Call "Bhotiyas" Are in Reality Not Bhotiyas', in M. P. Joshi, Allen C. Forger and Charles W. Brown (eds.), *Himalaya: Past and Present* (Vol. II), pp. 147–72. Almora: Shree Almora Book Depot.
———. 1994. 'Salt, Barley, Pashmina and Tincal: Contexts of Being Bhotiya in Traiil's Kumaon', in M. P. Joshi, Allen C. Forger and Charles W. Brown (eds.), *Himalaya: Past and Present* (Vol. II), pp. 218–37. Almora: Shree Almora Book Depot.
Cammen, S. 1951. *Trade through the Himalayas: The Early British Attempts to Open Tibet*. Princeton, NJ: Princeton University Press.
Channa, S. M. 2002. 'The Life History of a Jad Woman', *European Bulletin of Himalayan Research*, 22 (1): 61–81.
———. 2005. 'The Descent of the Pandavas', *European Bulletin of Himalayan Research*, 28 (1): 67–97.
———. 2010a. 'The Wilderness of the Civilization', in M. Lecomte-Tilouine (ed.), *An Exploration of the Categories of Nature and Culture in Asia and the Himalayas*, pp. 222–43. New Delhi: Social Science Press.
———. 2010b. 'A Ritual Transfer: From the High to the Low in Hindu–Tibetan Himalayan Communities', in G. Dharampal-Frick, R. Langer and N. Holger (eds.), *Transfer and Spaces*, pp. 43–64. Wiesbaden: Harrassowitz.
———. 2010c. 'Cosmology, Gender and Kinship: Role and Relationships of Himalayan Pastoral Women', *Nivedini: Journal of Gender Studies*, 16: 1–25.
———. 2013. *The Inner and Outer Selves: Cosmology, Gender, and Ecology at the Himalayan Borders*. New Delhi: Oxford University Press.
Dalton, E. 1872. *Descriptive Ethnology of Bengal*. Calcutta: Office Superintendent of Government.

Das, V. and D. Poole. 2004. 'State and Its Margins: Comparative Ethnographies', in V. Das and D. Poole (eds.), *Anthropology in the Margins of the State*, pp. 3–33. New Delhi: Oxford University Press.

Eliade, M. 1978. *A History of Religious Ideas: Vol. 1 – From the Stone Age to the Eleusian Mysteries* (translated by W. R. Task). Chicago: The University of Chicago Press.

Escobar, A. 2008. *Territories of Difference: Place, Movement, Life, Redes.* Durham and London: Duke University Press.

Evans-Pritchard, E. E. 1940. *The Nuer: A Description of the Modes of Livelihood and Political Institutions of a Nilotic People.* Oxford: Clarendon Press.

Fisher, W. F. 2001. *Fluid Boundaries: Forming and Transforming Identity in Nepal.* New York: Columbia University Press.

Francis, W. 1908. *Madras District Gazetteers: The Nilgiris.* Madras: Government Press.

Galey, J. C. 1994. 'Hindu Kingship in Its Ritual Realm: The Garhwali Configuration', in M. S. Joshi, Allen C. Forger and Charles W. Brown (eds.), *The Himalayas: Past and Present* (Vol. II), pp. 173–237. Almora: Shree Almora Book Depot.

Guha, S. 1999. *Environment and Ethnicity in India, 1200–1991.* Cambridge: Cambridge University Press.

Hutchinson, R. H. S. 1909. *Eastern Bengal and Assam District Gazetteer, Chittagong Hill Tracts.* Allahabad: Pioneer Press.

Joshi, M. P. and C. W. Brown. 1986. 'Some Dynamics of Indo-Tibet Trade through Kumaon Garhwal', in L. P. Vidyarthi and M. Jha (eds.), *Ecology, Economy and Religion of the Himalayas*, pp. 59–71. New Delhi: Orient Publications.

Levine, N. E. 1987. 'Caste, State and Ethnic Boundaries in Nepal', *The Journal of Asian Studies*, 46 (1): 71–88.

MacCormack, C. P. 1980. 'Nature, Culture and Gender: A Critique', in C. P. MacCormack and M. Strathern (eds.), *Nature, Culture, Gender*, pp. 1–25. Cambridge: Cambridge University Press.

Mazumdar, L. 1998. *Sacred Confluence, Worship, History and the Politics of Change in a Himalayan Village.* Unpublished PhD Thesis, University of Pittsburgh, Pennsylvania.

Ortner, S. 1974. 'Is Female to Male as Nature Is to Culture', in M. Z. Rosaldo and L. Lamphere (eds.), *Woman, Culture and Society*, pp. 67–88. Stanford: Stanford University Press.

Ramble, C. 1997. 'Tibetan Pride of Place: Or, Why Nepal's Bhotiyas Are Not an Ethnic Group', in D. Gellner, J. Pfaff-Czarnecka and J. Whelpton (eds.), *Nationalism and Ethnicity in a Hindu Kingdom: The Politics of Culture in Contemporary Nepal*, pp. 379–415. Amsterdam: Harwood Academic Publishers.

Rizvi, S. A. A. 1979. *Uttarkashi – Uttar Pradesh District Gazetteer.* Lucknow: Government of Uttar Pradesh.

Sax, W. 1991. *Mountain Goddess: Gender and Politics in a Himalayan Pilgrimage.* New York: Oxford University Press.

——. 2000. 'Residence and Ritual in the Garhwal Himalayas', in M. P. Joshi (ed.), *Himalaya: Past and Present, 1993–94*, pp. 79–114. Almora: Shree Almora Book Depot.

——. 2002. *Dancing the Self: Personhood and Performance in the Pandava Lila of Garhwal*. London: Oxford University Press.

Silverstein, P. A. 2002. 'The Kabyle Myth: Colonization and the Production of Ethnicity', in B. K. Axel (ed.), *From the Margins: Historical Anthropology and Its Future*, pp. 122–55. Durham: Duke University Press.

Smith, A. D. 1986. *The Ethnic Origins of Nations*. Oxford: Basil Blackwell.

von Fürer-Haimendorf, C. 1975. *Himalayan Traders: Life in Highland Nepal*. London: John Murray.

——. 1978. 'Preface', in J. F. Fisher (ed.), *Himalayan Anthropology*, pp. ix–xvi. The Hague: Mouton.

——. 1981. 'Introduction', in C. von Fürer-Haimendorf (ed.), *Asian Highland Societies in Anthropological Perspective*, pp. ix–xvi. New Delhi: Sterling.

Xaxa, V. 1999. 'Tribes as Indigenous People of India', *Economic and Political Weekly*, 34 (51): 3589–96.

2 The politics of census

Fear of numbers and competing claims for representation in Naga society[1]

Debojyoti Das

> *There has always been a close association between enumeration, the classification of people and state power.*
> Per Axelsson *et al.* (2011: 295)

Defining ethnic boundaries for official purposes is an inherently political task but one deemed necessary in many multi-ethnic states like India. The definition of indigenous identity – 'sons of the soil' – for official purpose is especially contentious in North-East India, given the intrinsic link between indigeneity (Arora 2007; Li 2000), politics of belonging (Middleton 2013), claims to territory, and self-determination, which are fostering the politics of ethno-nationalism (Lotha 2009). Although indigenous rights may be enshrined constitutionally or by treaty, the matter of who qualifies as indigenous for state recognition and reward is largely determined by bureaucratic rules and classifications. Official demographic sources, and the national census, in particular, are important forums where indigenous identities are constructed and circumscribed. As the flagship of enumeration, the census register is an influential site of inclusion and exclusion where the state selectively acknowledges collective identities within its borders. For this reason, among others, the census is deeply implicated in the nation's social and political order (Hoschild and Powell 2008). To understand how official enumeration practice reflects and constitutes indigenous identity, this chapter discusses the controversy surrounding the 2001 Census operation in Nagaland[2] that registered the highest decennial growth rate in the country and triggered an ethnic anarchy among the seventeen tribes officially recognised by the government's census operation. In this regard, I discuss how census enumeration is related to electoral representation in the State Legislative Assembly, the flow of developmental grants from the centre, and the inclusion of the most 'backward' tribes through policies of affirmative action-positive discrimination 'reservation' in government jobs.

Ideas of electoral democracy and political representation are indeed new to the Nagas. They were for centuries and until recently isolated in 'village republics' where both democratic and authoritarian descent groups functioned as robust political systems. For example, between the Konyak and Chang Nagas of eastern Nagaland, the *Angs* or village chiefs played the most important role as political and social heads of their clan and lineage. Conversely, the Tynemia Nagas (Angami, Chekeshang, and Phoms) have democratic dissent and village-level elected bodies. This is charted in the colonial ethnographic monographs and treaties produced by British administrators and anthropologists such as T. C. Hodson (1911), J. H. Hutton (1921a, b), J. P. Mills (1922, 1926), and Christopher von Fürer-Haimendorf (1969). The British government came into contact with the Nagas during the late 18th and 19th centuries when colonial tea gardens and mining leases came into conflict with the Naga land-use in the foothills. By 1880, the Naga Hills was annexed and made part of the Assam province as frontier tracts. The extension of colonial administration brought in technologies of surveillance that belittled the Naga people as 'noble savage' inhabiting the north-eastern Himalayas. Census enumeration was used as a grand design to establish the colonial gaze over its colonised people. In fact, Bernard Cohn (1966) has argued that the colonial census operations in British India were a crucial cultural technology of imperial rule. This is also true of the census being conducted in post-independent India, and Nagaland in particular.

Nagaland is a frontier state located in the north-eastern part of India, tucked between Assam and Myanmar and sharing political boundaries with Arunachal Pradesh and Manipur. The state is divided into eleven districts with a population of 1,980,602 (according to the 2011 Census) spread over 16,000 sq. km. Outside Nagaland, Naga tribes are scattered in parts of Assam, Manipur, and Arunachal Pradesh within India, and they also reside in neighbouring Myanmar. However, this chapter is concerned only with the Naga sub-tribes that are living within the contemporary state of Nagaland in India. The Nagas show their solidarity through ethno-nationalism based on their cultural and racial uniqueness from mainland India and an assertion of difference from their tribal and other ethnic neighbours. Nonetheless, the Nagas are internally divided by plural linguistic and sub-tribal identities. Nagamis is the creole language used by all the sub-tribes. Thus, they do not share a common language; this is quite unlike some of the Kuki tribes who have recently joined the Naga fold due to political reasons (Arora and Kipgen 2012).

Politically, the relation of the Nagas with the Indian state has been a troubled one. The Naga people led by their leader A. Z. Phizo began an armed struggle post-1947, as they failed to get independence with the end of British rule in India. The Naga People's Convention and the Government of India signed a sixteen-point peace agreement in July 1960. In December 1963, a new state was curved out of Assam and was named Nagaland. However, all these attempts did not lead to peace in Nagaland. Rather, it gave rise to insurgency and armed struggle for decades. In 1996, the Nationalist Socialist Council of Nagaland (Isak Muivah) (NSCN [IM]) faction agreed to a ceasefire agreement with the Government of India. This ceasefire is renewed annually. However, factional clashes, extortion, revenge killings, and inter-ethnic struggles continue to baffle the state till this day.

The electoral politics of mainland India made inroads into Nagaland in the early 1970s, as the newly created state had been kept under representation through a process of selection carried out by tribal elders in the Naga society. It is only in the early 1970s that full-fledged election was conducted for the Legislative Assembly in Tuensang and Mon, which are perceived as backward border districts of contemporary Nagaland.

* * *

In this chapter, first I examine the census as a project of objectification that is refashioned by the Naga sub-tribes to claim their share in development programmes and their representation in the electoral politics of the state following the 2001 Census. Second, I reflect on the contested claims provoked by census results that make the state 'legible' in everyday lives of Naga people. For readers unfamiliar with the political organisation of Nagas, I will explain the meaning of tribe and sub-tribe in this context. This will enable us to fully understand the importance of administrative recognition and of census to any recognition of tribal status, as has been elaborated elsewhere by Arora (2007) and Arora and Kipgen (2012). Under the census enumeration of the Government of India, there are seventeen recognised Naga sub-tribes. However, there are as many as thirty-six Naga sub-tribes living in India and Myanmar who claim to be part of the 'Nagalim', the united Naga homeland (Lotha 2007; Yonou 1974). Many of these sub-tribes who inhabit eastern Nagaland (namely Konyak, Phom, Sangtham, Yimchunger, Chang, Chekasang, Pichori, and Khiamungans) have been recognised as backward tribes in Nagaland, with reservations in government jobs and public services. Their backwardness is legitimised by a discourse of the late incorporation of eastern Nagas and of Tuensang districts in Nagaland State in 1963. Before 1961, the Tuensang district was part of North-East Frontier Agency, and in the colonial period, it was part of the un-administered area – blank space of the British Empire in Assam (von Fürer-Haimendorf 1938). The recognition of 'backward categories' within the State Legislative Assembly in the late 1990s as a measure of positive discrimination to uplift the underrepresented Naga tribes through reservation in public service and government education institutions has intensified new political rhetoric by the sub-tribes, who are territorialised by their ethnic boundaries and categories, 'developed as opposed to the less developed Naga tribes'. This explains the political context of my discussion.

The 2001 Census projected a 64.41 per cent population growth rate for Nagaland, which is the highest decadal population growth rate for any state of India.[3] This constitutes an alarming moment in the demographic history of the Nagas. The census statistics soon created an atmosphere of animosity between the seventeen major recognised sub-tribes of Nagaland who started debating the authenticity of census operation and its ambiguities. Civil society organisations from these sub-tribes lodged petitions, held rallies, and filed cases in the Guwahati High Court and the Supreme Court challenging the enumeration results and pleaded for an immediate halt to the government's Delimitation of Constituency Bill based on the census results. Pitched within the census politics were the electoral gain and loss and the development benefits that Naga civil society organisations felt were compromised through enumeration results. Some newly recognised sub-tribes were clearly to gain out of the enumeration results. The risk of underrepresentation meant exclusion from the state's development programmes while it gave political gains to others who were overrepresented. The recognition of backward categories, new sub-tribe status, and delimitation of new political boundaries (districts) and subdivisions within the existing districts have been critiqued as strategies for political appeasement of newly recognised sub-tribes by the ruling political parties in the past decade. This has brought in competition between sub-tribes and assertion of sub-tribal identities.

Until the mid-1970s, the people inhabiting Nagaland and living in eastern Nagaland, in particular, knew very little about elections, as the government continued the policy of representation based on selection and military power. This practice of selection of representatives was implemented for an interim period of ten years during which it was expected that the recently incorporated eastern Naga tribes would learn the values and imbibe the practices of democracy. Kiphire, Longleng, and Peren districts had remained outside the remit of colonial administration till 1947 as un-administered tribal areas of the India–Burma frontier; hence, they also remained outside the preview of the Indian Penal System and state legislation. During 1947–63, the administrative arrangement in these frontier areas witnessed several twist and turns with the creation of Tuensang Frontier Division (1947–57) and later Naga Hills Tuensang Area (1958–63) till 1963 to form the contemporary state of Nagaland. Post-1963, the government of Nagaland has followed a policy of 'interim period' in which the recently included 'frontier Naga territories' were kept outside of electoral politics. An interim period of ten years was decided upon before initiating direct elections in these areas. The general process was based on representation through selection in the Nagaland State Assembly. Hence, the Regional Council Members and Area Council Members were constituted under the Nagaland, Tribal, Area, Range, and Village Council Act 1966, in order to represent the various tribes and their areas of dominance (Angami 2008). This practice was abandoned after new legislations were passed in the late 1970s.[4]

What has changed in the past two decades of ceasefire that has made the Naga people so committed to electoral politics and state-building project pushed by the Government of India aimed at 'nationalisation and territorialisation of Nagaland'? This question allows us to understand how the Indian state apparatus has made its presence felt among the 'rebellious Nagas'.[5] The affirmative action policies of the Government of India for tribal welfare have made the state 'legible', to use J. C. Scott's (1998) term. James Scott refers to stateless pre-colonial highland societies in South and Southeast Asia as *zomia*. The post-colonial period has seen a reversal of this process as state apparatus such as the census, election, democratic representation, and reservation as positive discrimination policies guaranteed by the constitution has made the Indian state legible in people's everyday lives in the Naga Hills. This is evident in people's routine struggle for political representation and demand for share in state-directed development work whereby the state has increasingly been legitimised in North-East India (Arora 2013).

The 2011 Census results for Nagaland have caused an upheaval, as is evident in this news story circulated by the local daily *Nagaland Post*:

> Central census observer from Government of Nagaland, in-charge of Phek district, Norman Putsure IAS [Indian Administrative Service], visited and interacted with census charge officers, master trainers, supervisors and enumerators of Phek sadar, Khuza circle and Phek town on February 18, 2011. Later on the same day, he also visited Chizami and Pfutsero and held meeting with charge officers and other census functionaries. As part of his inspection tour, he also visited Meluri on February 17. On his visit, he called on census functionaries to be sincere and diligent in the mammoth census operation and to bring out a correct census report. He crosschecked on the works of the enumerators and hinted that he would be visiting places where census figures were inflated, stating that census enumeration should be differentiated from that of electoral enumeration. Deputy Commissioner Phek, Mikha Lomi and charge officer of Khuza circle SDO (C) [Sub Division Officer (Civil)], Razhouvolie Dozo also met census

enumerators and other village functionaries of Chepoketa, Khuza and Mutsale and had interaction.

Mon: Deputy Commissioner Mon, Dinesh Kumar IAS inspected Tizit and Naginimora circle on February 16 to verify the on-going census operation and conducted a meeting with enumerators and supervisors at Tizit, stressing on the importance of accurate and genuine data. He visited few households in Tizit town and Lapa Lampong for on-spot verification of already filled-in schedules while a team comprising of EAC [Extra Assistant Commissioner of a Circle] Tizit, EAC Mon and census nodal officer was sent to Neitong village and Yanpan village for spot verification. At Naginimora, after conducting a meeting with enumerators and supervisors, the DC also visited households in Hotahoti village to cross check census schedules. It was reported that few errors were detected in both the circles, for which, enumerators were directed to take corrective measures. DC meanwhile stated census operation was going on in full swing in the district and also appreciated the quality of work of the enumerators, supervisors and in charge officers. Jalukie: In Jalukie, a meeting of 2nd phase census, community monitors, village council and GBs [*Gauh Burha* or village headman] and enumerators was held at civil SDO office Jalukie.

(2011)

This news report demonstrates the critical role that the 2011 Census operations would play by the accurate enumeration of Naga tribal groups, which will have a significant bearing on the representation of different tribes in the State Legislative Assembly and in the distribution of development funds. The census observers were concerned about the mistakes that had been made during the 2001 Census and were trying to ensure that false or proxy enumerations would not recur in 2011, as it could potentially disrupt inter-tribal relations.

My informants shared how inter-tribal politics has increased factionalism and divisiveness within the Naga sub-tribes. The first general election to the State Legislative Assembly including Tuensang and Mon districts took place in 1976. Ever since, there has been a general rise in people's participation in electoral politics, which has shown phenomenal growth in the past decade with the rise of the Naga People's Front (NPF) and the Democratic Alliance of Nagaland (DAN) government headed by the charismatic Angami chief minister Neiphiu Rio (Rio 2012). During my fieldwork in 2008–9, one of my interviewees, who was the son of a former Member of the Legislative Assembly (MLA), recollected that during the 1970s when election was first introduced in these frontier districts (Tuensang and Mon), people had no idea of the power of secret ballot and of their votes. Elections carried very little meaning for these villagers as they were deeply committed to the age-old Naga practice of selection of their tribal elders.

The Government of Nagaland, while incorporating the eastern Nagas within the general electoral polity, introduced special reservations for these tribes as 'backward tribes' living in 'deprived frontier areas'. Policies aimed at establishing the 'backward status' of the Tuensang and the Mon people were legitimised by the Nagaland State Legislative Assembly in 1997 when it passed bills for the development of these 'backward areas' through the creation of the Backward Area Development Fund. After the 1997 legislation, 30 per cent of all government seats were reserved for the eight major sub-tribes of eastern Nagaland that included Kahimungen, Chang, Konyak, Yimchunger, Phom, Sangtham, Pichori, and Chekasang Nagas. Jobs in public institutions, civil services, and higher education institutions were reserved for the socio-economic uplifting of the historically marginalised and isolated Naga sub-tribes.[6] It must be noted here that marginality of these tribes has been defined by their 'administrative' and 'geographical' isolation from mainland India and the colonial-administered part of the Naga Hills inhabited by the Ao, Angami, Sema, and Lotha Nagas.[7]

Emergence of 'forward' and 'backward' Nagas

After 1997, the Nagas of Nagaland were categorised into backward and forward categories within the remit of the colonial 'excluded' and the present-day 'Schedule Areas'. During many interactions with my informants at Dimapur, Kohima, and Mokokchung (the most prosperous and developed parts of Nagaland), I gathered how they perceived the Mon and Tuensang groups as 'others', who were often described as being the 'wildest' and most 'aboriginal' of all the Naga tribes. The informants cited how these eastern tribes continued to observe 'authentic' Naga rituals, followed shamanic practices like animal sacrifice, and were unwilling to change, and therefore were relatively backward. Many learned Nagas and city dwellers cited that the Konyak Nagas are rigid and traditional and continued with the practice of *Angship* (village chief). The general perception of the urban people was reinforced by cultural events such as the 'Hornbill Festivals' that are now celebrated annually in December to showcase 'Naga culture, dance forms, and their way of life' to national and international tourists. Photographs of Naga men and women belonging to eastern Nagaland dancing wearing the traditional ceremonial dress show how the state objectifies the Nagas as 'timeless primitives' and, more so, the eastern Nagas with their 'authentic traditions'. However, a visit to Konyak village did change my own perception of *Angship* for good. The *Angs* (Konyak chief) these days feature in billboards of the Health Department, to popularise the government campaign promoting polio vaccination campaign for infants. In one instance, I discovered the *Ang* being photographed sitting on his couch in the centre and flanked by two village guards (Village Guard Silver Jubilee Souvenir 2008). These popular images indicate how the symbolic power of *Angship* has been appropriated by the state in order to promote its rural development programmes and to celebrate the presence of Village Guards who were established as a counter-insurgency police force in these frontier areas.

In real life, these days, the *Angs* act as rubber stamps and have no executive powers except being symbolic heads of their clan and villages in Konyak Naga villages. The real influence is exercised by MLAs, the *Dobashis*[8] who still act as mediators in settling disputes and as interpreters of the customary law. Electoral politics has grown stronger over the past few decades, with the regional and national parties vying with each other for the support of the people and the people actively voting and electing their representatives. The Congress (I), led by S. C. Jamir, the former chief minister of Nagaland, was the main contender in the past decades. The NPF-led DAN government has been in power since 2003, challenging the Congress (I). Both these political parties have used the ethnic divide for their electoral gains and contributed to the hardening of the division between the forward and backward Nagas by creation of special development funds at the district and subdivision levels.

The process of fake enumeration got reflected in the 1991 Census when the Nagaland State population recorded a spectacular decennial growth rate of 56.08 per cent. In a 2005 interview conducted by Sanjoy Hazarika of Jamia Millia Islamia, New Delhi, the chief minister of Nagaland, Neiphiu Rio, drew attention to the competitive inflation of population figures in 2001 due to the threat posed by the impending delimitation of state assembly constituencies. He argued that the hill districts dominated by Naga tribes feared a loss of five seats to Dimapur – the only plains district and the industrial and transport hub of Nagaland – and the subsequent losses in development grants made available through the Village Development Board (VDB) and village council in rural Nagaland (see Agarwal and Kumar 2012).

The 2001 Census enumeration caught nationwide attention, as Nagaland surpassed all other states with the highest decadal growth rate (64.14 per cent), as compared to the national average of 17.64 per cent. Demographers analysed the relevant demographic indicators but failed to explain why the state accounted for such a phenomenal rise in its population. Within Nagaland, people were alarmed at this spectacular growth rate. The representatives of the seventeen major sub-tribes challenged the 2001 Census results when the Delimitation of Constituency Bill was placed in Parliament in

2002. They claimed that some sub-tribes had manipulated their numbers in order to gain better representation in the State Legislative Assembly and legitimise claims for development grants. They, therefore, demanded fresh enumeration to ascertain the actual population of each group. The enumerators and the Census office maintained that it had been a free and fair census; the various civil society organisations representing the Naga sub-tribes, the Naga *Hoho* (Naga sub-tribal elders civil society groups), and others like the Chakhesang People's Organisation (CPO) saw it as a conspiracy by the newly recognised sub-tribes to fortify their numbers for electoral gains and to get a better share in the state development schemes.[9] Nagaland is a state inhabited by seventeen recognised Naga sub-tribes. Therefore, the possibility of ethnic conflict looms large on the political scene as each tribe contests to establish its identity, fortify community solidarity, and protect its land and property from other tribes.[10]

During the period of ceasefire (1996–2014), the central government deliberately pushed an agenda of intensive development that aimed at winning the 'hearts and minds of the Naga people'. One of the strategies followed by the central government was to fight insurgency by funding development activities (Arora 2013; McDuie-Ra 2008). The distribution of development funds is evident in the annual reports published by the North East Council and the Ministry of Development of North Eastern Region. The government-sponsored rural development programmes and various development missions have created further possibilities of appropriation of resources. During my fieldwork at Yimchunger Naga villages in 2008–9, the outreach of the Mahatma Gandhi National Rural Employment Guarantee Scheme was reflected in the number of village and agriculture-link roads that were built all over the Tuensang district. Simultaneously, the growth of electoral democracy has created forms of patron–client relations in the villages. The roots of such patronage can be traced back to the early 1970s when elections were first held in Nagaland.

Village councils and village development boards

In the early 1970s, the traditional practice of representation through selection of tribal elders among the Naga was replaced by popular representation through 'one-person one-vote'. Elections were presented as an integral part of democracy and a progressive form of governance. The villages formed the core of Naga politico-administrative structure, and the village heads were given special powers. The powers of the village council were reconstituted under the Village Council Acts, 1978, 1979, and Village Council Model Rule 1980s (Angami 2008). The 'village councils' were recognised as the main administrative authority in the Naga villages in line with the

Panchayati Raj System in non-Sixth Schedule states. In the 1980s, the village councils were reorganised and the VDB was incorporated for financial decentralisation and empowerment of Naga villages for rural development. Over the past three decades, VDBs have become the symbol of village governance in Nagaland. They are responsible for implementing legislations passed by the State Legislative Assembly and are responsible for the welfare and developmental activities of the village. It is through VDB and the village council that all development programmes are implemented in the village; they are the actual administrative and financial nodes that link the village with the state government. These initiatives of decentralised governance and development projects have brought the Naga people closer to the government and its apparatuses, Census being one of them.

During my fieldwork in Mon and Tuensang (2008–09), I documented the villagers' articulation of their backwardness. In one Yimchunger Naga village, a village guard explained to me how, historically, the Yimchunger tribe had been 'independent' Nagas who had never paid any tax to the state government. It is only after 1947 that they were merged with the state of Nagaland and brought under the Indian administration. This narrative of 'resistance to the state' and of being peripheral is often used to press claims or make the community eligible for development grants. He further added that the government should now allocate more for the development of the eastern Naga communities and make up for their earlier neglect. These remarks signal the agency of the individuals and how they have internalised the idea of 'backwardness' presented by the state through its schemes and programmes. The creation of reserve categories has generated a new consciousness of 'other/backward Nagas' based on economic and social marginalisation, which I shall return to later in the chapter.

Since the 1970s, successive elected governments have allocated for the people of Mon and Tuensang districts a special package in the form of Backward Area Development Fund. Similarly, during this period, the government also initiated crop subsidies for swidden cultivators in Mon and Tuensang under the Intensive Wet Terrace Rice Cultivation Programme. These projects established political patronage of the villagers, who slowly realised the gains and took part in these government-sponsored programmes. This led to the creation of the Department for Underdeveloped Areas in 2003–04, which was responsible for allocation of financial resources to Mon and Tuensang districts. These initiatives have also been complemented with administrative changes such as creation of three new districts, namely Longleng, Kiphire, and Paren. Two of these districts (Kiphire and Paren) have resulted from the division of the Tuensang district. Hence, many policies and projects that aimed at uplifting and integrating the backward areas have resulted in shaping new Naga identities. These are reflected in the growing consciousness of distinctive identity and struggles based on sub-tribal status and contestations over census enumeration. I will highlight the Yimchunger–Tikhir sub-tribal identity and the crisis following the row over the 2001 Census in Nagaland in the next section and discuss the role of the civil society and neo-tribal Naga elites in furthering ethnic divisions within the Naga community.

Village politics and the role of census

The census enumeration in 2001 showed that the natural growth rate of population, as reflected in the decadal growth rate, was skewed and many sub-tribes had overrepresented themselves in the hope that, by falsely inflating the household numbers, they would ensure increase in per capita central assistance through different development programmes implemented by VDB and the village council. The census operation was blamed by the Naga civil society and human rights activists for the irresponsible documentation of the population totals. However, census officials were not in a position to understand the complexity of the situation that led to massive proxy enumeration, which inflated the population figures of backward sub-tribes like Phoms and Pichori. The following is an account from my field visit to villages in Tuensang district in February 2009.

Tuensang village is located just on the fringe of Tuensang town and is one of the largest peri-urban centres in the district. It is divided into three *khels* (ward/colony). I visited the village with the principal of the Tuensang Government College. During our meeting with the villagers, my queries focused on the general levels of development, changing food habits of the people, and the economic activities in the village. The village council members and heads of households shared many interesting facts about their backwardness in poor medical, health, and educational attainments as compared to the more developed districts inhabited by Ao, Angami, Sema, Lotha, and Rengma Nagas in Dimapur, Kohima, and Mokokchung districts. They argued how the per capita state assistance to village settlements was more to small villages, which hence had prospered more than their village.

The college principal who accompanied me was an Ao Naga and hailed from Ungma village in Mokokchung district. He explained to me after the meeting that his village is also very large. However, it is well represented by three MLAs, who were influential in getting grants for their village. He explained that these MLAs looked after each ward and nobody had problems in being recognised as a beneficiary in different development programmes. Thus, his villagers never grumbled to outsiders like the Chang villagers did. At first, I could not comprehend his explanation. However, when I visited Ungma village in Mokokchung district, the levels of development it had attained were striking. Being an Ao village and the native place of S. C. Jamir, the former chief minister, majority of its inhabitants had government jobs, and those who did not have white-collar jobs were engaged in plantation farming and horticulture. Some were contractors in stone quarrying industry and had set up small-scale industries in Dimapur. In sharp contrast the Chang and Yimchunger villages of Tuensang district were predominantly dependent on slash and burn farming and had limited access to public sector jobs.

The depressing condition of the eastern Nagas can be gleaned from the Nagaland State Human Development Report – 2001 (2004). Among the then eight districts of Nagaland, Dimapur, with a Human Development Index value of 0.733, ranks the highest, whereas Mon, with a value of 0.450, ranks the lowest. With regard to the Gender-Related Development Index, Kohima ranks the highest, whereas Mon ranks the lowest. For the Human Poverty Index, while Mokochung has the lowest value, Mon has the highest. In fact, the districts of Mon and Tuensang are consistently respectively ranked eighth and seventh on all the three indices, highlighting the need for concerted strategies for the development of these districts. In relation to other parameters of human development, the eastern Nagas are far behind the advanced Naga tribes.

Many residents of Ungma village, like the college principal, have received good education, and some live as expatriates abroad[11] and others have made fortunes from tea plantations, cultivation of cash crops, and profitable quarrying of stones and chips for construction work. In contrast, people living in Tuensang village still depend on shifting cultivation, growing millets, and manual jobs. Their houses are built with thatched roofs, while other farmers who benefitted from assistance under the Indira Ahwas Yojana have received corrugated sheets for their roofs. To the marginalised Chang Naga villagers, the census enumeration has played a decisive role in defining their development aspirations.

The growing resentment about census results turned critical when the Constitution Delimitation Bill 2002 was placed before Parliament. Those Naga groups who felt that they would lose out their areas of influence started filing petitions in courts of law. I interviewed the president of CPO who was spearheading this campaign and had filed Public Interest Litigation in the Guwahati High Court to stop the use of 2001 Census data for the delimitation of constituencies in Nagaland. In his opinion, the Chakhesang tribe would politically suffer under the present seat-sharing arrangement in the state legislature. Other Naga tribes, who equally felt their rights of representation in the Legislative Assembly would be compromised, joined the Chakhesangs. The Naga tribes who were to gain from the census results started a countercampaign. They alleged in their petition to the government that they were being falsely accused of manipulating the census data. They maintained that the eastern Nagas had suffered alienation for a long time, and as they had been deprived of their legitimate right to representation in the Nagaland State Legislative Assembly, the government should seriously consider their plea. The census results shocked the Chakhesang community who would lose at least one seat if the government used the results of the 2001 Census to delimit constituencies. The Chakhesang had established their distinctive sub-tribal status by breaking away from the Angamis in 1947 and by merging three identities Chokri, Khezha, and Sangtham. The High Court gave some relief to the Chakhesang community by ruling in their favour.

Prior to the publication of the 2001 Census, in the 1980s, the eastern Nagas of Tuensang district had started a 'free land movement' for separate statehood. These eastern Nagas, who have now consolidated their voice through the Eastern Naga People's Organisation (ENPO), feel that they have been marginalised by their forward Naga brothers who had come into contact with the British and the missionaries much before them. Hence, they claimed they need more benefits and share of development grants than their advanced Naga brethren. In its pamphlets and public speeches, ENPO expressed their aspiration for a 'free land', endorsing the idea that they had historically been free and politically independent. Their movement did not become popular and died down in a couple of years, while their resentment continued to grow over time.

The decentralisation of financial powers and the reorganisation of the village council as the nodal village authority started with the Village Development Board Model Rule 1980s. This resulted in a new level of decentralised village politics, and this was further fostered in 2002 when the Nagaland State Legislative Assembly passed the Nagaland Commoditisation of Institutions and Essential Services Act. By this act villages were made directly responsible for managing their affairs in primary community health, elementary education, and electricity management. These laws, giving power to the community on the use of resources, have brought the people much closer to the state apparatus. Each village council is today responsible for managing health, electricity distribution, and primary health care in villages. Although the community control of essential services has not worked effectively in the Naga villages due to corruption and misappropriation of public resources, the process has heightened people's aspirations to improve them through social participation. Thus, the census headcount has become central to this process, with yearly developmental grants being decided by the size of the village population. The more the numbers, higher is the ratio of per capita central assistance primarily in the form of subsidies, loans, matching grant, housing schemes, and other benefits of economic empowerment.

Census statistics and basic facts

The enumeration errors of the 2001 Census have potentially created areas of serious conflict among the Nagas, and this is evident in the manner in which the civil society organisations have filed cases under Public Interest Litigation. When the first census was made available in 1901, the Nagas residing in the erstwhile Naga Hills district of Assam that had included the hills of Manipur State had a population of 100,000 persons. When the results of 2001 Census were published, their total population had risen to almost two million persons (see Tables 2.1 and 2.2). If we disaggregate the picture, we note how the decadal growth rate of individual sub-tribes has become the central point of debate and contestation in Nagaland. Some communities like the Phoms, Sangthams, and Pichori have registered 150 per cent growth in the past decade, which has raised serious debate about the credibility of the census among various civil society groups within Nagaland. The president of CPO observed that they are fighting this case unlike others as it has hit the very identity of the Chakhesang people and their representation in the electoral politics of the state.

Statistics presented in Tables 2.1 and 2.2 do not reflect the hidden ambiguities and controversies that are likely to emerge. A senior civil servant in the state secretariat told me during an interview in 2009 that the census

Table 2.1 Population of Nagaland, 1901–2001

Serial number	Year	Males	Females	Total
1	1901	51,473	50,077	101,550
2	1911	74,796	74,242	149,038
3	1921	79,738	79,063	158,801
4	1931	89,536	89,308	178,844
5	1941	93,831	95,810	189,641
6	1951	106,551	106,424	212,975
7	1961	191,027	178,173	369,200
8	1971	276,084	240,365	516,449
9	1981	415,910	359,020	774,930
10	1991	641,282	568,264	1,209,546
11	2001	1,041,686	946,950	1,988,636
12	2011	1,024,649	953,853	1,978,502

Source: Directorate of Economics and Statistics, Government of Nagaland, 2011.

Table 2.2 Projected population of Nagaland

District	2001	2002	2003	2004	2005	2006	2007	2008	2009	2010
Kohima	314,366	330,391	347,234	364,935	383,538	403,090	423,638	445,234	467,931	491,785
Dimapur	308,382	324,102	340,624	357,988	376,238	395,417	415,574	436,759	459,024	482,424
Phek	148,246	155,803	163,746	172,093	180,866	190,086	199,776	209,960	220,663	231,912
Mokokchung	227,230	238,814	250,988	263,782	277,229	291,361	306,214	321,824	338,230	355,472
Tuensang	414,801	435,946	458,170	481,526	506,073	531,871	55,984	587,480	617,428	648,902
Wokha	161,098	169,310	177,941	187,012	196,546	206,565	217,095	228,162	239,793	252,017
Zunheboto	154,909	162,806	171,105	179,828	188,995	198,629	208,755	219,397	230,581	242,335
Mon	259,604	272,838	286,746	301,364	316,727	332,872	349,841	367,675	386,418	40,6117
Total	1,988,636	2,090,010	2,196,554	2,308,528	2,426,212	2,549,891	2,176,877	2,816,491	2,960,068	3,110,964

Source: Directorate of Economics and Statistics, Government of Nagaland, 2011.

results have created nightmares for the planning department of the government, as the data is neither accurate nor reliable. This has virtually opened a Pandora's box raising serious questions about the factors that have resulted in inflated numbers.

While other officials tried to explain the massive growth rate due to the reduction in death rate and increase in birth rate because of better medical facilities, or even improved census coverage and also inclusion of migrants, they failed to convince anyone. To give an example of the abnormal growth rate in the population, an analysis of the 'Single Age Population Distribution' conducted on population growth shows that the number of persons born in 1991 (zero year) was 23,792, but in 2001 when they would have attained ten years of age, the figure shot up to 74,025 persons, which should have more or less remained the same barring minor corrections.

Likewise, the figures keep showing an abnormal increase in all specific age groups. In total, the number of children between zero and nine years in 1991 was 295,161 persons, and the number of this age group after ten years, in 2001, doubled to 549,323 persons. Where did the additional children come from? It is worth mentioning here that despite the influx of lakhs of illegal migrants over the past decades into Assam, which led to the massive anti-foreigners stir launched by the All Assam Students Union during the 1970s, the census of the state is still below the decadal growth of Nagaland for the particular period 1971–81. From 1971–81 to 1981–91 to 1991–2001, Nagaland achieved the dubious distinction of having the highest population growth ratio in the country. The dubious achievement has now landed Nagaland in a fix as it has serious ramifications for the next decade (*The Northeast Today*, 6 October 2009).

I will now discuss how local manipulations occur at the village level. During my fieldwork, many villagers reported how the census had exaggerated numbers since people did not share correct information with the census officials who came from Kohima and Dimapur. I found that the village heads who controlled the funds had given informal instructions to inflate the household numbers. During my fieldwork at a Yimchunger village, I also found that the village electoral roll statistics did not match with the census population data, pointing to the local manipulation of numbers.

The census debate and identity construction

The 'misleading' account of population growth for the 2001 Census is a good example of how and to what extent the census data can be manipulated. We need to relate this aspect to the identity claims advanced by those communities, which stand to benefit by inflating their numbers. This provides the context for my discussion on the 'politics of objectification' through census that has escalated identity contestations in Nagaland. Identity construction and claims to distinctiveness have fostered a politics of difference among the Nagas, and these are not specific to this context; for example, in neighbouring Manipur, some Kuki tribes have acquired a political identity as Nagas while culturally they belong to the Kuki category (see Arora and Kipgen 2012).

The ethnic turmoil witnessed in Nagaland is not an isolated phenomenon; it resonates with other ethnic struggles in the Greater Himalayan region – the Gorkhaland movement in the Darjeeling Hills, the Gaddi ethnic identity struggle, and the process of ethnic classification taking place in Nepal and the Himalayan state of Sikkim (see Arora 2007; Arora and Kipgen 2012; Guneratna 1998; Hanger 2001; Kapila 2008; Shneiderman and Middleton 2008). Nonetheless, the Naga ethnic struggle is distinctive on at least three counts. First, the emerging sub-tribal identity struggles are playing under a double bind of a struggle against the larger Indian state and the divided Nagas who are fighting for a separate nation 'Nagalim' (a united Nagaland) (Lotha 2009). Second, the ethno-genesis of Naga tribal identity as the 'savage other' has been validated and supported by colonial visual and textual ethnographic literature (von Fürer-Haimendorf 1938). The new consciousness for sub-tribal identities has been encouraged by the state government's protective discrimination policy, which has produced internal divisions among the Nagas as the forward and the backward Naga sub-tribes. Third, the provision for affirmative action is taking place within an already recognised 'scheduled tribe status'. Hence, reservation aims to create new categories within the already-existing categorisation. Unlike other Himalayan states where there is substantial non-tribal population residing in proximity, this is not the case in Nagaland, with Dimapur being an exception. Here the political struggle is among the Naga groups themselves, who measure their backwardness based on colonial contact, nature of historic administration, and the influence of the Baptist missionaries.

In an earlier section, I discussed the politics of census by analysing two important debates at the time of my fieldwork and explained identity construction and the politics of exclusion, objectification, and appeasement: first, the Yimchunger–Tikhir sub-tribal identity crisis in the Yimchunger-administered areas of Tuensang district where I conducted my preliminary research; and second, the increasing participation of Naga civil society groups in filing cases under Public Interest Litigation challenging the census results that had led to the freezing of delimitation of boundary in Nagaland till 2026. The contemporary struggle in Nagaland is muddled with identity politics that is simmering with new identities being formed and mediated by the state apparatus. In contemporary Naga society, there is a great fear of immigration from the plains, and particularly from Bangladesh;

this is true of many north-eastern states of India too (see Arora 2013). Often the political leadership in the state has tried to deflate the growing inequalities by placing the immigration question at the forefront (see Agarwal and Kumar 2012). Growing consumerism, changing land relations, and the emerging 'neo-tribal elite' who make fortunes through patronage and brokerage in development programmes try to keep the foreigner influx agenda alive, thus deflating the structural problems of the Naga society.

Ethnicity in historical context

If we study Naga history since the colonial encounters in the late 19th century, we find that the Assam ethnological surveys funded the survey of a handful of Naga tribes that automatically became the major sub-tribes of the Naga Hills – Ao, Angami, Sema, Lotha, and Thankgkul Nagas (Lotha 2007). British administrators/anthropologists and military survey parties who came to explore the Naga Hills often misrepresented the Nagas or grouped them under different names or called them as their neighbours, the Assamese people, knew them. Following this, Naga identity developed as the colonial administration took full control of the hills; similar was the case with the Kuki, as discussed by Arora and Kipgen (2012). The conflict over fixing or establishing Naga identities loomed large among the colonial administrators. To illuminate a few examples, the British termed the Nagas who lived beyond the Angami territory as 'Kacha Nagas' – the Rengma Nagas were known as 'Naked Nagas', while many Naga groups who lay beyond the Angami area were called Kacha Nagas. Similarly, the Kukis were subdivided into Old Kuki and New Kuki groups based on their trajectory of contact with the British (ibid.). The misrepresentation and clubbing in of identities continued till the last days of the British Empire.

Periodically, groups separated into new tribes, joined and left the 'Naga' entity, and depending on the context even fought bloody wars against their Naga brothers and sisters. The formation of local identities thus continues till date. Sometimes tribes even cease to exist, dissolving themselves into other ethnic constructs. In the late 1930s, von Fürer-Haimendorf (1938) collected artefacts and wrote about the Kalyo Kengyu Nagas, and later H. E. Kauffmann (1939: 12) mentions the Razìamià-Angamis. The Kalyo Kengyu are the present-day Khiamniungan, and the Razìamià-Angamis are possibly a group that is now considered part of the Zeme (or Jeme). The latter united in 1947, a few months before Indian independence, and joined with the Liangmei and Rongmei to form a new tribe, the Zeliangrong (von Stockhausen 2009).

A similar move happened in the 1960s when the former Eastern Angami, consisting of two language groups – Chakri and Khezha, aligned with the

Southern Sangtham to form a new tribe, the Chakhesang (Lotha 2009). The Sangtham were later to leave the alliance, as did the Pochury, who had originally been part of it too (von Stockhausen 2009). The latter were named by the British the Eastern (or Naked) Rengma, in contrast to the Western Rengma, who, for their part, now distinguish three sub-tribes: the Northern and Southern Rengma in the Kohima district of Nagaland, and the Western Rengma, a small group living in geographical isolation from the main tribe in the present-day Karbi Anglong district of Assam. These Western Rengma refer to themselves as Njang (Oppitz *et al.* 2008: 15).

Such multifarious and diffused sub-tribal identities are constantly being constructed and re-constructed in present-day Nagaland, and there are ever-growing claims for new sub-tribal identities. The Tikhits of Tuensang district present one such case (Das 2012; Lotha 2009). They inhabit small pockets of Yimchunger tribal area in Samatur subdivision of Tuensang and Kiphire districts. Colonial records mention only the Yimchunger in the tour diaries and travel reports of government officers. Even von Fürer-Haimendorf, who joined J. P Mills, the then deputy commissioner of the Naga Hills, talks of the Yimchunger in his tour reports (see Mills 1995) and journal publications while describing the events that led to the Pangsha anti-slavery expedition in 1936–37. In this context, the Tikhirs emerge as a new category, out of the Yimchunger fold.

The Yimchunger community is divided into four linguistic sub-groups Tikhir, Mikori, Yimchunger-Langa, and Chir. The Chir-speaking people mostly inhabit the Myanmar Naga territories. During my fieldwork, I witnessed hostility between the Tikhir and the Yimchunger, each trying to establish its unique and independent identity. The Yimchunger–Tikhir conflict over the past decades has evolved from what was based on social exclusion to an economic one when backwardness was rewarded by affirmative action and reservation. In the past decade, this conflict led to bloody feuds between the militias of Yimchunger and Tikhir.

One of my interlocutors, who represented the Yimchunger Naga *Hoho* and was also a member in the Yimchunger Tribal Council, the apex body of the Yimchunger people, explained while displaying documented records that the Yimchunger were united with the Tikhirs and both were considered blood brothers. A resolution passed in 1947 confirmed that all Yimchunger villagers agreed to speak Langa as their common language and stay united. This position taken by Yimchunger elders was bitterly disclaimed by Tikhir villagers and tribal council leaders who claimed different lineage, kinship, and migration history. The contest of difference is quite obvious if we look at Naga history of identity construction. B. B. Kumar describes that the history of the individual Naga tribe is 'also the history of a thousand Naga village republics' (2005: 20). Naga identities are now constructed based on their ethnic and social differences. The Tikhir claim for a sub-tribal status has, in the past, been registered through public protest, vandalism, revenge killings, and their registration as Tikhirs in birth certificates and other demonstrable public spaces (*Newsonline*, news.oneindia.in, 8 January 2007 [accessed on 1 July 2014]). The Naga identity problem resurfaced during the 2011 Census enumeration when the Tikhir-Yimchunger sub-tribes enrolled themselves as Tikhirs. It created massive public protest by Yimchunger civil society groups calling it unjust and unfair (*Nagaland Post* [Kohima], 3 March 2011). The Tikhir and Yimchunger elders have established armed militia and promoted their civil society groups to assert their distinctive identities.

Tikhir villagers complained that the elected Yimchunger MLAs deny them jobs and opportunities to take the benefits of reservation. This, in turn, further marginalised them. While the Yimchunger claim such arguments as propaganda by Tikhir tribal elite and explain that the Mikori and the Chir linguistic groups never contest over their identity, on the ground, the reality is different. The Chir and the Mikori do not fall in the same electoral constituency; neither of them is dependent on the Yimchunger for development grants and employment. More important, they have not been historically ridiculed as 'lazy and dirty', like the Tikhirs. The social exclusion of the Tikhirs from mainstream Yimchunger fold has translated their marginality and deprivation, sharpening their demand for 'major backward tribal' status in the state. The Tikhirs feel themselves trapped in small villages surrounded by the Yimchunger majority. The Yimchunger elders further noted in their interviews that the Tikhirs are spread over few villages in the Yimchunger area and their number is too small to claim a sub-tribe status in Nagaland.

The electoral politics has further sharpened the divide and brought the identity question in the forefront of the debate. While reservation is intended to reduce backwardness, it has, in turn, created concerns for tribes who see it as a problem affecting their development. The Tikhir tribal leaders have mobilised their community to fight for their tribe, and protect their identity, while the Yimchunger tribal elders have moved the case to the High Court for justice.

The genesis of the Yimchunger–Tikhir identity crisis simmered over a dispute during the 1990s while naming the Shamatur village Baptist Church in Shamatur subdivision of Tuensang district. The Tikhir-dominated Shamatur villagers announced that it should be called Tikhir Baptist Church, which the Yimchunger Tribal Council rejected as an action by Shamatur village to disregard the pan-Yimchunger identity. This led to violent protests and clashes between the Yimchunger and Tikhir elders as well as the respective students' unions. Violence ravaged the sub-district headquarters of Shamatur for nearly a decade till 2007, when some hope of reconciliation emerged between the two groups and a ceasefire was declared. The fresh standoff between the Yimchunger and the Tikhirs during the census enumeration of 2011 has rekindled the debate. The census standoff has yet again reflected the economic foundations of identity construction.

The larger picture of the census enumeration lies in Yimchunger fears of underrepresentation if Tikhirs were to count as a separate sub-tribe in the census. The Yimchunger tribal elders fear this will legitimise Tikhirs' demand for separate sub-tribal status. The Yimchunger leaders further fear such an action would allow other tribes to influence the Tikhirs and set them up against them. These discussions were persistent and emotionally charged in villagers' everyday talk in the Shamatur subdivision, the heart of Yimchunger and Tikhir tribal area. A local newspaper covering the census enumeration of 2011 reports that the Tikhirs were enumerated by the NSCN (IM) faction at gunpoint, which the Tikhirs later disclaimed and blamed the Yimchunger for causing hindrance towards Tikhirs' legitimate right to become a sub-tribe (*Nagaland Post* [Kohima], 26 February 2011).

The identity debate has sharpened in Nagaland, with new identities emerging and advancing claims to sub-tribal distinctiveness as the government rolls out its policies for affirmative action, access to development resources, and empowerment of the underrepresented communities in the state through reserved seats. The fluid identities of the Naga sub-tribes based on kin relations and 'oral history' are thus contested and constantly rearticulated to support their politics of identity construction. This process of fusion and fission of new identities has also brought complexity to the process of census enumeration, and this explains the contestations around its data. In the case of Tikhirs, both language and discrimination have become markers of their ethnic identification. In the 1991 Census, the Tikhirs were enumerated separately, and this becomes a part of their claim for sub-tribal backward status. Both the Tikhirs and the Yimchungers have used their history and tradition to establish their position as a major sub-tribe. Similarly, the census results continue to affect the Delimitation Bill, although it has been temporarily frozen till 2026. In his interviews, the CPO president observed that the Chekasang community would fight it till the very end. In a 2012 Guwahati High Court verdict, CPO won a major battle on recruitment in public sector jobs. These cases and many others have made it clear how contested the reservation policy is and the way fresh debates on defining sub-tribal status are raised.

For many indigenous Naga scholars, such conflicts are normal in a competing multi-ethnic Naga society (Pangerungba 2008). But we need to understand the micro-politics and agency of the political elites who mobilise people and define community's identity through symbolic and material capital. In these struggles, the Naga community leaders have played a critical role in establishing community collective identity through associations. Today, each Naga major sub-tribe is represented by a tribal council of Naga elders (*Naga Hoho*), student unions, and women's association (Naga Mothers Association). Besides, the Naga Student Federation and the Eastern Naga Students Federation work for the welfare of their own community within Nagaland. The privileged Naga elders act as village heads or chiefs or have achieved their social position to represent themselves in various bodies through education, participation in politics, and their involvement as brokers in state-driven development and welfare programmes.

The elites play an important role in shaping the agenda of community struggle. For example, in the Yimchunger–Tikhir conflict, the tribal elders from both communities who come from influential walks of life have been negotiating over reconciliation. The Yimchunger elites have tried to persuade the pan-Yimchunger identity as the only way out of the crisis. However, this position is contested by the Tikhir Tribal Council. The Yimchunger elites see their interest protected if pan-Yimchunger identity prevails. They fear the 'small numbers' of the Tikhirs can potentially damage their electoral mandate and narrow their claims over reservation and benefits currently enjoyed by the community. This validates Arora's (2013) emphasis on the role of political elite in crystallising fissions and escalating separatism. Simultaneously, it would lead to territorialisation of the community and reduce their area of jurisdiction and control over Legislative Assembly seats. The Tikhirs fear that they would be backward as a result of their identity being subsumed with the pan-Yimchunger fold. All this feeds into the electoral politics of the state in contemporary Naga society.

The politics of census enumeration and people's participation raises further questions on the ephemeral stability of a 'pan-Naga identity', in the sense that different ethnic identities become more central to the idea of a community than the pan-Naga identity, which casts a shadow over the idea of a unified Nagalim. With numerous social differences, the dilemmas of reservation can be clearly felt in Nagaland.

The Naga struggle for independence is today undermined by active engagement with census data as it can often distort their representation. Is this seen as a political strategy of divide and rule of the Indian government? Reservations and demarcation of new territories to appease the newly recognised backward tribes have created their new set of problems in the Naga society polarising along tribal identities that have been rearticulated through emergent discourses of and categories of backwardness and 'underdevelopment'.

Notes

1 This chapter was developed during my PhD fieldwork in Nagaland (2008–09). I would like to acknowledge the following fellowships and grants that have funded my fieldwork in Nagaland: Felix Scholarship, Christopher von Fürer-Haimendorf Anthropology Fund, ATREE Small Grant, University of London – Central Research Fund, and OKDISCD Resident Fellowship. This chapter is not part of my doctoral thesis submitted to and defended at the Department of Anthropology and Sociology at the School of Oriental and African Studies, University of London, in 2012. I am grateful to Vibha Arora for helpful comments and numerous suggestions that shaped the writing of this chapter.
2 Nagaland is a Sixth Schedule state under Article 370 of the Indian Constitution. Therefore, the state enjoys special privileges.
3 See the news report, 'Nagaland Records Negative Growth in Decadal Population', *The Hindu*, 2011, www.thehindu.com/news/ national/.../ nagaland...in.../article1590652.ece (accessed on 4 April 2014). Nagaland is the only state to have experienced the highest decadal growth rate during 1991–2001. In 2011, the census recorded negative growth rate, thereby questioning the figures arrived at by the previous two censuses.
4 See The Nagaland Village Council Act, 1978, and the Nagaland Village and Area Council (Second Amendment Act), 1990.
5 The nationalisation of frontier space has been explored by Baruah (2003). His analysis focusing on Government of India's development policy in Arunachal Pradesh is relevant for Nagaland, where electoral patronage and vote bank play a crucial role in representation of various tribes in the Nagaland Legislative Assembly.
6 It must be noted here that there are many Naga sub-tribes who are still fighting for new sub-tribal status. The policy of reservation and affirmative action has heightened these claims that are often based on ethnic exclusiveness and linguistic differences.
7 The generic term *adivasi*, coterminous with global terminologies like indigenous, is not used in the context of the Sixth Schedule–listed tribal groups of Nagaland state because they were never part of the caste hierarchy or British Land Revenue administration (see Arora 2007). Instead the village go-between or tribal chiefs played a lead role in facilitating control over the administered and un-administered tracts in the Naga Hills. Revenue collected at nominal rates in the form of house tax was used as an instrument of political control over the colonised Naga swidden and terrace rice cultivators.
8 *Dobashi* is a government-appointed Naga man who can act as assistant in the deputy commissioner's office assisting in customary law and act as go-between in local village disputes in Naga villages.
9 In order to avoid ethnic conflict, the central government deferred delimitation to 2031, while the state government rejected the 2001 Census and demanded re-conducting the Census.
10 In Nagaland, there is conflicting account on the actual number of Naga sub-tribes. While the government currently recognises seventeen major sub-tribes, some claim there are fifty-two Naga sub-tribes. The policy of protective discrimination and electoral representation has provided incentive for new ethnic formation (see Lotha 2007).

11 Educated Nagas today live in cities and urban areas and have made their presence felt all over the globe, including mainland India. The prime drive for out-migration of the villagers is the need for employment and better education and their aspiration for improvement.

References

Agarwal, A. and V. Kumar. 2012. 'Number Game in Nagaland', *The Hindu*, Chennai, 17 July.
Angami, Z. 2008. *Nagaland Village Empowerment Laws*. Kohima: Novelty Printing Press.
Arora, V. 2007. 'Assertive Identities, Indignity, and the Politics of Recognition as a Tribe: The Bhutias, the Lepchas, and the Limbus of Sikkim', *Sociological Bulletin*, 56 (2): 195–220.
———. 2013. 'The Paradox of Democracy in the Northeast and the Eastern Himalayas', in V. Arora and N. Jayaram (eds.), *Routeing Democracy in the Himalayas: Experiments and Experiences*, pp. 101–32. New Delhi: Routledge.
Arora, V. and N. Kipgen. 2012. 'The Politics of Identifying and Distancing from Kuki Identity', *Sociological Bulletin*, 61 (3): 401–22.
Axelsson, P., P. Skolkd, J. P. Ziker and D. G. Anderson. 2011. 'From Indigenous Demographics to an Indigenous Demography', in P. Axelsson and P. Skolkd (eds.), *Indigenous People and Demography: The Complex Relation between Identity and Statistics*, pp. 295–308. New York and Oxford: Berghahn.
Baruah, S. 2003. 'Nationalizing Space: Cosmetic Federalism and the Politics of Development in Northeast India', *Development and Change*, 34 (5): 915–39.
Cohn, B. S. 1966. *Colonialism and Its Forms of Knowledge: The British in India*. New Delhi: Oxford University Press.
Das, D. 2012. *Contested Development: Problems and Dilemmas in Sustainable Jhum Redevelopment in Nagaland*. PhD Thesis in Anthropology, School of Oriental and African Studies, University of London.
Guneratna, A. 1998. 'Modernisation, the State and the Construction of Tharu Identity in Nepal', *The Journal of Asian Studies*, 57 (3): 749–73.
Hanger, S. 2001. 'Creating a "New Nepal": The Ethnic Dimension', *East West Center Policy Studies*, Working Paper No. 34. Hawaii: East West Center.
Hodson, T. C. 1911. *The Naga Tribes of Manipur*. London: Macmillan.
Hoschild, J. and B. M. Powell. 2008. 'Racial Recognition and the United States Census 1850–1930: Mulattoes, Half-breed, Mixed Parentage, Hindoos, and the Mexican Race', *Studies in American Political Development*, 22 (1): 59–96.
Hutton, J. H. 1921a. *The Angami Naga*. London: Macmillan.
———. 1921b. *The Sema Naga*. London: Macmillan.
Kapila, K. 2008. 'The Measure of a Tribe: The Culture Politics of Constitutional Reclassification in North India', *Journal of the Royal Anthropological Institute*, 14 (1): 117–34.
Kauffmann, H. E. 1939. 'Kurze Ethnographie der nordlichen Sangtham Naga (Lophomi), Assam', *Anthropos*, 34 (1): 207–45.

Kumar, B. B. 2005. *Naga Identity*. New Delhi: Concept Publishing Company.
Li, Tania Murray. 2000. 'Articulating Indigenous Identity in Indonesia: Resource Politics and the Tribal Slot', *Comparative Studies in Society and History*, 42 (1): 149–79.
Lotha, A. 2007. *History of Naga Anthropology, 1832–1947*. Kohima: Chimpo Museum Publication.
———. 2009. *Rearticulating Naga Nationalism*. PhD Thesis in Anthropology, New York University, New York.
McDuie-Ra, D. 2008. 'Between National Security and Ethno-nationalism: The Regional Politics of Development in Northeast India', *Journal of South Asian Development*, 3 (2): 185–210.
Middleton, T. 2013. 'Anxious Belongings: Anxiety and the Politics of Belonging in Subnationalist Darjeeling', *American Anthropologist*, 115 (4): 608–21.
Mills, J. P. 1922. *The Lotha Naga*. London: Macmillan.
———. 1926. *The Ao Naga*. London: Macmillan.
———. 1995. *The Pangsha Letters: An Expedition to Rescue Slaves in the Naga Hills*. Oxford: Pitt Rivers Museum.
Nagaland Post. 2011. 'Census Review Meetings in Every District', www.nagalandpost.com/ShowStory.aspx?npoststoryiden... (accessed on 3 December 2014).
Nagaland State Human Development Report. 2004. hdr.undp.org/en/content/nagaland-state-human-development-report-2004 (accessed on 29 April 2014).
Oppitz, M., T. Kaiser, A. von Stockhausen and M. Wettstein. 2008. *Naga Identities: Changing Local Cultures in the Northeast of India*. Gent: Snoeck Publishers.
Pangerungba, Richard. 2008. *The Naga Peoples Struggle for Creative Integration: Competing Moral Versions of 'Ali Romgsen' (Cultural Economy) and 'Sen' (Moral Economy)*. PhD Thesis in Philosophy, Princeton Theological seminary, Princeton, New Jersey.
Rio, Neiphiu. 2012. *Speeches of Neiphiu Rio*. Kohima: Directorate of Information and Public Relations.
Scott, J. C. 1998. *Domination and the Art of Resistance: Hidden Transcript*. New Haven, CT: Yale University Press.
Shneiderman, S. and T. Middleton. 2008. 'Reservation, Federalism and the Politics of Recognition in Nepal', *Economic and Political Weekly*, 43 (19): 39–44.
von Fürer-Haimendorf, C. 1938. 'Through the Unexplored Mountains of the Assam Burma Border', *The Geographical Journal*, 91 (3): 201–16.
———. 1969. *The Konyak Nagas: An Indian Frontier Tribe*. London and New York: Holt, Rinehart and Winston.
von Stockhausen, A. 2009. 'Naga: Lineage of a Term', Paper presented on Writing the North East Conference, Jawaharlal Nehru University, New Delhi, 14–16 January 2009.
Yonou, Asoso. 1974. *The Rising Nagas*. New Delhi: Vivek Publishing House.

3 The making of the subaltern Lepcha and the Kalimpong stimulus

Vibha Arora

Dominance/subordination is always produced historically in specific contexts and may be altered and even transcended historically. The subaltern is, by definition, a political category, a relational, interactive, and fluid group.[1] Gyanendra Pandey (2006) forcefully argues how the relationship of subalternity is a complex one and is always negotiated between citizens. Subalternity is not an autonomous domain or a position of absolute exteriority and agency in relation to power structures (Chatterjee 2004; Pandey 2006). Political struggle is an intrinsic feature of subalternity, and subaltern politics ranges from everyday forms of resistance to peaceful rights-based campaigns and participation in electoral democracy to armed struggles (Nilsen and Roy 2015: 1–5). The emergence of a subaltern Lepcha (replacing the trope of Lepcha, a vanishing tribe) in the eastern Himalayas highlights their ability to negotiate, rebel, or resist the hegemonic power of the postcolonial state and engage with democratic institutions. This is a corollary of their extended political engagement with other ethnic groups inhabiting the region, various political parties, and civil society, and shaped by the acquisition and production of a cultural repertoire. The subaltern engages with the structures of domination, acquires consciousness, frames ideologies of oppression, and negotiates social transformation(s) through their expressive practices. Following Partha Chatterjee (2004), the 'politics of the governed' is visible in various domains. I recognise the efforts of their 'organic intellectuals' to ceremonialise and invent cultural symbols to unify, awaken the consciousness of a geographically dispersed religiously divided Lepcha community, and enable them to communicate their subjectivity. The organic intellectuals residing at Kalimpong have given creative direction to these political processes and ceremonial events, which I term the 'Kalimpong stimulus'. I show how this stimulus has furthered the politicisation of Lepcha identity, the recovery of collective subjectivity, and this resistance has taken a distinctly spatial turn.

Subalternity does not preclude agency, although this agency arises and develops within and in relation to dominant discourses and political forms (Chatterjee 2004; Nilsen and Roy 2015). The Lepchas have resisted and engaged with the extant structures of power relations and multiple forms of their marginalisation and subordination. I agree with Sammadar (2012: 126) in that 'it is the double nature of politics, which gives birth to the political subject, and leaves its imprint on the subject position in politics'. The chapter historically documents and explains the cultural experiments, the simulation of experiences, and political engagement whereby a scheduled tribe recovers subjectivity in a democratic India – becomes a subaltern Lepcha.

The subaltern's mobilisation within political society impregnates the possibility of both mobility and change (ranging from compromise to tact to active resistance), and once subaltern groups are able to challenge and overcome hegemonic power then they will cease to be a subaltern group. The political will of Lepcha elite to engage with electoral politics in postcolonial India, struggle with competing ethnic groups, and to ensure their success in negotiating with the state indicates their political mettle. Democracy has enabled their agency but simultaneously been transformed by their emergence. This has shaped the form, extent, and process of their political engagement, and the direction of their social mobility, and transformed the very meaning of democracy within. The emergence of a subaltern Lepcha (as opposed to the idea of a vanishing subaltern) signals the consolidation of democratic institutions, and the emergence of political space for representing marginalised groups and furthering inclusive politics. The assertion of the subaltern citizen marks democratic change and the redistribution of power, and signals the deepening roots of a participatory democracy in the eastern Himalayas. After all any test of democracy is revealed in the meaning it has for the people engaging with it and their willingness to engage and struggle for greater agentive capacity (Harriss, Stokke and Tornquist 2004). Will the Lepchas be able to transcend their subalternity?

Among the many exponents, it is largely the perspective of Chatterjee (2004), Pandey (2006), and Rosalind O-Hanlon (1988) that guides my historical and ethnographic analysis (while I am aware of the tension between their individual positions). The struggle of the Lepcha subaltern is not merely to engage or reclaim the mythic and get their small voices heard, but affirm their agency and signal their political moment to history and anthropology. But do they cease to be a subaltern with their political mobility? O-Hanlon emphasises how central to the process of 'recovery of the subject' was the ability of the historian to listen; uncover subaltern myths, ideologies, and cults; and understand their revolts.[2] Using the Lepchas as a case, I show how our ability to listen and document the subaltern depends not only on their capacity to speak but also on our capacity to comprehend the undertones and sensitively follow their expression. Significantly, our 'hearing' varies with our ability to comprehend their praxis, analyse the production of (counter)culture, and decode the metaphors deployed by their spatial practices.

The argument of this chapter is substantively organised into five sections and contributes to subaltern studies,[3] and analysis of 'local' democratisation. I begin by introducing the Lepchas to an unfamiliar reader. The second section foregrounds the dominant trope used to describe and politically frame the Lepcha community as a disappearing, threatened, and vanishing group in the region. The third section differentiates between the Lepchas of Sikkim and Lepchas of Darjeeling Hills, and shows how political history has impacted their respective political consciousness and struggles. The fourth section focuses on the 'Kalimpong stimulus' and the role of organic intellectuals in producing spatial practices to assert their uniqueness, declare their indigenieity, and proclaim their prior rights over resources. I discuss three manifestations (worship of 'sacred' Mt Tendong, the anniversary celebrations to memorialise the birthday of *Pano*[4] Gaeebo A-chyuk, and transformation of Dzongu into a holy land), which have enabled the emergence of a Lepcha subaltern and their transformation into an eco-warrior guarding the fragile Himalayan environment. The fifth section highlights the aspirations of the political elite to carve political space in two democratic contexts (Sikkim and Darjeeling Hills), the negotiations with the state, and the outcome of their local struggles over power, meaning, and control over resources for development.

Who are the Lepchas?

Etymologically, the term 'Lepcha' is not an ethnonym but derived from the derogatory reference to the group in Nepali language, namely *lap-che*, meaning vile-speakers (cf. Waddell 1978: 433). Their autonym in the Lepcha language is *Rong-pa* (meaning ravine-folk, the dwellers of the valley), and they describe themselves as *Mutanchi Rongkup*, meaning beloved children of mother (or creator), or *Mutanchi Rumkup*, meaning children of the God.[5] I begin by briefly introducing the Lepchas inhabiting the eastern Himalayas of India, although by now the reader already knows that they are geographically spread in the two Indian states of West Bengal and Sikkim.

According to the 2001 Census, there are 40,568 Lepchas residing in Sikkim, and the largest concentration is in North district, especially Dzongu, which is a reserve exclusively inhabited by them. They are largely a rural-based ethnic group (merely 4.5 per cent was urban) now having a literacy rate of about 65.7 per cent.[6] Around 14,700 Lepchas live in Darjeeling district of West Bengal. In addition, they reside in small numbers in the

Illam district of Nepal and Samtsi and Chukha districts of Bhutan. Politico-economically, they are concentrated in the primary sector (farming, horticulture, and animal husbandry), and a small minority is employed in the tertiary sector (government administration, teachers, clerks, nurses, tourism and hospitality, the army, police, self-employed in business, etc.).

Following the founding of the Buddhist kingdom in the 17th century, many converted to Buddhism, while others continue to follow shamanism (original religion) in Sikkim. In the 19th century, a large section residing in the Darjeeling Hills became Christians, while only a small minority of Lepchas of Sikkim are Christians. The Christian Lepchas are subdivided by different denominations. In brief, the ethnic community is fragmented and internally differentiated by class, education, religious affiliation, and geographical dispersion, and many have inter-married with other ethnic groups (Bhutia, Limbu, Tibetan, etc.). The unity of the group has been compounded by its marginalisation by other economically advanced ethnic groups (e.g. Bhutia, Nepali, and Bengali). The indigenous natives have been reduced to a numerical and politically insignificant minority following waves of migration. Since 1978 they are recognised as scheduled tribe.

The population figures for the Lepchas residing in Sikkim and in neighbouring Darjeeling do establish their numerical minority status but not any real or possibility of extinction. Over the past fourteen years of my fieldwork in the region, I have documented the circulation of the trope of the vanishing Lepcha in many contexts, albeit not persuaded by its veracity. Culturally, linguistically, and politically the Lepchas continue to be a vibrant ethnic community of the eastern Himalayas, and considerable sustained effort has gone into ensuring this position.

Foregrounding the vanishing Lepcha trope

G. B. Mainwaring (1876) and G. Gorer (1938) authored the colonial trope of vanishing Lepcha during the period of widespread immigration and settlement of the Nepalis in Sikkim and the Darjeeling region of Calcutta Presidency. Witnessing their rapid marginalisation, Mainwaring declared, 'To allow the Lepcha race, and language to die out would indeed be most barbarous, and inexpressibly sad' (1876: xx). Half a century later, Gorer (1938: 37) had commented how examples of Lepcha society could be found only in Zongu/Dzongu, and those residing in Kalimpong had completely forgotten their language and lost corporate unity. Thereafter, the trope of disappearing Lepcha gained currency and became a defining one for the contemporary. The perceived threat of cultural extinction and fear of being marginalised by the domination of the majority community (Nepali culture, or Bengali culture, or Indian culture) have prompted the leaders and members of the community to become self-conscious and introspect on strategies to revitalise the tribe.

The endangered social future of the Lepchas inhabiting the eastern Himalayas was evocatively projected in *Lepcha, My Vanishing Tribe*, published by the late Arthur Foning in 1987. His auto-ethnographic account has become a politically influential volume about the social life and culturally unique heritage of the Lepchas. For Foning (1987), the conversion of Lepchas into Christianity had a very detrimental impact on their cultural continuity and customary practices, as the converts became Westernised, leading to cultural extinction. He declared Jongu/Dzongu to be a utopia and admitted, 'Many of our customs and usages that are still practiced there [in Jongu/Dzongu] have become memories this side [in Kalimpong]' (ibid.: 264). For him, Jongu/Dzongu represents the last bastion of undiluted uncontaminated Lepcha culture (ibid.: 260). I was repeatedly told during fieldwork in 2001–2 how the 'really real' and 'the authentic Lepcha' were now only to be found in Dzongu in North Sikkim.[7] Statements like these intrigued me and encouraged me to make short trips to the Darjeeling Hills of West Bengal, and Kalimpong, in particular. Essentially, to be a 'Lepcha' was to cling to certain iconic images such as nature-worshipping, forest-dependent, or forest-dwelling agriculturists living on the margins of the state having little interaction with the wider world. I would be sometimes tutored on how Lepchas living in urban spaces were not representative of their community, as many had inter-married with non-Lepchas (the Bhutias, the Limbus, and the Nepalis) and thereby lost their cultural moorings. However, were they becoming less Lepcha due to this? While interacting with the Lepcha ideologues in Sikkim, I realised that there was much more than religious conversion that explained the extent of difference between them and the Lepchas of West Bengal.

Imperial India had drastically altered the demography of the region to serve colonial interests and marginalised the indigenous people. However, democratic post-colonial India has facilitated the cultural revival of the indigenous/scheduled tribes and earmarked resources for uplifting the historically marginalised. Foning was an influential Kalimpong Lepcha, who not only held positions in the Mutanchi Rong Shezum as general secretary but also established the Lungten Chok Lee (the Lepcha Cultural Centre) at Kalimpong in 1967 with grant-in-aid from the Scheduled Castes and Tribes Welfare Department of the Government of West Bengal (ibid.: xix). Foning's book attained iconic status after the leaders and ideologues of the Lepchas of Kalimpong realised how important it was to preserve culture, to signal their tribal identity, and obtain preferential treatment and resources under the Indian Constitution.

I will briefly mention some other concurrent and later studies on the Lepchas that indicate the differences between the Lepchas of Sikkim and the Lepchas of Darjeeling Hills. R. N. Thakur's book *Himalayan Lepchas* published in 1988 drew heavily on the insights and fieldwork conducted by Thakur in 1978 in Darjeeling Hills and in Sikkim with the help of Sonam Wangdi Lepcha, whom I interviewed during my fieldwork in 2002.[8] This book also emphasised how, with modernisation, they were getting de-tribalised and Lepcha culture was decaying (Thakur 1988: 4, 143), although they had not been assimilated. Simultaneously, Thakur emphasises the trend of forming ethnic associations and revitalising Lepcha language and culture through them. He outlined how, due to modernisation, they had become more conscious of the need to preserve their language and cultural heritage, and began to assert their identity as the *Mutanchi Rongkup* (ibid.: 16, 148–51).

On the other hand, Veena Bhasin's book *Ecology, Culture and Change: Tribals of Sikkim Himalayas* published in 1989 followed an ecological perspective in understanding the Lepchas and Bhutias of Sikkim and their inter-relationship. Bhasin's fieldwork was conducted between September 1981 and December 1983 in Dzongu and in Lachen-Lachung only a few years after the kingdom of Sikkim was incorporated into India (Bhasin 1989: 19). Bhasin describes 'the Lepchas to be a race of hunters and food-gatherers, roaming in dense forests and remote mountains' (1989: 19–20). The inhabitants of Dzongu *still* hunted, gathered, fished in the streams, and engaged in slash-and-burn cultivation with some animal husbandry (ibid.: 20), even though they had contacts with the outside world, sold cardamom, and visited markets for making necessary purchases (ibid.: 85). Bhasin also noted how 'the Lepchas of Dzongu are considered wild, uncivilised, and very primitive by other Lepchas and ethnic groups of the state' (ibid.: 82).

A decade later, *Lingthem Revisited* was published in 1995 by Rip Roshina Gowloog based on her doctoral research in Lingthem village of Dzongu, where Gorer had collected data for his book. She documents the social and cultural changes and how the process of de-tribalisation had occurred here. More recently, she has emphasised how the Lepchas had been reduced to a marginalised insignificant minority in Sikkim (see Gowloog 2013). She states that they have been rapidly losing their material culture, language, and costumes, and altering their food habits, while many traditional ritual practices were slowly being replaced by Buddhist practices, and shamanism was declining.[9]

Contextualising the regional differences among the Lepchas

Following Nilsen and Roy (2015: 12–15), the heterogeneity within the Lepcha category highlights the dynamic, relational and inter-sectional character of subalternity. I would like the reader to know the differences between the Lepchas of West Bengal and the Lepchas of Sikkim, which have been shaped by their specific political history and historical interaction with the former colonial government, the erstwhile *Chos-rgyal* dynasty of Sikkim, and the post-colonial Indian state. These divergent histories foreground my central argument, so I briefly detail them here.

The politico-economic context of Lepchas living in the erstwhile kingdom of Sikkim that was incorporated into India in 1975 has radically differed from the Lepchas inhabiting the Darjeeling Hills that were annexed by the British in 1835 and included in India in the 19th century. The British annexed Darjeeling Hills from Sikkim in 1835, while Kalimpong was annexed from Bhutan in 1865; subsequently, both Kalimpong (British Bhutan) and Darjeeling Hills (British Sikkim) were merged into the Indian state of Bengal. In the mid-19th century, both Kalimpong and Darjeeling rapidly developed into famous hill stations for the Europeans seeking a reprieve from the heat and humidity of the Indian plains, and were transformed into educational hubs for the children of British officers serving in India, the Anglo-Indians, and the Indian elite, with several notable missionary schools and colleges being opened here. The demographic profile of the region changed drastically with the settlement of Nepalis, who became casual labourers in these hill towns or were employed in the numerous tea gardens. The forested areas adjoining these towns were rapidly transformed into commercial tea plantations. The industrious Nepali peasants terraced the hill slopes and introduced new crops (cardamom, wet rice cultivation, etc.) and indelibly altered the landscape (White 1909). The Lepchas were unable to economically compete and lost most of their land to these immigrants.

Within a span of two decades or so of the British policy encouraging settlement of Nepali immigrants, the indigenous Lepcha became a minority in their homeland. The original habitation of Lepchas continues to be indicated by the numerous Lepcha villages that surround these hill towns wherein they continue to be farmers. The first chapter of Foning's (1987) book provides an insider account of this history. Under the influence of the Christian missionaries, many of the Lepchas converted to Christianity, and they became colonial citizens of the British Raj in the 19th century; few were employed as servants, and the educated few became colonial officers, and some even joined the Gorkha regiment. As Nepali became the lingua franca of the region, the use of Lepcha language diminished, and youth increasingly shifted to Nepali. Gradually, the Lepchas lost their literati, and their rich linguistic heritage dwindled, which prompted Mainwaring (1876) and Mainwaring and Grundwell (1898) to compile a grammar and a dictionary.[10] The Kalimpong and Kurseong Lepchas are now largely Christians. The Church strictly prohibits them from attending any ceremonies or following their ancient religious practices. Hence, they have gradually and thoroughly lost their original Lepcha cultural practices; they have de-tribalised and Westernised (Foning 1987; Thakur 1988). Many elders living in Darjeeling Hills regaled me with stories of how Christian missionaries had civilised and Westernised the erstwhile forest-dwelling Lepchas.

The Lepchas of Darjeeling and Kalimpong in West Bengal were exposed to the modern world much before the Lepchas of Sikkim. After 1947, this region underwent drastic socio-economic and political changes. Hence, the Lepchas acquired the political capacity to negotiate the different institutions and safeguards of Indian democracy far ahead of the Sikkimese Lepchas. As one of the tribes of West Bengal, the Lepchas have been vigorously fighting for cultural protection and competing for accessing resources with the ethnically diverse and numerically dominant Nepali groups. The West Bengal government does not officially promote their culture or provide official space for their explicit expression. Lepcha festivals are not recognised as a state holiday. Provisions of funds specifically earmarked for preserving their culture and development are non-existent (unlike in Sikkim). Their long-standing demand for introducing Lepcha language in schools of Darjeeling Hills has not been accepted. Here the Lepchas have also been dealing with the political upheavals and development chaos ushered by the violent Gorkhaland[11] movement for the past three decades. The Nepalis who migrated here are demanding an ethnic homeland,[12] which they are superimposing on Lepcha-land, wherein the Lepchas have been rapidly reduced to an insignificant minority.

In contrast, Himalayan Sikkim's isolation and geographical remoteness and Dzongu's status as an ethnic reserve had afforded protection and forestalled cultural assimilation of the Lepchas. Sikkimese Lepchas were often defensive about their subjugation by the ethnically dominant Bhutias and economically advanced Nepalis, and stressed how they had been politically marginalised over the past few centuries. The Lepchas had been part of the ruling nobility and enjoyed higher status and political privileges than the Nepalis. North Sikkim was protected from Nepali immigrants after the passing of Land Revenue Order Number 1 of 1917 that prohibited the alienation of land from the Lepchas and Bhutias to other ethnic communities. In other parts of Sikkim, the Nepalis settled rapidly and altered its demographic profile. Sikkim's polity continued to be dominated by the Lepcha–Bhutia elite until the 1950s, when the clamour for equal rights by Nepali citizens shook the foundations of the Sikkimese kingdom. Politically, the Sikkim government has rhetorically expressed its commitment to preserve Lepcha culture as part of its constitutional mandate. The government policies have been supportive and recognised the importance of preserving the Lepcha heritage.

On the cultural side, the Lepchas were converted to Buddhism around the 17th century when the kingdom of Sikkim and a number of monasteries were founded. Lhatsun Namkha Jigme (one of the patron saints who crowned Phuntsog Namgyal at Yoksum) played an important role in this. Barring a small minority, most Lepchas continue to follow a combination of their traditional shamanism and Tibetan Buddhism, without any major contradictions being manifest in subscribing to these two systems,[13] excepting recent abhorrence of animal sacrifice by the shamans and death ceremonies.[14] This explained why the Buddhist Lepchas of Sikkim retained some of their Lepcha cultural traits and their lifestyle. The number of shamans is declining, but simultaneously there is a strong current of revival shamanism as part of Lepcha identity politics (Arora 2004). Although the Christian missionaries entered Sikkim in the 19th century, large-scale conversion did not take place. The royal family of Sikkim neither facilitated nor welcomed the Christian missionaries. Culturally, the Lepchas of Sikkim did not face any identity crises or lose their cultural heritage, as was the case in neighbouring Darjeeling. Hence, the Lepchas are neither de-tribalised nor comparably Westernised in Sikkim.

The Lepchas' engagement with democratic politics in Sikkim has been more recent than that of their siblings living in West Bengal, and in Sikkim seats have been reserved for them in the Legislative Assembly despite being a numerical minority. Protected as a scheduled tribe since 1978 along with the Sikkimese Bhutias, this indigenous group has not struggled or been forced to compete with other groups until the Limbu and Tamang were also recognised as schedule tribes in 2002 (Arora 2004). Lepcha is one of the official languages and has been taught in schools since 1975. Books and periodicals are being published in that language. The Lepcha cultural association has been supported to promote Lepcha culture, organise archery contests, promote trainings in Lepcha handicrafts, and organise song and dance performances. Sikkim Radio and television regularly broadcast their literary activities, songs, dances, and dramas. In 2005, the Sikkim Legislative Assembly declared the Lepcha to be a Most Primitive Tribe and gave them further protection and special status for uplifting them from their backwardness. This reinforced their trope of being a vanishing tribe.

My engagement with the region reveals how the Lepchas living in urban areas – East Sikkim, South Sikkim, and West Sikkim – have more experience of multicultural settings and inter-ethnic competition. Many of them have also inter-married with other communities and been exposed to mass media, and democratic institutions, and accessed educational facilities provided by the state government. Lepcha youth in Sikkim, many of whom have benefitted from modern education, moved away from the villages and farming, and settled in urban areas, have started to value their traditions and heritage. They are increasingly helping the elders living in villages think about the future of their community. While traditional Lepcha livelihood practices were becoming economically unsustainable or even considered desirable, many youth who have lived outside Dzongu for their education in hostels are aspiring to assert their Lepcha-ness without its forest-dependent or agricultural foundation. By 2007, the remoteness of Dzongu had been sufficiently undermined not by any improvement in its road infrastructure but by the spread of modern telecommunication facilities and Tata Sky television.

While the Kalimpong Lepchas are making concerted efforts to re-tribalise, the Sikkimese Lepchas were never insecure about their cultural heritage. The upcoming possibility of construction of hydropower projects, and acquisition of land in Dzongu, placed it at the centre of global capitalism and shattered its idyllic image. It has become an intensely contested landscape (Arora 2009). This was vividly narrated by an elderly Athup Lepcha to me at Passingdon, Dzongu:

> We have to carefully preserve our land for our future generations. If we lose our land and livelihood, our community will be scattered. Then, our culture will be lost. How can you have Lepcha identity without Dzongu, this is our homeland of culture, religion, identity, of everything.

The launch of protests and rise of Affected Citizens of Teesta (ACT) and Joint Action Committee to organise a movement and pressurise the state government of Sikkim divided the residents into those who wanted to preserve Dzongu from those wanted it to modernise. The first generation of this educated class hailing from Dzongu and other remote areas of North Sikkim is making definite efforts to articulate its development demands and acquire a vocal presence in Sikkim's polity. This explains why the youth led and joined the Save the River Teesta movement opposing the construction of hydropower projects in Dzongu and North Sikkim. The fear of losing cultural traits associated with 'being Lepcha' has motivated many Lepcha youth to value them and to evolve strategies to preserve their language and celebrate rituals and markers of identity (e.g. cuisine and costumes), including decisions about whom to marry. For many of them, the movement enabled cultural rediscovery and political awakening (Arora 2014). Many ethnic associations have sprung up in North Sikkim, and some of these are actively organising various activities (literary, cultural events, publications, political decisions) in which elders and youth participate.

If one compares the Sikkimese Lepchas with the Kalimpong Lepchas, then there persist inter-generational differences in their exposure to modern democratic processes, acquisition of political agency, and access to development resources. The Sikkimese Lepchas admitted having learnt significantly from their Kalimpong siblings and leaders. I elaborate this historical process in the next section.

The Kalimpong 'stimulus' in cultural production

Relations of subordination do not automatically produce consciousness of being a subaltern group. The unity of the subaltern has to be produced and creatively constructed through various cultural practices. The restoration of subjectivity is a dynamic process for any subaltern group. Following Antonio Gramsci (1971), the organic intellectuals have struggled to change the mindset of the members and provide the group with a certain degree of homogeneity and awareness of their socio-economic position. The subaltern group needs to be energised and transformed into a politically conscious group, and this requires the deployment of icons, invention of symbols and historic images, and the spatial enactment of rituals in landscapes.

To know about Lepcha culture, social change, and the recent cultural revival, the Lepcha leaders of Sikkim constantly directed me towards Kalimpong back in 2001–2. As one commented:

> Our leaders at Kalimpong can educate you more, as they are actively working to preserve Lepcha heritage. The Lepchas of Dzongu are not as concerned or politically motivated to value their heritage, as yet. Circumstances may change and we are demanding government patronage, but we are not politically as effective as the Kalimpong Lepchas.

Many of the notable Lepcha teachers working in the schools of Sikkim (e.g. Dorji Wangdi and Lha Tsering) who are credited with revitalising the Lepcha language and rejuvenating the Lepcha literature in Sikkim indeed were indoctrinated at the Lungten Chok Lee at Kalimpong and migrated from the Darjeeling Hills for employment.

I first visited Kalimpong with members of the Sikkim Lepcha Youth Association in December 2001 to attend the Gaeebo A-chyuk celebrations at Damsang Fort, and this visit enabled me to establish contacts with the Lepcha ideologues based at Kalimpong and see the famous Lepcha museum. At Kalimpong, the Lepcha leaders fondly remembered Siiger and had copies of his two volumes. I also interviewed Major Lyangsong Tamsang, the eldest son of K. P. Tamsang (1915–85; he had worked at the School of Oriental and African Studies, London, and collaborated with the British linguist Richard Keith Sprigg. I interviewed Sprigg several times during 2003–4 in England). I stayed at P. T. Lepcha's house located on the outskirts of Kalimpong a few times for short durations and interviewed him at length and, with his help, interacted with other Kalimpong Lepchas during 2001–2. Thereafter, I interviewed and interacted with some Kalimpong Lepchas when they visited Delhi in connection with litigation and staging *dharna*s, or at Gangtok during my fieldwork in 2007–9. I have retained touch with them some via blogs and Facebook. I visited Kalimpong briefly in March 2013 and interviewed some of the emerging young leaders. Let me summarise the background of their political awakening and highlight the role of language revival in forging a common Lepcha identity independent of religion.

The first Lepcha associations (Mutanchi Rong Shezum) were established in Kalimpong back in 1925 but were not functioning effectively. An independent Lungten Chok Lee was established in 1967 by Foning to revive the Lepcha language and culture. During the 1970s, the Mutanchi Rong Shezum became quite active under K. P. Tamsang, and he motivated his son Lyangsong Tamsang to continue his legacy and work for uplifting the Lepcha community. The Indigenous Lepcha Tribal Association (ILTA)[15] was launched in the 1990s and formally registered in 2004. This association has played a critical and strategic role in preserving and promoting Lepcha language and literature by publishing textbooks (primary to higher secondary school level), Lepcha primers, Lepcha–English dictionary, books, and magazines. Lyangsong Tamsang highlights how, based on donations, ILTA has been managing about forty night schools to impart basic education and Lepcha language and culture.[16] ILTA has been demanding the introduction of Lepcha language in school curriculum in Darjeeling so that Lepcha children can be educated in their mother tongue. Since 1996, ILTA has instituted the 'Aathing K. P. Tamsang Lepcha Language and Literary Award' for the conservation, safeguard, and fostering of the Lepcha language, literature, and culture. It is given to either a person or a night school.

The activities of organic intellectuals residing at Kalimpong have played a critical role in mobilising and shaping the political agency of the Lepcha community over the past few decades. The democratic percolation of the association at the village level and its active promotion of school education, language learning, cultural education, and welfare activities have ensured that Lepchas are unified into a strong community. In the past few years, to deal with the crises of dwindling number of shamans, they have initiated training on learning shamanism and the art of performing traditional prayers and rituals. They have creatively instituted cultural events to periodically assert their identity, symbolically resurrect their subaltern past, and proclaim their unity (not the religious ones where the Church may raise objections) across the geographical boundaries invoking an erstwhile Lepcha-land and their mythical *mayel-lyang* (hidden paradise). The bilingual magazine *Aachuley* has played an important part in disseminating and writing their oral culture, showcasing their linguistic heritage, and perpetuating knowledge of their past history; recently, a blog for the magazine has also been started. The Lepcha subaltern have created their own forum in print and online (blogs and Facebook groups) to fashion their identity and imaginary for local and global consumption. As Azuk Tamsang, who despite being Christian has learnt to become a *bongthing* (shaman), explained: 'We are Lepcha foremost. We are at home in nature. For us our nature and culture is inseparable.' Many Kalimpong Lepchas give prominence to being Lepcha over their religious affiliation.

I am struck by the major difference and substantial efforts of the Kalimpong Lepchas to preserve their rich folk culture using meagre personal resources to establish a commendable museum at Bom Busty, promote language learning, market Lepcha handlooms and crafts, and ingeniously institute rituals to revitalise the community. Sikkim does not have any Lepcha museum, although the chief minister of Sikkim has been promising the establishment and grant of resources for the same for many years. Many of my Lepcha interlocutors in Sikkim time and again clarified how the dynamic political impulse emanating from Kalimpong significantly contributed to their self-awakening, revitalised their linguistic heritage, and regenerated their dying cultural traditions. Cultural revival in Sikkim is state-dependent and sponsored, while in Kalimpong it has been a bottom-up process.

In the course of my extended research, I have documented three perspectives on this engagement between the Lepchas of Sikkim and the Lepchas of Darjeeling Hills. First, it is those who would 'romanticise' and reiterate the state of harmonious co-existence and healthy ethnic alliance between the Lepchas and Bhutias based on the tradition of inter-marriage, Buddhism, and shared political privileges as indigenous inhabitants. They were indifferent to the Kalimpong group and treat them as outsiders. Second, it is those who emphasise the metamorphosis of the Lepchas living in the Darjeeling Hills (often termed 'Kalimpong Lepchas'), as compared to those of Sikkim. The Kalimpong siblings were considered more Westernised, exposed to democratic politics, and better organised to pressurise for achieving their demands. The Bhutias looked down upon the backward Lepchas and argued that common religion was not sufficient to bestow an equal status on them. This group also emphasises the internal differences between Lepcha and Bhutia material culture and socio-economic life. Third, it is a vocal group that continually denounces the Kalimpong influence. Many Sikkimese Bhutia leaders would blame the Kalimpong Lepchas for poisoning the minds of the Sikkimese Lepchas and instigating ethnic tensions between the two communities. They explained how,

> Our docile Sikkimese have become assertive, started questioning 'joint' decisions made on behalf of the two ethnic groups. They have now started defying the decisions taken by SIBLAC [Sikkim Bhutia Lepcha Apex Committee] under the influence of the politically aggressive Christian Lepchas of Kalimpong.

The emergence of ethnic leadership and political agency of the Lepchas of Sikkim is attributed to exogenous influences.

The organisational success of ILTA owes to its teamwork and strategic leadership. Let me acknowledge the role of three eminent senior leaders who have framed the Kalimpong stimulus. First, Major (retired) Lyangsong Tamsang (b. 1946) of the British Gorkha regiment is the eldest son of the renowned Lepcha linguist, writer, and thinker, the late K. P. Tamsang (1915–85). He has been writing extensively on various cultural themes and has played a major role in the revival of Lepcha language and culture. Serving as general secretary and later as president of the ILTA, Lyangsong has politically galvanised the Lepcha community. He is the most popular and prominent face of the Lepcha leadership at Kalimpong and has received several awards at the state and national levels (Lok Bhasha Samman 2001 and Vir Birsa Munda National Award 2003). He has promoted Lepcha literature at the Sahitya Akademi and very effectively represented the Lepchas as indigenous people to the United Nations Educational, Scientific and Cultural Organization (UNESCO).

Second, Sonam Tshering Lepcha (an ex-service man of Gorkha rifles) has been serving as the cultural secretary of ILTA for a long time and is regarded the backbone of Lepcha culture and its revival.[17] He is an adept poet who has composed more than 500 songs, a classical singer (renowned for his Aprya von [extempore poetic composition]), a dramatist, a maestro of traditional Lepcha musical instruments, an authority on folk culture (who has composed prayers for worshipping the Himalayas, worshipping nature, Mt Tendong, Mother Earth), and a *bongthing* (Figure 3.1). In 1967, he started bringing out *Aachuley* to disseminate information about Lepcha culture and heritage to the youth and others. The Lepcha museum located at Bom Busty is an outcome of his singular efforts to preserve Lepcha literary texts and cultural and musical heritage. He has received several state and national awards such as Sangeet Natak Akademi Award in 1996 and Padma Shri in 2003. His wife Hildamit Lepcha is an acclaimed singer and poetess, and also received the Padma Shri in 2013.

Third, P. T. Lepcha, who is an acclaimed Lepcha scholar, arranges marriages and is a *bongthing*. He received the Bhasha Samman Award in 2002 for

Figure 3.1 Sonam Tshering Lepcha offering prayers at Mt Tendong, 2002
Source: Vibha Arora.

Figure 3.2 P. T. Lepcha, 2002
Source: Vibha Arora.

his literary writings and recently translated parts of Rabindranath Tagore's *Gitanjali* into the Lepcha language. He has retired from the Central Intelligence Department of Bengal and lives in a village near Kalimpong town.

Many strategic decisions have been taken with the help of senior leaders and youth leaders who are active at various levels and in diverse forms. The tragic trope of Lepchas dissipating has been supplanted by a self-affirmative subjective presence. I will share a relevant extract from the English translation of a song composed by Sonam Tshering Tamsang titled 'Who Says the Lepchas Are Vanishing?' published by the Sahitya Akademi.[18] Using the historic figure of the slayed Lepcha king, the poet rouses the Lepchas to rally together:

> King Gaeboo Achyok did not die in vain
> From the Bhutanese swords,
> He's summoning and warning
> From his fort Damsang
> 'Quick, you Lepchas, come out from your houses;
> black clouds are gathering on four sides'
> Who says Lepchas are vanishing?

Lepchas are now a strong and awakened community, asserting their emplaced belonging – they have become a subaltern.

> It is true that Lepchas who are born and brought up in the urban areas are not practicing their culture but recently if we see the youth of these places, they are already seeking their identity by reconstructing their indigenous cultures.
>
> (Lepcha 2014)

The educated Lepcha youth of Sikkim and West Bengal are yearning for and practising their religious traditions and culture in a journey to recover their self; many have expressed that performing cultural rituals and offering prayers in their mother tongue helps them reclaim their roots. Their identity and what S. Feld and K. H. Basso (1996) term 'senses of place' have got deeply intermeshed with each other. The following three ceremonial occasions testify this.

A Lepcha sacred mountain: crafting ethnic unity

Identity, locality, and spatial practices have engendered a cultural politics of place. Traditionally, the Lepchas revere Mt Kanchenjunga and locate their hidden paradise or *mayel-lyang* in its five peaks and slopes. They define themselves as progeny of ancestors who lived in *mayel*. Mt Kanchenjunga is the place of origin and where their souls return upon death. However, the prominence of Buddhist connotations and rituals followed in worshipping Mt Kanchenjunga have gradually symbolised the ethnic unity of the Lepchas and Bhutias, and its nationalist association with the kingdom of Sikkim (Arora 2004, 2008; Steinmann 1996). To overcome the loss due to its incorporation into the Buddhist pantheon, the Lepchas of Kalimpong instituted the worship of Mt Tendong (2,652.9 m) that is located in South Sikkim. The ideologues cleverly upgraded Mt Tendong to a sacred mountain by insisting its seminal position in Lepcha folklore.

Lyangsong Tamsang (1997) details the mythology of a great deluge that occurred in River Teesta. With the drowning of great many fauna and human beings in the rising waters of the River Teesta, Mt Tendong was the only hill peak that gave refuge to humans and wildlife. It is only after a hill partridge offered millet beer to the creator that the waters subsided and normal life resumed. *Tendong Lho Rum Faat*, as its worship is termed in Lepcha language, originated as a ritual performed at Kalimpong and was later disseminated to Sikkim, where it gained wider recognition as a state-sponsored Lepcha cultural festival in the 1990s. Every year on 7 August, the Lepchas of Sikkim and Kalimpong jointly worship Mt Tendong at the summit, and later in separate cultural events on 8 August at Gangtok and 22 August at Kalimpong. Namgyal Lepcha, a former president of the Sikkim Lepcha Youth Association and member of the committee, explained to me (in 2002) that they decided that a shaman or *bongthing* would officiate at the prayers, since their original religion is a form of shamanism. The inventor and chief composer of prayers is identified to be Sonam Tshering Tamsang, who reads prayers from a book composed by him; Mt Tendong also happens to be the place of origin of his clan (*putso* in Lepcha). The Sikkim government declared 8 August as a state holiday to acknowledge the importance of this cultural festival for the Lepchas (ibid.: 23). This cultural event communicates an essential message of ecological harmony and propitiating mountains and revering nature.

It is widely proclaimed now that Mt Tendong is a sacred mountain and its worship is an ancient Lepcha festival.[19] However, this is not the case; it is an example of an invented tradition.[20] While the myth of deluge is mentioned in many books on folklore and mythology (Foning 1987; Kotturan 1976), there is no record of community prayers being organised for its worship in the past. When I traced the origins of this festival, I documented how it was invented by notable singer-writer Bhasha Samman awardee Sonam Tshering Lepcha (also of Tamsang family of Kalimpong), who has retired from the Department of Culture of Sikkim.

To offer prayers, I travelled with him and others to the summit of this mountain in August 2002 and have detailed my experience elsewhere on

Figure 3.3 Group that went to Mt Tendong to offer prayers and construct a shrine, 2002

Source: Vibha Arora.

the construction of a shrine (Arora 2008). Back in 2002, many a Sikkim Lepcha confessed to me that it was about ten years or so since they had started celebrating it. Mt Tendong has got 'mythologised in collective memory' over time, and the active construction of this invented tradition is being elided or forgotten (Connerton 1989; Hobsbawm 1983). A recent news report equally highlighted and reminded the public that this festival began to be celebrated on a large-scale only since 1993 and the Sikkim government declared 8 August to be holiday in 1997.[21]

An article published online by Azuk Tamsang in 2012 refreshes our memory and educates others: 'Lepchas are nature-lovers and nature-worshippers . . . the offering of Lepchas to Mt Tendong has a universal appeal and truth in it.'[22] Even Christian Lepchas participate actively in literary elocution competitions, perform traditional songs and dances, and so on. The organisers have reported how the enthusiasm of the Lepcha youth has been given a new direction with the organisation of this annual event. The Sikkimese Lepchas have embraced the symbol of Mt Tendong and the trope of being nature-worshippers with great enthusiasm.

Making of subaltern Lepcha and Kalimpong stimulus 97

The presence of the subaltern is constructed and refracted through their practices (O-Hanlon 1988: 202–3), and this explains why Mt Tendong has become the 'new' symbol of Lepcha culture and rejuvenated the divided community. This form of cultural production indicates, in Gramscian terms, the subversive power of subaltern organic intellectuals to challenge ethnic hegemony of the dominant others (Bhutias, Nepalis, Indians). It clearly represents Lepcha awakening, the rise of their self-consciousness and resilience of the circulated trope of worshipping nature. Its wider dissemination has affirmed their 'nature-worshipping' tribal identity and enabled the organic intellectuals to re-unite the members of the tribe and re-create borders with other ethnic groups. In August 2014, a large 4-metre-long rock (*lung-chok* in Lepcha) sourced from West Sikkim was installed at the summit of Mt Tendong. The chief minister himself trekked 7 km uphill to the summit from Damthang village and announced that a ropeway would be constructed in the near-future.

The legendary Gaeebo A-chyuk: memorialising the last Lepcha king

I often wondered about the political leaders and their legendary shamans. However, no authoritative account is available; based on Lepcha literature and oral history recordings, some were attempted but have not been completed. Nearly every Lepcha person is familiar with the prowess and wisdom of Tekong Tek (affectionately termed grandfather or *Thi-kung* in Lepcha). Foning offers an extended explanation where he insists on the egalitarian ethos of the Lepcha community. In his opinion, Mainwaring and other Europeans who spoke of Lepcha kings who ruled in the 15th century were grossly misled or mistaken: 'These are nothing but figments of imagination; they may be nothing more than dramatizing of some legendary figures by some of our own tribesmen, and given out to eager and enthusiastic foreigners' (Foning 1987: 8). Hardly any Lepcha elder ever narrated legends of any Lepcha chief or king during my fieldwork in Sikkim, excepting few who spoke of the Lepcha chief and an eminent *bongthing* (shaman) Men Salong who authored the Lepcha script and the *lazaong* (syllabic scheme) and his fort in West Sikkim.[23] Nevertheless, in Kalimpong, Gaeboo A-chyuk[24] occupies an important position in Lepcha collective memory. I was amazed to hear about Gaeebo A-chyuk from Lepchas at Kalimpong, who recounted his heroism and martial prowess in numerous conversations.[25] Foning (ibid.: 275) emphasises that Sikkimese history has ignored Gaeebo A-chyuk and done injustice to this valiant Lepcha.

Gaeebo A-chyuk is memorialised as a mighty legendary warrior who defended Lepchas and was killed treacherously by the wily Bhutanese around 1730. Written sources mention how this famous military commander or chief/king was assassinated by the Bhutanese and had resisted the third Sikkimese king's influence (Dolma and Namgyal 1908: 24; Foning 1987: 268–69; Risley 1894). Foning (1987: 8) credits him with constructing many forts in the Kalimpong region. While admitting his military prowess, he is remembered to have defied the king of Sikkim, 'This man, A-chyuk, could never have been a Lepcha, as understood in the real sense. At most, he was a half-breed, cultured, moulded and fashioned in the style of the [Sikkim] rulers themselves' (ibid.). This statement is self-contradictory as Foning devotes an entire chapter to him in the same book. There are numerous stories about his ancestry given to me during interviews, which are quite confusing; these are documented in Foning (ibid.: 265–80).

We make our spaces in the process of our identities (Massey 1995: 285), and these places reinforce our identities and demarcate territory. Damsang Fort is located about 15 km from Kalimpong town near Algarah, which is a scenic junction from where roads lead towards Kalimpong, Doars, and Sikkim.[26] The Lepchas claim the Damsang Fort was built by Gaeebo A-chyuk around 1690 and served as the headquarters of the Lepcha principality. Kalimpong (or Damsang)[27] was believed to be an independent country or region governed or ruled by the Lepcha warriors such as Gaeebo A-chyuk who defended the Lepcha community from being destroyed by successive attacks of the aggressive Bhutanese. After he was murdered, the Bhutanese ruled the area from Damsang Fort. In 1864, the British captured the fort and annexed Kalimpong; early reports submitted by British officers mention how this fort was under the Bhutanese in their reports. This fort and other nearby ruins of forts attributed to Gaeboo are built in traditional Lepcha architecture. This historic site contains the ruins of a fortress, or a palace, as it is termed, which includes sentry posts, stables for horses, rooms for guards, granary, rooms of the king and queen, and their bathing chambers; the site is protected by the Archaeological Survey of India (Foning 1987: 274–76). This fort is hailed as a 'historical holy place' where the Lepchas assemble every year to pay homage to their 'last Lepcha king' (Roy 2011).

I am guided by the argument how 'histories and identities are necessarily constructed and produced from many scattered fragments, fragments which do not contain the signs of any essential belonging inscribed in them' (O-Hanlon 1988: 197). There is very little written record of Lepcha history, and much of what is claimed to be history has been transmitted in the oral tradition. History and mythology creatively interlace with each other to historicise the living culture of the Lepchas of the eastern Himalayas. Historically, King Gaeebo A-chyuk may be fiction or reality. The recent scheduling of an annual celebration by ILTA in December underscores this iconic elevation. Every year on 20 December the Lepchas of India along with representatives of Lepcha communities living outside India in neighbouring Nepal and Bhutan gather at the ruins of the Damsang Fort to celebrate his birthday, publicly recount the legends of their mighty chief/king Gaeebo A-chyuk, and proclaim the message of their ethnic unity. On the morning of 20 December, Lepcha shamans go to Damsang Fort and offer prayers with traditional millet beer with elders, notable leaders, and others. A cultural festival is held later wherein dance troupes perform and singing contests and archery competitions are held. I attended the celebrations back in December 2001, and those ceremonies have gathered momentum since then. Now the Lepcha association organises a huge assembly at the *mela* ground (venue of festivities) in Kalimpong (some contests are now held here) and from there they take out a rally.[28]

The celebration of this festival indicates how the subaltern possesses the creative capacity 'to appropriate and mould cultural materials of any provenance to his own purpose and discard those that no longer which no longer serve them' (O-Hanlon 1988: 197). Why is only Gaeebo A-chyuk remembered? I was often intrigued about the political history of the Lepchas and their loyalty towards the kingdom of Sikkim and if there were other legendary figures.

I conducted extensive fieldwork at Kabi village of North Sikkim, which was the historic site of the ethnic alliance between the Lepcha shaman Tekong Tek and Khye Bumsa of Kham (Tibet) enacted in the 14th century. Kabi served as the residence of the influential Lepcha chieftain Karwang (progeny of Tekong Tek), who later became prime minister of the fifth *Chos-rgyal*, and his daughter married the sixth *Chos-rgyal*. The *History of Sikkim* (Dolma and Namgyal 1908) narrates the challenges of safeguarding Sikkim's borders against the more aggressive Gorkhas of Nepal and the Bhutanese, especially the reign of the fifth *Chos-rgyal* Namgyal Phuntsog (1734–80) and sixth *Chos-rgyal* Tsugphud Namgyal (1790–1863). In fact, Bho-lod's son, Chothup, excelled as military commander and repelled the Gorkhas and earned the sobriquet of Satrajeet. Kabi was also the site where Bho-lod, the Lepcha prime minister, was murdered in 1826. Despite the historical presence of these legendary figures, they are hardly remembered or their exploits narrated within Sikkim despite notable presence of their descendants even today.

The historic assassination of the Lepcha prime minister in 1826 led to a Lepcha rebellion and their exodus under Kotra Kungha to Illam in Nepal, escalating greater dependence of the king on Tibet. It led to the political decline of the Lepchas and prompted the entry of the British into the region as peace-makers (ibid.: 53; see also Sprigg 1995: 88–89, 1999). The Lepchas were employed in great numbers in the Sikkim militia and considered extremely loyal to the ruling family. The borders between Sikkim and

Nepal, and Sikkim and Bhutan, were ultimately fixed with the help of the imperial powers. Nonetheless, the image of the martial Lepcha has all but faded in contemporary memory.

The legacy of Gaeebo A-chyuk does provide them with mythological raw material of how Lepchas have not always been docile but were brave warriors in the past, maybe as a counterpose to the trope of the martial Gorkha. The leading tropes highlight the docility and servility of Lepchas rather than their bravery or combative competence. Lepcha marksmanship is remarkable and established every year in the archery festivals and contests held at Kalimpong and in Sikkim.

The institution of the birth anniversary celebrations of Gaeebo A-chyuk indicates political creativity and desire to recover a subaltern past. Needless to say, the legend of King Gaeebo A-chyuk has established the historic fact of Kalimpong being an original Lepcha-land once ruled by brave warriors such as Gaeebo A-chyuk. It is important to note that Lyangsong Tamsang (retired from the British Gorkha regiment) and many of the key office-bearers of ILTA are retired pensioners from the army and the police (e.g. Pasang Tshering Lepcha, Nubu Tshering Lepcha, Palden Lepcha, O. T. Lepcha, Posong Tshering Lepcha). Hence, showcasing a martial heritage is a strategic way in which the Lepcha community is signalling to others, especially the Gorkhas, that they are not weaklings.[29] Many politically important decisions and programmes for the Lepcha community have been launched and broadcast to the public from Damsang Fort, a historic venue on his birthday. An annual commemorative volume and the Lepcha lunar calendar are released every year on this day at Kalimpong. Culture is inherently political and, simultaneously, the political is encultured for resistance and self-affirmation.

Long March and transformation of Dzongu into a holy land

The opposition to the hydropower projects over River Teesta took an organisational form in 2007, and the Lepchas of Sikkim played a prominent part therein (see Arora 2009, 2014). The agitated activists organised under the banner of ACT assert that the Lepchas belong to the land and the land belongs to them. They have voiced strong objections on cultural, religious, ecological, and political grounds. The peaceful nature-worshipping Lepchas have used non-violent methods of agitation as part of their protest campaign (Arora 2007, 2014). Located at the heart of Sikkim, Dzongu, regarded the cradle of their civilisation, became the epitome of an endangered indigenous culture. It was transformed into becoming the heart of Lepcha community, and the homeland of their belonging in the landscape. Dzongu was transformed into the battleground for defending the future of Lepcha culture during this movement (Arora 2009, 2014).

An emphasis on the cultural politics of space underscores the simultaneity of symbolic and material struggles over territory (Massey 1995). 'Dams over Dzongu will be built over our dead bodies', proclaimed the banner on 6 January 2008 that marked the 200th day of their relay hunger strike and public opposition. A small contingent of Lepchas led by Lyangsong Tamsang dressed in traditional attire came to Gangtok on this momentous day, and shamans performed traditional prayers for the well-being of the activists. They sang a Lepcha song titled *Rumlyang*, declaring Dzongu to be their 'God's land', their ultimate 'holy land'. This song eventually became an anthem for the activists. Sharing the dais with the ACT leaders, Ren Lyangsong Tamsang gave a rousing memorable inspiring speech. He roused the Lepchas to unite under the Lepcha flag and recognise their moral duty and willingness to sacrifice their sweat, blood, and even soul for it. Despite living outside Sikkim, the Kalimpong Lepcha delegation expressed their strong connection with Dzongu and their unwillingness to compromise their emplaced identity. Overall, the West Bengal Lepchas supported the Sikkimese activists in manifold ways – organising rallies,[30] participating in the relay hunger strike at Gangtok, signing of memorandum, sharing resources, and formally pressurising the government to reconsider its decision and abandon the proposed projects. The activists have jointly demanded the complete scrapping of all projects located in Dzongu (Arora 2009, 2013, 2014) and rapidly disseminated the idea of it being a sacred landscape/holy land.

The activists have been campaigning among the local villagers since 2004–5 and sensitising the local villagers about the impact of the project. Prior to 2007, the Lepcha activists did admit the location of sacred sites within Dzongu but never ever termed it to be a pilgrimage centre, excepting the Tholung monastery (Arora 2006). For the Kalimpong Lepchas, who only had heard of Dzongu and never lived here, it rapidly acquired the status of a sacred complex by 2007. They declared that they would not allow it to be desecrated by any landscape-altering development projects. After celebrating the 200th day of the movement at Gangtok, a group of about 30 Kalimpong Lepcha pilgrims went to Dzongu to perform traditional prayers and reconnect with their ancestral cultural homeland, to see the landscape of their folk tales. Loden Lepcha (who has married the daughter of the former president of the Lepcha Association at Darjeeling), who hosted them, shared how after crossing the bridge they kissed the holy ground and took samples of soil and stones and carefully kept it in their bag as keepsake. Gyatso Lepcha of Passingdon village, who accompanied them during their visit to Tingvong and Lingza waterfalls, shared how Dorjee Lepcha and others baptised themselves and took Lepcha names. Being a Lepcha became a 'religion' superior to their Buddhist or Christian faiths. Leaders such as Sherap Lepcha, Pema Lepcha, Gyatso Lepcha, and Tseten Lepcha[31] shared with me how other Dzongu Lepchas reacted when these Lepcha pilgrims started shouting *Aachuley*, singing songs loudly, and declaring Dzongu to be a holy land during their journey to different sacred sites located in Dzongu. During this visit, the pilgrims had a small verbal exchange with some locals, who complained about them to the administration and police. Thereafter, they were asked to leave Dzongu immediately.

Angry and upset, the pilgrims went back to Kalimpong and burnt the effigy of the Dzongu MLA (Member of the Legislative Assembly), which angered the ruling party supporters even further. The ILTA leaders decided to use their political skills to challenge the Sikkim government's control over the locality and counter their inherent right to undertake a pilgrimage by making plans to revisit Dzongu on a larger scale. Lyangsong Tamsang applied directly to the Sikkim government seeking permission for a large contingent of Lepchas to undertake a pilgrimage to Dzongu and perform traditional rituals and offer prayers at holy places. The April 2008 'Long March 1' included Lepcha men and women, elders and youth, and shamans and *lamas* who walked in rain from Tribeni Ghat in Kalimpong towards Sikkim. On crossing into Rangpo at Sikkim, they were welcomed by the Sikkimese Lepchas and a group of policemen. They walked to Singtam and

Figure 3.4 River Teesta flowing through Sikkim
Source: Vibha Arora.

found that the ruling party had forced all shops to shut down. Hungry, wet, and tired the pilgrims were also locked out of their rented accommodation in lodges. The ACT activists were very upset and wanted peace to be preserved. As the government imposed Section 144 at Gangtok, they diverted the Long March 1 towards Dikchu. Here, local Lepchas who were pro-dam supporters and party activists pelted stones at the Lepcha pilgrims who were declared dangerous outsiders who were disrupting the tranquillity of Sikkim. Many stood at the bridge connecting Dikchu to Dzongu, and declared their intention to thwart entry of the pilgrims. The cultural/religious purpose of the march was completely sidelined by the politically charged context, so the Kalimpong Lepchas were persuaded to abandon their march. With tears in their eyes, disheartened and confused at this reception, they were bundled into vehicles and forced to return to West Bengal. Intra-Lepcha clashes would have undone and undermined their ethnic unity. At Rangpo, they were addressed by Medha Patkar who then travelled to Gangtok to meet the activists at Bhutia – Lepcha house and Dawa and Tenzing in the hospital.[32]

During an interview, Azuk Tamsangmoo Lepcha declared,

> Dzongu is a holy place, and it's the holy land where our souls rest after their death. It is the only place where our ancient culture and traditions are still intact, so we cannot afford to let it be desecrated and destroyed. To protect our mother-land, our holy-land, we will do everything that we can do to ensure its sanctity is not undermined.

The transformative cultural politics of a pilgrimage (*Faokraam-Takraam*, in Lepcha language) undertaken by the Kalimpong Lepchas' foot-march in April 2008 to save Dzongu fortified this conception of Dzongu. However, the resistance offered by the Lepchas of Dzongu in thwarting the Kalimpong Lepchas' plans to perform their pilgrimage (Long March 1) in April 2008 categorically establishes the contours of this recent social construction of Dzongu as a holy land.

Not all Lepchas of Dzongu are comfortable with the transformation of their reserve into a holy land or opposing the projects. Duncan McDuie-Ra (2011: 89–98) discusses the dilemmas of pro-development Lepcha citizens and non-governmental organisations such as Mutanchi Lom Aal Shezum,[33] which has been involved in cultural preservation, yet ironically are supporting the ruling party and the government's decision to construct the hydropower projects. Most of the gram panchayats of Dzongu have consistently supported the government. Despite massive political campaigning against the ruling party by the ACT activists in Dzongu, they voted them back in power in October 2007 and 2014. These pro-dam supporters want

Dzongu to be opened up for development and overcome its infrastructural backwardness. They are persuaded by the promise that the company would invest a percentage of the profit from the sale of power for their welfare and socio-economic development (opening of hospitals, modern schools with computing facilities, scholarships for education, funds for monasteries, banking facilities, etc.). In November 2009, when ILTA and Kalimpong Lepchas wanted to take a 'Long March 2', they wrote to the Ministry of Tribal Affairs, Government of India, and insisted their rights under the Indian Constitution to do so.[34] Their requests were countered by the delegation of Dzongu panchayat representatives and Lepcha residents, who formally submitted to the Sikkim government and administration that this permission be denied. They insisted that they did not want the peace and tranquillity of Dzongu to be disturbed by these outsiders – Lepchas of West Bengal.[35] The coalescing of pilgrimage and political practices indeed embattled Lepchas against each other, divided families, embittered neighbours, shattered the close-knit communities, and affected social life in the Lepcha reserve.

A young woman graduating from the Government College, Gangtok, during an interview in 2009 explained, 'Everyone is talking about saving Dzongu. I am born there, so it's my motherland. How can the government destroy and illegally acquire my motherland. How can I sit quietly? We have to protest and speak up against this injustice.' A Dzongu youth studying in the Tashi Namgyal Academy of Gangtok elaborated at Bhutia – Lepcha house,

> I have now started thinking more and more about my unique culture as I cannot assume it will be there for my children. It's rooted in the land. It is part of my identity and I have to fight for its future. I have to support these valiant leaders. This movement has made me value my land and my heritage.

As another stated, 'I did not value Dzongu before, and its importance for my self-identity. Because of this movement, and the way the Kalimpong Lepchas attempted a pilgrimage to Dzongu, I can neither ignore my heritage and a responsibility to safeguard it.'

Activists sat on an indefinite relay hunger strike at the Bhutia – Lepcha house in Gangtok for 915 days, and three activists undertook two rounds of unbroken fasts. These exerted moral pressure that culminated in pressurising the government into withdrawing four projects in Dzongu. However, other hydropower projects such as Panang located in Dzongu and Teesta Stage IV (520 MW) adjoining Dzongu have been given clearance (Arora 2009). The protests subsided in 2010 due to various reasons, but the sentiments of belonging continue to live a life of their own. As another stated, 'ACT has made us rethink and chose to act or die.' What are the other options before the struggling youth? A few educated youth and former anti-dam activists (lawyers, teachers, graduates) have decided to settle back in Dzongu and contribute to its socio-development by opening private schools and handicraft centres and are offering trekking services to tourists.

The rise of the subaltern Lepcha citizen

Rapidly marginalised in their Himalayan homeland numerically dominated by the ethnic Nepali, the Lepchas have been democratically struggling, campaigning for allocation of resources to preserve their cultural heritage and further socio-educational development after joining the Indian Union. The identity crisis of the Lepchas of West Bengal is partly due to their embracing Christianity and distancing themselves from shamanism and Buddhism and partly shaped by a wider politico-economic context wherein the Nepali groups have marginalised them ethnically and overpowered them politico-economically in their homeland since the colonial period. The Lepchas of Darjeeling Hills had to compete with other tribes of the state and contour the distinctive symbols in response to processes and structures of a post-colonial India and other tribal exemplars. This explains why the recovery of a subaltern past and cultural production of symbols to reinforce tribal unity largely arose in West Bengal and subsequently transferred to a recently democratised Sikkim. The organic intellectuals based at Kalimpong shaped the subaltern Lepcha praxis and subsequently influenced the praxis of Sikkimese Lepchas. The Lepchas of Sikkim and other ethnic groups duly recognise and acknowledge the power of the Kalimpong stimulus in organising and galvanising the Lepcha subaltern.

The Kalimpong Lepchas have claimed their rights as equal citizens and demanded their subaltern status be acknowledged to enable them to transform themselves. They have not yet transcended their subaltern position by deploying the discourse of the rights of indigenous and citizens of India; affirmation of subaltern position and acknowledgement by the state is an important way by which the community is seeking protection and access to development resources. The three examples of cultural production I have discussed in the chapter have been deployed to evoke subjectivity, spatially claim ethnoscapes, astutely utilise and create political opportunities, engender cultural ceremonies to assertively emphasise citizenship, and mobilise themselves to express their belonging. The first, the rise of worship of Mt Tendong as a cultural festival, facilitated re-unification of a religiously divided and geographically dispersed Lepcha community, and gave credibility to their identity as nature-worshippers. The second, manifestation in the form of King Gaeebo A-chyuk's birthday celebrations, has played an important role in resurrecting Lepcha political vanity and establishing their martial abilities. The third indicates how the Lepchas of Darjeeling Hills have played a pivotal role in politically galvanising public opinion (nationally and internationally using the indigenous people networks, including that of UNESCO) in support of and to oppose construction of hydropower projects in Dzongu, which they proclaimed to be their *rumlyang mo* (like heaven, in Lepcha) and their *mayel-lyang* (hidden paradise, in Lepcha). Thanks to the Long March of the Lepchas from Kalimpong in April 2008 where they attempted (but were prevented) to visit the land of their ancestors, Dzongu was elevated to a holy land.

The Kalimpong stimulus culturally (re)produced and invented Dzongu as a centre for pilgrimage, which enhanced the emotive appeal of cultural-ecological resistance to hydropower projects during 2007–10. Due to the prominent role played by the Lepcha leaders in campaigning on environmental issues affecting their livelihood, they are increasingly being recognised as a bio-centric group or eco-warriors. The ascendancy of the Lepcha community as environmental custodians of the Himalayas has now achieved local, regional, and international attention because of their combined networking efforts and outreach. After the anti-dam agitations weakened and formally subsided in Sikkim in 2010, the Lepchas of West Bengal were aggrieved and demoralised by the real possibility of losing their cultural bastion. They have not given up hoping or struggling for citizenship, asserting their rights as the indigenous, and differentiating themselves from the Gorkhas.

The subaltern leaders and political elite have acquired the ability to politically advance their interests as part of the state and civil society. Civil society comprises the space for organising political struggles for the recognition of new needs and interests, and asserting rights as citizens. Following Pandey (2006), the Lepchas have become 'subaltern citizens' and demonstrably engendered a subaltern elite. Applying Nancy Fraser's (1990: 66–67) conceptualisation, drawing on their oppositional identities, advancing their ethnic interests, and asserting their development needs, the Lepchas have managed to not only create subaltern counter-publics but even enter the public sphere. The persistent assertiveness as an indigene was finally rewarded in February 2013 when the Lepchas of Darjeeling Hills were granted a Lepcha Development Board by the state government of West Bengal.

I was conducting fieldwork in Dzongu, so I travelled to Kalimpong to interview some Lepcha leaders in February 2013. At this time, within Sikkim, former ACT leader Dawa Lepcha had decided to take a political route by contesting state-level elections from Dzongu as a candidate for the newly launched political party – Sikkim Krantikari Morcha. Dawa Lepcha had aspired to become an MLA of Dzongu so that he could formally oppose hydropower projects in the Sikkim Legislative Assembly and get a better deal for his tribal community. Effective organisation of political opposition in civil society may not necessarily or easily translate into electoral success. This is precisely why, despite his popularity, Dawa Lepcha did not win the elections, but lost to another Dzongu Lepcha who is affiliated with the pro-dam Sikkim Democratic Front (the ruling party).[36]

On 3 September 2013, Lepchas dressed in traditional attire lined up the streets of Kalimpong to give a hearty welcome to Mamata Banerjee, the West Bengal chief minister. The streets of Kalimpong reverberated with *Aachuley* (a Lepcha slogan meaning hail to the Himalayas) as Lepchas steadily streamed out of their homes while the Nepali confined themselves to their homes in response to Gorkha Janmukti Morcha's (henceforth GJM) call for a *ghar bhitra janta* (literally, people should be inside homes, in the Nepali language, a shut-down).[37] Later in the day, a large gathering of Lepchas congregated at the *mela* ground to participate in a ceremony organised to felicitate Mamata Banerjee with the title *Kingchum Darmit* (goddess of fortune, in Lepcha language). Ren. Lyangsong Tamsang (the former president of the ILTA and now the president of the Lepcha Development Board) conferred this honorary title on her person in recognition of her pivotal role in granting them a development board. As the chief minister of West Bengal, Mamata Banerjee proclaimed how the state government would facilitate the setting up of 'a Lepcha Heritage Centre, Lepcha Academy, a Community Centre, a library and introduction of Lepcha language in the primary classes from next academic year, besides construction of a building for Lepcha Development Board' and enhanced their ecstatic pleasure.[38]

On her part, Mamata Banerjee addressed the gathering and indirectly conveyed a political message to upset the GJM leaders:

> Lepchas are the original, first and the oldest inhabitants of Darjeeling. But you all have always kept peace and unity and struggled to stand by yourself, and that is why I respect you all a lot. You all are truly brave. Your population is not less, almost 1.5 lakh Lepchas are residents of Darjeeling.[39]

She ended her speech by emphasising how Darjeeling, Kurseong, and Kalimpong are and would remain a part of West Bengal and she would rather embrace death than witness the partition of the state.

The Lepchas of West Bengal have never opposed the demand for Gorkhaland while pressing forth their own ethnic interests. Subalternity, by definition, signifies the impossibility of autonomy (Prakash 1994: 1480). The

Lepchas had no intention of antagonising or offending the economically advanced, politically powerful, numerically preponderant Nepali residents of Darjeeling and GJM, but they inevitably did so by organising the 3 September 2013 function to felicitate Mamata Banerjee. The GJM-led Gorkha Territorial Administration (GTA) has interpreted the grant of a Lepcha board as a clever ploy of the state government to counteract their demand for a separate Gorkhaland and ethnically divide the hill communities. By January 2014, other ethnic groups such as Tamang, Sherpas, Limbus, and Bhutias had also initiated demands for development boards. Explicitly, subalternity and ethnic identities are contextual and relational identities. Hence, a subaltern Lepcha may be dominated in a relation yet also undermine this dominance and be dominant in relation to others in multi-ethnic contexts. It will be erroneous to perceive the Lepcha as a vanishing tribe or even an exemplar of the wretched of the earth who is always going to be located at the receiving end, dominated, and placed at the bottom.

The emergence of subaltern counter-publics has widened the scope and nature of democratic participation and promoted decentralisation in the eastern Himalayas. They have also become the foundation of the possibility of subaltern elite joining the public sphere and transforming it. The making and rise of the Lepcha subaltern illustrates the democratic inspiration from below, the local interaction of marginalised groups with democratic institutions and their participation in civil society, the interpenetration of the past and the present, and the creative re-working of these by actors.

To conclude this chapter, realising an ethnically specific Lepcha Development Board is a laudatory achievement and a positive outcome of sustained campaigning by the ILTA of Kalimpong and showcases their leaders' prowess in negotiating and pressurising both the national and state governments. It is the result of a combination of well-coordinated teamwork and political timing wherein the state government of West Bengal is determined to preserve its territorial integrity. The triumphant Lepcha leaders renamed their board as 'Mayellyang Lepcha Development Board', with Kalimpong as its headquarters. The nomenclature is not an inconsequential one, as they cope with the possibility of losing their beloved *mayel-lyang* (paradise identified with Dzongu in Sikkim) to hydropower projects. The political achievement of the Kalimpong Lepchas has ignited the imagination of Lepcha leaders in Sikkim, and they are accordingly transforming their political strategy.

Notes

1 Conceptually, 'subaltern' originated in the Italian Marxist Gramsci's writings and referred to subordination in terms of race, class, gender, and language, and to signal the centrality of dominant–dominated relationship in history. The idea of a relational subaltern who had an autonomous domain

in history has profoundly shaped historical discourse and post-colonial criticism after the launch of the subaltern studies by Ranjit Guha (1983). Recent scholarship pays greater attention to developing 'the emergence of subalternity as a discursive effect without abandoning the notion of the subaltern as a subject and agent' (Nilsen and Roy 2015: 12–15; Prakash 1994: 1481). Gyan Prakash (1994: 1476) highlights how the idea of subaltern is frequently appearing in other geographies (Latin America, Africa, etc.) and addressing questions of tribe, race, and gender.

2 Spivak (1988) provocatively problematises the production and retrieval of subaltern speech due to subaltern's dependence on and relative (in)ability to use dominant discursive fields. She emphasises muting and doubts their ability to speak or be heard, while Guha (1996) counters this by arguing how statism authorises and shapes the criteria of the historic. He, therefore, instructs us to 'choose to listen' and make extra effort to cultivate the disposition to hear and interact with the small voices that are constantly drowned in the noise of statist commands (ibid.: 1–3, 9).

3 Acknowledging how subaltern agency is doubly besieged, Sivaramakrishnan (1995) criticises the way subaltern consciousness is treated ahistorically and as static in subaltern studies. I make a modest attempt to historicise the emergence of the Lepcha subaltern.

4 Lepcha word meaning 'king, chief'.

5 See http://aachulay.blogspot.in/2010/07/mayel-lyang-lepchas-about-sikkim-and.html (accessed on 10 November 2014).

6 See Cesnsusindia.gov.in (accessed on 10 November 2014). The figures for 2011 are not available as yet.

7 My doctoral research (Arora 2004) largely focused on politicisation of numerous sacred sites and rituals of the sacred landscape among the Buddhist Lepchas and Bhutias in Himalayan Sikkim.

8 Sonam Wangdi Lepcha was then a judge in the Sikkim High Court.

9 I will mention some notable authors who have also contributed to the study of Lepchas, although the purpose of this is not to compile a bibliography. Many Lepcha writers such as K. P. Tamsang, Lyangsong Tamsang, Sonam Tshering Tamsang, Pasang Tshering Lepcha, Azuk Tamsang, and Gautam Rongkup have been publishing books and articles to disseminate information about the rich culture and language of the community. There have been a few other publications such as Chattopadhyay (1990) and Dolma (2010). Articles on various aspects of Lepcha life by R. K. Sprigg, Heleen Plaisier, Kerry Little, D. C. Roy, Jenny Bentley, and me have highlighted change and cultural revival among the Lepchas in the two states.

10 Fascinated by the Lepchas, Mainwaring declared, 'To allow the Lepcha race, and language to die out would indeed be most barbarous, and inexpressibly sad' (1876: xx).

11 'Gorkhaland' is the term coined by Subhash Ghising, who led the militant Gorkha National Liberation Front movement in the 1980s to demand statehood for Darjeeling Hills inhabited predominantly by the Nepalis.

12 The Gorkhas assert their politico-economic marginalisation at the hands of the dominant Bengali groups while they dominate other ethnic groups within the Nepali category, and other ethnic groups such as Lepchas, the *adivasis*, and the peasant groups residing in the hills and the Doar region.

13 The Lepchas used to bury their dead but stopped doing so after their conversion to Buddhism, and the priests gradually became more powerful than the shamans in the rites of passage. The death rituals of the Lepchas have changed drastically with the abandonment of burial and shamans no longer guiding the souls of the departed to their place of origin, thereby obstructing possibilities of rebirth. The Buddhist practice of cremation is believed to prevent the reincarnation of souls of shamans, and there is a recent movement towards burying the bodies of the shamans in Dzongu than burning them.
14 Gorer (1938: 180–81) was quite impressed with this syncretism.
15 This association has a website of its own: http://lepchaassociation.blogspot.in/ (accessed on 14 November 2014).
16 http://aachulay.blogspot.in/2010/06/safeguarding-of-indigenous-lepcha.html (accessed on 21 December 2014).
17 For more information, see http://aachulay.blogspot.in/2011/03/lepcha-songs-in-book.html and http://lepchaassociation.blogspot.in/2010/07/chapter-iv-old-lepcha-folk-songs.html (accessed on 14 November 2014).
18 See http://aachulay.blogspot.in/2010/07/who-says-lepchas-are-vanishing.html (accessed on 14 November 2014).
19 See, for instance, a recent *Aachuley* article at http://aachulay.blogspot.in/2012/07/tendong-hlo-rum-fat-and-its.html (accessed on 8 December 2014).
20 Hobsbawm (1983: 1) explains that the term 'invented tradition' includes both 'traditions' actually invented, constructed, and formally instituted and those emerging in a less traceable manner within a brief and dateable period.
21 See 'CM at Mt Tendong', http://sikkimnow.blogspot.in/2014/08/state-level-tendong-lho-rum-faat.html (accessed on 8 December 2014).
22 See http://aachulay.blogspot.in/2012_07_01_archive.html (accessed on 14 November 2014).
23 The figure of Men Salong is surrounded with controversies as he is supposed to have countered the Sikkimese king.
24 'Gaeebo' or 'Gaybu' in Lepcha means the 'victor'. 'A-chyuk' is a composite of 'A' meaning 'that' in Lepcha and 'Chyuk' meaning 'which is permissible'. Hence, A-chyuk means 'that which is permissible', indicating the capacity of the governor to act independently and take decisions (Foning 1987: 267, 276).
25 I knew about him from reading Foning (1987: 265–80).
26 In September 2014, Chief Minister Mamata Banerjee declared that the state government was planning to build a 'New Darjeeling' here to attract tourists and decongest influx in Darjeeling and Kalimpong towns. See http://kalimpongnews.net/2014/09/05/new-darjeeling-plan/ (accessed on 8 December 2014).
27 Hence the Lepchas of the region are called Damsangmu.
28 See http://darjeelingtimes.com/archive/main-news/98-citizen-news/1948-279th-birthday-anniversary-of-lepcha-last-king-gaeboo-aachyok-celebrated-in-kalimpong.html (accessed on 8 December 2014) and http://aachulay.blogspot.in/2011/04/279th-birth-anniversary-celebration-of.html (accessed on 12 December 2014).
29 Employment in some regiments of the Indian army continues to be on ethnic lines.

30 For example, http://www.kalimpong.info/2007/10/08/lepcha-rally-in-kalimpong-draws-thousands/ (accessed on 24 November 2014).
31 Interviews conducted in Dzongu in 2013.
32 Interview with ACT leader Tseten Lepcha, who escorted Medha Patkar during her Sikkim visit.
33 I interviewed the president of Mutanchi Lom Aal Shezum residing at Passingdon village three times between 2007 and 2013.
34 See http://sikkimnews.blogspot.in/2009/11/long-march-2-by-lepchas-from-darjeeling.html (accessed on 23 December 2014).
35 See http://sikkimnews.blogspot.in/2009/11/lepchas-from-dzongu-demand-diversion-of.html (accessed on 23 December 2014).
36 With the help of lawyers, some Lepcha activists of ACT have finally managed to challenge the environmental clearances given to Teesta IV and obtained a valuable chance to file a counter-petition at the National Green Tribunal in August 2014. See ACT press release dated 4 May 2014, http://www.actsikkim.com/projects.html (accessed on 8 December 2014).
37 For the past few decades, the Darjeeling Hills has been aflame and witnessed much violence with the Nepali demand for a separate ethnic state and sub-division of the West Bengal state. To appease the agitating Nepali, a Gorkha Territorial Administration (GTA, a semi-autonomous administrative council for Darjeeling Hills) was established in March 2012 after a memorandum was signed between representatives of the state government, central government, and GJM in July 2011. The GTA is empowered with administrative, executive, and financial powers. However, it does not have any legislative powers. The GTA replaced the Darjeeling Gorkha Hill Council that was formed in 1988.
38 See https://aitmc.org/news_details.php?nid=1552 (accessed on 14 November 2014).
39 See https://aitmc.org/news_details.php?nid=1552 (accessed on 14 November 2014).

References

Arora, V. 2004. *Just a Pile of Stones! The Politicisation of Indigenous Knowledge, Identity and Sacred Landscapes among the Lepcha and Bhutia Tribes of Contemporary Sikkim, India*. DPhil Thesis, University of Oxford, Oxford.

———. 2006. 'The Roots and the Route of Secularism in Sikkim', *Economic and Political Weekly*, 41 (38): 4063–71.

———. 2007. 'Unheard Voices of Protest in Sikkim', *Economic and Political Weekly*, 42 (34): 3451–54.

———. 2008. 'What Is Sacred about That Pile of Stones at Mt Tendong? Serendipity, Complicity, and Circumstantial Activism in the Production of Anthropological Knowledge of Sikkim, India', in N. Halstead, E. Hirsch and J. Okley (eds.), *Knowing How to Know: Fieldwork and the Ethnographic Present*, pp. 130–50. Oxford: Berghahn Books.

———. 2009. '"They Are All Set to Dam(n) Our Future": Contested Development through Hydel Power in Democratic Sikkim', *Sociological Bulletin*, 58 (1): 94–114.

———. 2013. 'The Paradox of Democracy in the Northeast and the Eastern Himalayas', in V. Arora and N. Jayaram (eds.), *Routeing Democracy in the Himalayas: Experiments and Experiences*, pp. 101–32. New Delhi: Routledge.

———. 2014. 'Weepingsikkim.blogspot.com: Reconfiguring Lepcha Belonging with Cyber-belonging', in G. Toffin and J. Pfaff-Czarencka (eds.), *Facing Globalisation in the Himalayas: Belonging and Politics of the Self*, pp. 344–68. New Delhi: Sage Publications.

Bhasin, V. 1989. *Ecology, Culture, and Change: Tribals of Sikkim Himalayas.* New Delhi: Inter-India Publications.

Chatterjee, P. 2004. *The Politics of the Governed: Reflections on Popular Politics in Most of the World.* New York: Columbia University Press.

Chattopadhyay, T. 1990. *Lepchas and Their Heritage.* New Delhi: B. R. Publishing Corporation.

Connerton, P. 1989. *How Societies Remember.* Cambridge: Cambridge University Press.

Dolma, Y. 2010. *Legends of the Lepchas: Folktales from Sikkim.* New Delhi: Westlands Publications.

Dolma, Y. and T. Namgyal. 1908. *The History of Sikkim* [English translation]. Gangtok: Namgyal Institute of Tibetology.

Feld, S. and K. H. Basso. 1996. *Senses of Place.* Santa Fe: University of Washington Press.

Foning, A. 1987. *Lepcha: My Vanishing Tribe.* London: Tavistock.

Fraser, N. 1990. 'Rethinking the Public Sphere: A Contribution to the Critique of Actually Existing Democracy', *Social Text*, 25 (26): 56–80.

Gorer, G. 1938. *Himalayan Village: An Account of the Lepchas of Sikkim.* London: Michael Joseph.

Gowloog, R. R. 1995. *Lingthem Revisited: Social Changes in a Lepcha Village of North Sikkim.* New Delhi: Har-Anand Publications.

———. 2013. 'Identity Formation among the Lepchas of West Bengal and Sikkim', *Studies of Tribes and Tribals*, 11 (1): 19–23.

Gramsci, A. 1971. *Selections from the Prison Notebooks.* New York: International Publishers.

Guha, R. 1983. *Elementary Aspects of Peasant Insurgency in Colonial India.* New Delhi: Oxford University Press.

———. 1996. 'The Small Voice of History', in S. Amin and D. Chakraborty (eds.), *Subaltern Studies – IX: Writings on South Asian History and Society*, pp. 1–12. New Delhi: Oxford University Press.

Harriss, J., K. Stokke and O. Tornquist. 2004. 'Introduction: The New Local Politics of Democratisation', in J. Harriss, K. Stokke and O. Tornquist (eds.), *Politicizing Democracy: The New Local Politics of Democratisation*, pp. 1–28. London: Palgrave Macmillan.

Hobsbawm, E. 1983. 'Introduction: Inventing Traditions', in E. Hobsbawm and T. Ranger (eds.), *The Invention of Tradition*, pp. 1–14. New York: Cambridge University Press.

Kotturan, J. 1976. *Folk Tales of Sikkim.* New Delhi: Sterling Publishers.

Lepcha, D. 2014. 'Is Lepcha Really a Vanishing Tribe?', *Aachuley*, November, http://aachulay.blogspot.in/2014/11/is-lepcha-really-vanishing-tribe.html (accessed on 23 December 2014).

Mainwaring, G. B. 1876. *A Grammar of the Rong (Lepcha) Language, as It Exists in the Lepcha and the Darjeeling Hills*. Calcutta: Baptist Mission Press.

Mainwaring, G. B. and A. Grunwedel. 1898. *Dictionary of the Lepcha Language*. Berlin: Unger Brothers.

Massey, D. 1995. *The Conceptualisation of Place*. Oxford: Oxford University Press.

McDuie-Ra, D. 2011. 'The Dilemmas of Pro-development Actors: Viewing State – Ethnic Minority Relations and Intra-ethnic Dynamics through Contentious Development Projects', *Asian Ethnicity*, 12 (1): 77–100.

Nilsen, A. G. and S. Roy. 2015. 'Reconceptualizing Subaltern Politics in Contemporary India', in A. G. Nilsen and S. Roy (eds.), *New Subaltern Politics: Reconceptualizing Hegemony and Resistance in Contemporary India*, pp. 1–27. New Delhi: Oxford University Press.

O-Hanlon, R. 1988. 'Recovering the Subject: Subaltern Studies and Histories of Resistance in Colonial South Asia', *Modern Asian Studies*, 22 (1): 189–224.

Pandey, G. 2006. 'The Subaltern as Subaltern Citizen', *Economic and Political Weekly*, 41 (46): 4735–41.

Prakash, G. 1994. 'Subaltern Studies as Postcolonial Criticism', *American Historical Review*, 99 (5): 1475–90.

Risley, H. H. (ed.). 1894. *The Gazetteer of Sikkim*. Calcutta: Bengal Secretariat Press.

Roy, D. C. 2011. 'Damsang Gree: A Historical Holy Place of the Lepchas', *Aachuley*, May, http://aachulay.blogspot.in/2011/05/damsang-gree-historical-holy-place-of.html (accessed on 14 November 2014).

Sammadar, R. 2012. 'The Politics of a Political Society', in A. Gudavarthy (ed.), *Re-framing Democracy and Agency in India: Interrogating Political Society*, pp. 125–52. London: Anthem Press.

Sivaramakrishnan, K. 1995. 'Situating the Subaltern: History and Anthropology in the Subaltern Studies Project', *Journal of Historical Sociology*, 8 (4): 395–429.

Spivak, G. 1988. 'Can the Subaltern Speak?', in C. Nelson and L. Grossberg (eds.), *Marxism and the Interpretation of Culture*, pp. 271–312. Urbana: University of Illinois Press.

Sprigg, R. K. 1995/1826. 'The End of an Era in the Social and Political History of Sikkim', *Bulletin of Tibetology* (n.s.), Seminar Volume, 88–92.

———. 1999. 'An Appeal to Captain Lloyd by Kaji Gorok of Illam (1828)', *Aachuley*, 3: 5–11.

Steinmann, B. 1996. 'Mountain Deities, the Invisible Body of the Society', in A. M. Blondeau (ed.), *Reflections of the Mountain: Essays on the History and Social Meaning of the Mountain Cult in Tibet and the Himalaya*, pp. 179–217. Vienna: Verlag Der Österreichischen Akademie Der Wissenschaften.

Tamsang, A. 2012. 'Tendong Hlo Rum Fat and Its Significance', *Aachuley*, July, http://aachulay.blogspot.in/2012_07_01_archive.html (accessed on 14 November 2014).

Tamsang, L. T. 1997. 'Offering to Mt Tendong and Its Significance', *Aachuley*, 1: 22–23.

Thakur, R. N. 1988. *Himalayan Lepchas*. New Delhi: Archives Publisher Distributors.

Waddell, L. A. 1978. *Among the Himalayas*. Kathmandu: Ratna Pustak Bhandar.

White, J. C. 1909. *Sikkim and Bhutan: Twenty Years on the North-East Frontier (1887–1908)*. London: Edward Arnold.

Part II
Negotiating democracy

4 Monks, elections, and foreign travels
Democracy and the monastic order in western Arunachal Pradesh, North-East India

Swargajyoti Gohain

This chapter explores the participation of monks in elections in Tawang and West Kameng, two districts located in western Arunachal Pradesh, inhabited by the Monpas, a Tibetan Buddhist ethnic minority. I highlight the central role played by monks in electoral politics in postcolonial India; but rather than seeing this as reflecting an increasing democratisation of monasteries, I argue that monks' participation in electoral processes is linked to livelihood and authority issues in a system where traditional means of sustenance have been substantially reduced and the leadership role of monks in society has been diluted. Participating in electoral politics constitutes one among several other livelihood options or strategies that include migration to foreign shores, which has been adopted by novice monks as well as high-ranking monastic personnel in order to cope with their relative loss of prestige and authority in modern social milieus.

In principle, participatory democracy, with its ideal of governance by and for the people, appears to be at odds with the Tibetan (Buddhist) state system, which was traditionally based on an elite leadership with a strong monastic composition and was sustained by a system of manorial estates and taxation (*khre*). In this chapter, drawing on Ayesha Jalal's (1995: 3) distinction between the formal and substantive aspects of democracy I am more interested in showing how monks in Monyul utilise the formal procedures of electoral democracy in order to retain their authority in non-monastic spheres. The *formal* implies the norms guaranteeing the right to vote and freedom of expression, while the *substantive* is democracy in its empirical aspect; and any democracy is a compound of its formal and substantive meanings. I argue that monks engage with electoral institutions not to change but to preserve the monastic authority structure. Participation of monks in elections is a means to sustain a presence in social and public affairs through engagement with, rather than abstinence from, state structures. I focus on the specific examples from Monyul, and especially on the career of the late T. G. Rinpoche, the head of Ganden Rabgye Ling monastery (also known as Upper Gonpa) in Bomdila, West Kameng, to illustrate this process. This case compares to the role of *sangha* (monastic body) representative that Vibha Arora (2006) discusses in her article on the interface between democracy and secularism in Sikkim.

Tawang and West Kameng districts are collectively known as Monyul, a Tibetan-origin term meaning 'lowland' (*mon* means 'low' and *yul* means 'land' or 'settlement'). Previously, Monyul referred to all low-lying territories in the Tibetan borderlands, and Monpa referred to the people living in the lowlands. Currently, Monyul is mainly used to refer to the westernmost districts of Arunachal Pradesh, with a population of 113,523 (Government of India 2001). Once described as 'an outlying district of Tibet' (Kingdon-Ward 1938: 613), Monyul came under Tibetan rule in 1681 through a decree of the Fifth Dalai Lama, which declared that, henceforth, Tawang (La'og yul sum) and its neighbouring areas would be ruled by the 'king' (Dalai Lama) of Tibet (Aris 1980). In the same year, work on the imposing Ganden Lhatse Namgyal or Tawang monastery began, and Monpa villagers in and around Tawang started paying taxes to the monastery. While all four sects of Tibetan Buddhism – Nyingma, Kagyu, Sakya, and Gelug – are followed in Monyul, the Tawang monastery, which is of the Gelug order, was established as a Gelug military outpost in 17th-century sectarian wars between Tibet and Bhutan, with an administration directly linked to the religious Government of Tibet.[1] Besides political and spiritual rule by Tibet, the Monpas shared trade ties, kinship connections, and cultural relations with both Tibet and Bhutan, and Monyul functioned as a corridor (ibid.) in this trans-Himalayan traffic of goods and people.

Monyul became a part of India in 1914 following the demarcation of the McMahon Line as the Indo-Tibetan boundary by the British colonial rulers, but Tibetan authorities continued to collect taxes from this region until 1951, when, in response to the imminent Chinese takeover of Tibet, the postcolonial Indian government sent an expedition to Tawang to put an end to Tibetan tax-collection. However, Monyul remained part of the trans-Himalayan trade networks until the border war between India and China in 1962 led to all passages between Monyul and Tibet being militarily closed and cross-border contact curbed. Along with the Monpas, many other Tibetan Buddhist communities on the Indo-Tibetan border were detached from their previous monastic networks and absorbed into the new democratic framework of India (see Arora 2006). The Monpas were listed as one of the twenty-six scheduled tribes of the North-Eastern Frontier Areas, a tract that was originally an administrative division of Assam State but was established into the separate state of Arunachal Pradesh in 1987.

As the governance of Tawang monastery changed hands from that of the Tibetan to the postcolonial Indian state, and Monyul was merged into the social and politico-economic networks of India, the impact of the political transition was felt most keenly by the monastic populations who now had to negotiate with administrative structures very different from those of the previous system. The Panchayat Raj Regulation for village-level governance came into effect in Arunachal Pradesh in 1967 (Mathew 1995); the first assembly elections were held in February 1978 after Arunachal Pradesh evolved into a union territory, and the first state elections for all sixty constituencies were held in February 1990.

This chapter is based on data collected through participant observation in Dirang in West Kameng district during the fifth assembly elections conducted in Arunachal Pradesh in 2009, when the Congress party swept to power.[2] While in residence in Dirang constituency, I was drawn into the fractured, inflamed public sphere of elections. I listened to heated political debates conducted in sundry living rooms and offices, heard partisan stories of support or impassioned denouncement of disfavoured candidates, and was treated to the personal histories of not only the two main candidates contesting from Dirang but also their wives, brothers, cousins, and friends. I witnessed the frenzied campaigning, and the nightly public feasts that were part of the campaigns, the rioting and sporadic outbreaks of violence before elections, and finally the post-election jubilations (of the winning camp) and gloom (of the losing camp).

I noted how monks actively participated in the election practices and even helped shape the public discourse around elections. However, while monks justify their entry into politics as social work, I argue that popular criticism reinstates the boundary between monastic and electoral spaces by rejecting monks in politics. In this regard, I discuss lay perspectives regarding monkhood, and especially the role of gossip, in framing a dissonance between monkhood as an ideal type (i.e. what it should be) and monkhood as a lived reality today. As monks strive to retain grip over a slowly vanishing mode of authority by expanding the frontiers of activity to non-traditional modes of authority, they paradoxically give rise to a critical popular discourse on an ideal-typical monkhood, from which ordinary monks in the present are seen to deviate. Despite the increased visibility of monks in the electoral arena, popular gossip limits the extent to which monks can transfer their authority from the monastic to the lay public sphere.

Politics as social work and Buddhism in the margins

Historically, the relation between Buddhism and politics has differed according to national context as well as the particular variant of Buddhism. In the Tibetan state, especially from the reign of the Fifth Dalai Lama onwards, the relation between Tibetan Buddhism and politics was spelled out through the notion of '*chosi nyitrel* [a Tibetan phrase] which translates as religion and political affairs joined together', where the government was committed to upholding the Tibetan Buddhist religious ideology (Goldstein 1989: 2). What I am discussing here, however, is the role of monks in Arunachal Pradesh in democratic political processes of independent India. While the phenomenon of monks in secular[3] (for lack of a better term) politics can be traced back to anti-colonial struggles of the 19th century which later morphed into nationalist struggles (Harrison 2008; Tambiah 1992), I am interested in the particular relation between the Buddhist clergy and democratic politics in a context (Arunachal Pradesh) where Tibetan Buddhists are a minority.

In other words, Buddhism from the margins presents a picture very different from that of regions where Buddhism has been a dominant political force and where members of the Buddhist order have assumed leadership roles in organising popular protest. For example, in countries such as Sri Lanka, Thailand, and Myanmar or the erstwhile kingdom of Sikkim and the former Tibetan nation, members of the clergy have commanded public support and openly influenced the shape of the country's politics; they have articulated a distinctive form of religious nationalism. Stanley J. Tambiah (1992) shows how in Sinhalese nationalism, religion (Buddhism), race (Aryan), and territory (Sinhaladwipa or the island of Sri Lanka) were conflated by the monk leadership. Many predominantly Buddhist societies have also witnessed militant movements led by members of the Buddhist order, prompting much discussion on what motivates followers of a faith that advocates other-worldly values, even world renunciation, to participate in worldly activities such as politics. Paul Harrison, professor of Buddhist Studies at Stanford University, stated during an interview that 'in many Buddhist countries where previously things were not so bad in terms of political oppression and so on . . . members of the Sangha feel obliged to take up [political] struggle in order to improve the situation, for the people' (2008).

The situation is different in Monyul, as here Buddhism is a minority religion in relation to the rest of Arunachal Pradesh, where a substantial part of the population are Christians converted during the colonial period. Hence, in Monyul, monks engage with state institutions in order to ameliorate their progressive marginalisation by adopting a strategy of accommodation rather than confrontation. Yet accommodating democratic politics in monastic life is a means to an end, here the end being a greater space for manoeuvre for the monastic community that is struggling to hold on to a gradually shrinking cultural universe in a Tibetan enclave.

Monpa monks frequently allude to their time in politics as social work. As Harrison (2008) remarks, some members of the Buddhist order consider it their duty to engage in social work in order to improve the lot of the people, rather than simply devoting themselves to their own enlightenment; and, in several past instances, many Buddhist monks have justified their participation in politics by folding the latter into the monastic vocation. Let me illustrate my argument by discussing the personal career trajectory of the now-departed Thirteenth Tsona Gontse Rinpoche of West Kameng, or T. G. Rinpoche (henceforth Rinpoche), as he was popularly known.

Rinpoche was born on 19 August 1967 in Tawang in Arunachal Pradesh as Jetsun Tenzin Jampal Wangchuk. Right after his birth, he was recognised by His Holiness the Fourteenth Dalai Lama as the Thirteenth reincarnation of the Tsonawa (Master of Vinaya) – the Buddhist code of discipline laid down in the canonical text, *Vinaya Pitaka*.[4] Like many monks in Monyul, he went to the Drepung Loseling Monastery in South India for his monastic studies, graduating with the degree of Geshe Lharampa – the highest monastic degree equivalent to a doctorate in Buddhist philosophy. After returning to Monyul, he became active in social work and politics, and served as state minister of industry, textile and handicrafts, and hydropower and cabinet minister of tourism in his different tenures with the Congress government in Arunachal Pradesh, before withdrawing from politics in 2009 (Figure 4.1). People who knew Rinpoche during his younger days say

Figure 4.1 Late Tsona Gontse Rinpoche giving blessings in his chamber at Dirang, 2008

Source: Swargajyoti Gohain.

that he decided to join electoral politics once he realised that only political power would help him bring about cultural reforms in Monyul.

In 2009, Rinpoche, incumbent minister, did not run for re-elections. A pamphlet was circulated with the title 'Buddhist Monk Exits Politics' by the Buddhist Culture Preservation Society, the cultural organisation he had founded. Despite its title, which suggests a discussion on Rinpoche's motives for quitting electoral politics, the pamphlet focused more on the monk's biography, where his stint in politics was merged with his personal history. We find a similar merger of the personal and the social/vocational in Rinpoche's own explanation for renouncing politics during one of my interviews with him:

> I have used political power as the medium – delivering something to the people. I have not accepted *kursi* [chair or seat implying political position in electoral parlance] as my destination. . . . I have divided my life into parts – one part devoted to studies, the second part, 20–50 years devoted to work – social, religious. Later part, [there will be] less travel, less work and preparation for next life.

Rinpoche refers to his years in politics as being a passing phase of life during which he devoted himself to social and religious work. The equation between politics and social work, however, gets an added component in his statement here, where we discern a position of accommodation to state structures:

> In earlier times, religious *guru* [teacher] had so much responsibility to look after the public. They did not govern directly, Maharaja used to be head of state. [But] Maharaja would be acting according to the *guru*. Because of that people were shown the correct direction. After India became a republic, there is no place for *rajguru* [royal advisor]. According to Indian constitution, there is no role for the *guru*s. Monks only can become *dost* [friends] according to constitution. I have few friends among MLAs [members of legislative assemblies]. I can influence them, share my views and serve for the betterment of our country. So I took a decision to become the *friend* of the MLAs. (Emphasis mine)

According to Rinpoche, the downsizing of the role of monks in Arunachal Pradesh as part of the Indian republic with its democratic values and procedures has had adverse consequences for Monpa society as a whole. In earlier times and polities such as in the Tibetan state and Sikkim (Arora 2006), when monks as religious teachers had advisory powers, social and moral values were preserved, as 'people were shown the correct direction'. In order to preserve the moral fabric of people in present Monyul, therefore, monks must take leadership positions once again. However, since the Indian constitution professing secular values has no place for any specific political role for religious teachers, a monk leader must transform himself from being a 'teacher' into a 'friend'. Then his functions and capacities for giving advice and influencing popular opinion will remain constant, and his presence in society will be preserved through a role displacement.

Friendship here is not simply about moving from an earlier role of a teacher to non-hierarchical modes of mentorship in order to accommodate democratic structures. It indicates a positive attitude to state processes where collaboration, rather than antagonism, is stressed. As an (former) elected MLA himself during the late 1990s and early 2000s, Rinpoche was not situated outside the state apparatus or in opposition to it, but was working from within.

In the context of Monyul's location, it is not surprising that Rinpoche, despite his forceful and forthright character, projects himself as a 'friend', not only of the people but also of the state. Monyul is a border in which the Indian state has huge investments in security and surveillance, and people here have to be mindful of how they position themselves. Any stance that contains a critique of government policies may possibly be construed as anti-national sentiment, as I realised during my fieldwork period. Those who perceived my interview work to be similar to that of government representatives conducting surveys for state-related projects were careful to praise the government for all the good work it has done for the people of this region.

Second, though Rinpoche has a large following within Monyul (and in other Tibetan Buddhist cultural regions outside Monyul), he is not the accepted spiritual leader in the state-wide circuits of Arunachal Pradesh. The deficit in his spiritual influence was filled through his political clout – something that was acquired only by campaigning and contesting for state-level elections. People close to Rinpoche recalled to me during elections how the monk had been very disturbed at the lack of development and gradual erosion of Buddhist customs in Monyul when he returned home after monastic studies in 1987. Rinpoche decided to join politics out of a wish to have greater say in decision making, since his position, however elevated, as spiritual leader of a Buddhist community, did not give him a voice in matters of the state.

During his tenure as politician, Rinpoche not only built and renovated many Buddhist monasteries, *chortens* (Tibetan word meaning *stupa*s), and other religious monuments but also encouraged public reflection on the importance of Buddhism through organisations he personally formed or helped foster. He encouraged a trend of organising weekend religious teachings on Buddhism at the Ganden Rabgye Ling monastery in Bomdila, West Kameng. In 2003, he formally launched the Mon Autonomous Region Demand Committee, which is an organisation to lead the movement for the formation of an autonomous council for the two districts of West Kameng and Tawang. A dominant narrative within the discourse of local autonomy is the preservation of (Tibetan Buddhist) culture. While the demand for autonomy is popular among Monpas from different quarters, its more vocal proponents come from the monastic sections. A main agenda of the Mon Autonomous Region Demand Committee is to gain official recognition for *Bhoti* (the Tibetan script) as mother tongue in schools and offices of Monyul. In 2009, Rinpoche did not contest the state elections but was placed in charge of a new state department called the Karmic and Adhyatmik Affairs, which is managed by the Union Ministry of Culture. He may have withdrawn from the world of electoral politics, but his leadership in public affairs has been recognised widely and continues.

The transition from the monastery to the world of democratic politics, however, was not necessarily a smooth one. I was once witness to a small incident while seated in Rinpoche's chamber in November 2009. Rinpoche sat in the centre surrounded by high-ranking monks from Monyul or visiting from the Ganden monastery at Mondgod, Karnataka. He suddenly picked up his phone and made a call to an administrative office in Itanagar, the state capital, but the moment he identified himself as 'TG', as if those were his secular initials, I noticed looks of discomfiture on the faces of the other monks. Rinpoche himself appeared to have taken in stride the pragmatic aspect of the address used for him. The reason behind the palpable discomfort of the other monks in his chamber was explained to me in another conversation with a woman from Tawang, who commented, 'We regard him [Rinpoche] as god', and according to her, one who is god or has god-like qualities should not move about or rub shoulders with ordinary mortals. Yes, that is exactly what Rinpoche must do in lay political and social circles.

Elections at Dirang, October 2009

> Peculiar also to the postcolony is the way the relationship between rulers and ruled is forged by means of a specific practice: simulacrum (*le simulacre*). This explains why dictators can go to sleep at night lulled by roars of adulation and support only to wake up the next morning to find their golden calves smashed and their tablets of law overturned. The applauding crowds of yesterday have become today a cursing, abusive mob.
>
> (Mbembe 1992: 10)

Dirang is a small town in West Kameng at an altitude of 4,911 feet. Situated between Tawang and Bomdila, the district headquarters of West Kameng, Dirang is inhabited by Monpa and Sajalong (formerly known as Miji) indigenous communities along with traders and military populations from other parts of India. In Dirang, I witnessed the contested terrain of the public sphere during the 2009 elections. This small town, which otherwise presents a placid character, becomes extraordinarily fired up with strong passions during the elections. Elections are infamous for creating rifts between family or kin members supporting rival candidates. In 2009, the two main candidates for the Dirang constituency were the incumbent minister of the Indian National Congress and his young contender and former protégé contesting with a People's Party of Arunachal ticket. Supporters of both candidates openly declared their allegiance and campaigned for the candidate of their choice, and high school, college, and university-going youth were sucked into the whirlpool of election campaigning.

The contest in Dirang, compared to the other towns, was particularly intense as the stakes were said to be between the conservative figure of the incumbent and the revolutionary outlook of the younger candidate standing in opposition. During the Dirang elections, both candidates vied with each other to offer medical services, transport, and such facilities to supporters. For villagers, elections are a time to get as much as possible from the contesting candidates before they cast their votes, since politicians are famous for retracting their given word later. The candidates, who also know

Figure 4.2 Monastery under construction in Dirang, 2013
Source: Swargajyoti Gohain.

this, bend over backwards to please voters. A person injured after being thrown from a tractor was taken to Itanagar on an all-expenses-paid trip sponsored by one of the candidates. This kind of distribution of largesse before elections (and also post-elections for select people) is common in Arunachal Pradesh. Where candidates did not have money themselves, they need to have rich supporters as benefactors and sponsors. Villagers, thus, look forward to elections with festive expectations, and money, gifts, and local liquor (*ara* and *chang* in the Tibetan language) flow freely and openly (*khulle aam* in the Hindi language) during this time.

In fact, elections are almost a new kind of enterprise or business wherein the unemployed youth seek lucrative returns. Politicians use local young men as henchmen during election time in order to cajole, coerce, or secure voters. These young men may later be nominated as village headman or be aided in getting elected as *anchal* or *zilla samiti* (Hindi word for village-level councils) members. Politicians are treated like celebrities, for people depend on their largesse in order to rise socially (through jobs) or materially. Conversely, if politicians do not help their supporters or fulfil their expectations after elections are over, those very same supporters might turn against them or jump to a rival side in the next elections. There is usually a huge turnout of voters on election day, for candidates bring in their supporters from distant villages in cars requisitioned for that specific purpose.

Elections are a charade in which both voters and politicians participate, although both know the stakes involved. Elections are less about issues and agendas, and more about raw money and power. What changes do you expect the leaders to bring in this society? This was the wrong question to ask, as I realised progressively. What do you expect to get (in terms of monetary and service benefits) in the present, preferably even before the vote is cast, is the correct question that explains popular attitude. Perhaps, this is not the wrong attitude but the appropriate one in a context where voters are willing to sell their votes. The practices of *khulle aam* (open bribes) to voters hint at what is carried on, perhaps in more muffled tones, in other parts of India.

As my friend Namang (name changed) reasoned, there is nothing wrong in taking what the politicians give, because the voters are only getting back what is rightfully theirs ('Everything belongs to the public, after all,' was his argument). If, as Harry West argues, 'democracy necessarily resides within the languages and terminologies used by "the people" to assess power's workings in their midst' (2008: 118), then the discourse of rationalisation that surrounds the system of open give and take during election time in Arunachal Pradesh only illuminates how people can interpret one of the ideals of democracy. That is, at the end of the day, politicians, as representatives, depend on people's votes to remain in power and that vote-giving is ultimately about fulfilling the, often pecuniary, interests of the people. Whereas in other states one gets to hear stories about unfulfilled promises, as politicians promise to pay back later, in Arunachal Pradesh, people are smart enough to grab what they can before the politician has any chance to renege.

The support shown by the monks to political candidates in the Dirang elections was similarly conditional, resting on expectations of gains after the elections were over or repayment for favours already shown. The politicians, on their part, were in need of the moral authority that the support of a religious leader could give them in a society where religion dominates daily life. During election time, monks are thus encouraged to exercise their traditional roles of *rajguru*. In Dirang, both the candidates had their own monk advisor, who attempted to influence the outcome of electoral results. Both monks had aspirations that they considered would be fulfilled only with the help of political allies. In 2009, one monk was overseeing the construction of a monastery at Dirang that would provide boarding for monk students as well as for old and destitute people. This monk was grateful for the generosity of the incumbent minister in providing funds for building the monastery, and supported his patron's candidature. The other monk supporting the opposition candidate was of the view that the minister had not done much for the monastic populations, while the opposition had promised to allot a substantial sum to him for constructing a monastery in Dirang as well as fulfil other conditions of pressing concern for monastic sections in the present such as regularising the position of monks teaching *Bhoti* language in schools. When the election results were declared, the younger contender emerged the winner to the jubilation of his monk advisor, who was proud that his candidate won through the force of his prayers. As we passed the house of the defeated minister, sounds of a ceremony being conducted wafted to us, and the monk looked at me and shrugged, saying that these ceremonies (held to propitiate protector deities) were now futile, since the minister had already lost the elections this time.

The principle of give and take that involved politicians and the common men thus also extended to these monks. The material and social power that accrues to politicians in the current set-up attracts a section of the monks who are eager to reclaim their declining authority among the public. The participation of monks in elections, directly or indirectly, shows aspirations that have to do with advancing agendas that would have practical benefits for the monastic populations or some aspect of the monastic system. Participation in electoral practices thus becomes a means of achieving pragmatic benefits or returns for the monastic communities.

Monks, cars, and foreign travel: gossip in the lay–monastic interface

When monks come out from within the monastic walls to take part in democracy's processes, they are, however, brought into sharper public scrutiny. There is increasing questioning by the laity today of monastic interest in materialistic values. In a public question–answer session during the visit of His Eminence Sakya Trizin Rinpoche to Tawang in April 2010, a young man, who introduced himself as a Buddhist, asked the following question:

> Our Buddhists monks today are very materialistic – they have their own houses and cars. How far are they practising renunciation? Lord Buddha practised non-attachment – he left his own house, all his worldly possessions, but our monks have everything.

Sakya Rimpoche's answer to this was as follows:

> One must renounce attachments. Even if you have lots of possessions, and you do not have attachments, then it does not affect . . . but if you have a small thing, and you have strong attachments [to it] then it is a great hindrance. Of course, not all monks are perfect. They are just like our fingers . . . all kinds of different levels. But there are great Boddhisattvas who own lots of possessions, but they do not have attachments, and so it does not affect the renunciation.

Later, Dawa (name changed), another friend, confided in me that while the question had been a very good one, Rinpoche's answer had not been satisfactory. He reasoned that if attachment does not arise, then it is all very good. But how can attachment not develop towards one's worldly possessions? The aforementioned question and my friend's comment mirror a common perception among lay Monpas today regarding the lifestyle of monks in contemporary Arunachal Pradesh. It is widely said that *lamas* are materially very well off. Most monks have their own houses, cars, and expensive technical gadgets. A lot of gossip abounds in lay circles on the clandestine activities of monks that are in violation of their monastic vows.

A particular anecdote, discussed as an exemplar of how the monastic vows are breached, narrates the story of a nun and monk who got married and had children. A favourite topic of gossip-mongers is to discuss the carnal objectives of certain robed individuals. A female friend Drema (name changed) once furtively pointed out to me that an ex-monk, a *Bhoti* teacher, fell in love with his ward's mother and later married her. The ex-monk is apparently very rich for he has foreign sponsors, who, as mischievous talk would have it, are unaware of his activities. In gossip circles, people talk, often with a tinge of envy, about the rich and lavish lifestyles of monks. When monks flaunt their wealth, local girls who crave expensive, imported goods fall in with their plans. 'My own wife's sister's daughter has a *lama* friend now based in Taiwan who chats with her on cell phones, and also sent her a digital camera,' Tsering, a government employee, told me, and his wife added that her sister knows a *lama* in Karnataka who sends her expensive handsets, shawls, and clothes. The common conclusion is that *lamas* have become materialistic and corrupted now. Monks' interest in politics is similarly viewed as unhealthy and driven by lust for money.

The gossip concerning the deviant behaviour of Buddhist monks is based on an idealised perception of how monks as spiritual figures should be behaving. 'Earlier monks used to sleep on wooden cots and now they sleep on imported mattresses and use imported blankets,' Dawa said ruefully. The behaviour of monks today is seen to depart from an ideal set of behaviours by which the laity measure and pass judgement on the former. While the context and circumstances in which monks live today are changed, the monks themselves are expected to behave in conformity with an older ideal. Censorious gossip thus creates a division between monkhood as an expected ideal and its lived realities.

The dissonance between monastic traditions and the changing realities is also reflected in the concerns expressed in a document brought out during a workshop on Tawang monastery (Approach paper n.d.), which draws attention to the problems in maintaining continuous ties between monastery and village society in a changing milieu. As in other parts of the Buddhist world, it was previously customary for each family in the surrounding villages of Tawang, having three sons and more, to send their second son (*Bu-sum Barma*) to become a monk in the Tawang monastery, the breach of which custom resulted in community fines. In the traditional system, each family had to contribute food grains to the Tawang monastery twice a year, once in summer and once in autumn, and had to provide firewood to the monastery in rotation.

With the change in political system, former links between monastery and lay society gradually eroded. Families today mostly prefer to pay cash as donations rather than participate in voluntary service for monasteries. On their part, monasteries are sometimes forced to recognise the difficulty of holding onto ancient customs in a rapidly modernising society. For example, one of the peculiar problems faced by Tawang monastery today is the immoral tendencies fostered in impressionable young *lamas* sent for caretaker duties in subordinate monasteries for a period of three years at a stretch, where outside the disciplining spheres of the Tawang monastery, they 'get spoiled' by 'getting attracted to women and alcohol' (Approach paper n.d.).

Young monks, on their part, appeared to be aware of the aspersions cast on their conduct by the laity, but they argue back that monkhood in its ideal form must be adapted to the constraints and challenges faced by monkhood as a lived reality in the present. Sonam (name changed), a monk at Tawang monastery, remarked that if people acquired more knowledge about Buddhism, they would be better able to understand and empathise with the plight of monks in modern times. Many of the monastic customs are out of sync with present realities. For example, out of the 253 vows that a *lama* has to take in order to progress to *gelong* (Tibetan word for fully ordained status) one concerns a certain physical and social distance to be maintained from women. Such conditions are difficult to maintain in today's world. He gives another example from his own experiences. When he goes on duty to monasteries outside town, he has to halt one night at the marketplace so that he can catch an early morning vehicle back to Tawang. But then people spread the slander that a monk is staying at a market accommodation when he should, in fact, be staying at the monastery premises. According to this monk, if people really knew how strenuous his duties were and that it involved a long trudge uphill to the monastery, they would look more kindly upon his staying in the market for one night. As for using private vehicles for transportation, he argued that monks use taxis not out of a desire for comfort but out of a simple wish to save time.

Critical public opinion, however, holds that nowadays monks are too enamoured of material goods, craving, just like any other teenager or young man, all the latest gadgets in the market and carrying in their cloth bag much more than necessity dictates. This is not to say that lay people are losing their faith in religion. People still have unswerving faith in the Dalai Lama and regularly go to *wang* (Tibetan word for blessings). While they may be more questioning of the modern *lamas'* lifestyles, their religious faith has not abated. It is simply that they are losing faith in monks as their spiritual guides. Even Rinpoche admits, 'Earlier monks used to be respected. Nowadays, people are not respecting monks. So that is why we need support of the people.' A reassertion of monastic authority is thus incumbent on monks, especially those in the upper ranks of the monastic hierarchy. Participation in elections becomes a way to adapt to new modes of commanding authority.

Popular gossip regarding the increasingly materialist bent displayed by contemporary monks extends also to foreign travel by the latter. If running for elections or advising electoral candidates constitutes one avenue for expanding opportunities for *lamas*, equally, if not more, desirable is foreign travel, meaning travel to richer countries such as Japan, Taiwan, and the United States. Many monks have foreign sponsors and are given their stipend in foreign currency and hence are rich, while many others try to go abroad after passing the final monastic exams, and if they succeed there, they start amassing money by performing ceremonies in the houses of wealthy patrons. Since *lamas* staying abroad do not incur much personal expenditures, they save up or send money to their relatives back at home, and once they return, they sometimes even start businesses of their own.

A critical popular discourse has now developed on why monks choose to go abroad. According to Dawa, monkhood has become a kind of enterprise today. The notion of monkhood as business in public discourse once again calls attention to the gradual professionalisation of monkhood. While this component might always have been present to an extent, where parents regarded monkhood as a way of moving out of poverty, earlier it was veiled, whereas nowadays it is visible and open to public criticism. Second, earlier monkhood was a 'culturally valued' mode of earning an income (Goldstein 1989: 21), whereas today many see the income part of monkhood being subservient to the cultural values that it encodes.

My monk acquaintances admit that while it is true that many *lamas* desire to go abroad because they earn good money, it is also important to note what is done with such money. The money should be excused if it is put to good use, such as construction of monasteries. While monasteries in India receive money from the central government for maintenance, the construction of monasteries of the kind that are seen today requires huge sums of money which are certainly flowing in from abroad.

It is important to note that during their foreign trips, monks are rewarded in terms of not only money but also prestige, in circles much wider than those possible in the small towns of western Arunachal Pradesh. Senior monks speaking at public gatherings frequently remark on the social respect accorded to them in the West as a measure of how appreciation of Buddhism has travelled, even doubled, in foreign contexts. If elections are one means for fulfilling monastic aspirations for authority, foreign travel points to another modality of adaptation to modernisation by monks. Not every monk has the will or opportunity to participate directly or indirectly in elections. Foreign travel thus constitutes an alternative avenue for mobility by monks.

Conclusion

The question why do monks participate in politics should be accompanied by the rider, what is the factor that allows their transition from a monastic sphere to the domain of democratic politics? According to some social scientists (see Jalal 1995; Nugent 2008), elections mask and reinforce systems of inequality whereby members of socially privileged groups successfully manipulate the electoral apparatus to exercise a personalised style of rule. For Ayesha Jalal (1995), Indian electoral politics since its beginnings has been organised around the lines of caste, community, and region, and therefore, while electoral democracy might pay lip service to participatory politics, in actual fact the affairs of the state are run by a coalition of political leadership, bureaucracy, and a privileged class. From this perspective, democracy fosters, unlike its ideological claims, systems of patronage. Other writers have argued that while democratic politics in India has followed diverse trajectories in different regions, the overall trend has been towards greater democratisation of society in the sense of having equal access to political power (Varshney 2000). In south India, especially, Tamil Nadu and Kerala, universal franchise led to the democratic empowerment of lower castes by the 1960s, while in the north, lower-caste politics took hold of the public sphere in the late 1980s and 1990s (ibid.).

From the first point of view, which sees elections as masking inequality, the social and financial privileges to which monks had been privy in an earlier traditional structure might be seen to have a bearing on how monks find themselves in politics today. Monks have a tradition of literacy and access to material resources that facilitate their entry, although in terms of having an available platform from which to launch into the electoral arena or possessing the necessary resources to fund election campaigns, some monks are better placed than others. Yet it is the conditions of democracy that compel monks to convert to monk-politicians. That is, monks, no matter how high ranking they are, feel emboldened and empowered to initiate social changes only by entering electoral politics. Despite having mass support, therefore, T. G. Rinpoche could introduce the reforms he sought only by becoming a politician.

However, when monks enter politics, they are sucked into the game for power, position, and money, and, consequently, expose themselves to public criticism. So while the ability to run for elections, and influence election mandates, might be enhanced for certain monks, it is checked and circumscribed by an articulate and speaking public. Many people agree that it is a different matter for Rinpoches who join politics out of a desire to bring about positive change. That is, unlike the ordinary, individualistic agendas of some monks, Rinpoches have extraordinary aims of social welfare. But even Rinpoches may be tainted through association. They may personally eschew the violence or illicit money laundering during election time, but they cannot account for the actions of their supporters, who might use the same means as that of other electoral candidates. Further, public reverence for Rinpoches as 'god-like' and situated outside ordinary, lay circuits keeps alive the tension between the two spheres of the monastery and democracy.

In this chapter, I have attempted to show that when people perceive the participation of monks in politics as being contrary to monastic principles of renunciation, they critically intervene in a monastic discourse that rationalises monks' presence in politics. Politics, in lay perception, does not add to the monastic vocation but 'spoils' it. Thus, a critical public discourse on monkhood, circulated as gossip, circumscribes monks' abilities to cross monastic bounds and reduces the effect of elections as a channel for restoring monastic authority.

Notes

1 While most monks of the Nyingma or old order are householder monks, monks of the Gelug order are celibate. Tawang monastery has 500 monks and is in charge of the administration of eleven smaller monasteries. During Tibetan rule, Tibetan representatives of Tawang monastery deputed from Tibet collected taxes from different Monpa villages, which would then be carried by porters all the way to Tsona in Tibet, the headquarters for Mon areas.
2 I conducted fieldwork in Tawang and West Kameng between 2008 and 2010 for my doctoral dissertation, but the subject of this chapter is different from the contents of my dissertation. It emerged out of my observations of, and a sense of wonder at, the local election processes. I thank my PhD advisors Professor Bruce Knauft and Professor David Nugent of Emory University for commenting on earlier drafts of this chapter.
3 By the use of the term 'secular', I wish to distinguish between the phenomenon of monks in monastic power struggles and monks involved in political conflicts outside the monastic sphere. The former was common during the ascendancy of the Tibetan state when monks participated in political intrigues in order to maintain individual supremacy or for influence of monastic sections over other secular organisations such as the military (Goldstein 1989). Although the boundary between the two phenomena is not always clear, since monastic life seldom precluded political battles, I wish to draw attention to the specific cases of monks' involvement in non- or extra-monastic political processes.
4 *The Concise Biography of the Great Tsonawa*, published by the Buddhist Culture Preservation Society of West Kameng, was handed to me during one of my visits to the Ganden Rabgye Ling Monastery at Bomdila.

References

Anonymous. n.d. *Approach Paper for the Workshop on Traditional System and Functioning of Tawang Monastery*. Centre for Buddhist Cultural Studies, Tawang Monastery, Tawang Arunachal Pradesh, India.
Aris, M. 1980. 'Notes on the History of the Monyul Corridor', in *Tibetan Studies in Honour of Hugh Richardson*, Proceedings of the International Seminar on Tibetan Studies, Warminster, England, 20 September.
Arora, V. 2006. 'Roots and the Route of Secularism in Sikkim', *Economic and Political Weekly*, 43 (38): 4063–71.
Goldstein, M. C. 1989. *A History of Modern Tibet, 1913–1951*. Berkeley, CA: University of California Press.

Government of India. 2001. 'Census of India 2001', www.censusindia.gov.in (accessed on 10 August 2011).
Harrison, P. 2008. 'Buddhism and Politics', 9 April, http://www.cfr.org/religion/buddhism-politics/p15969 (accessed on 10 August 2011).
Jalal, A. 1995. *Democracy and Authoritarianism in South Asia*. Cambridge: Cambridge University Press.
Kingdon-Ward, F. 1938. 'The Assam Himalaya: Travels in Balipara', *Journal of the Royal Central Asian Society*, 25: 610–19.
Mathew, G. 1995. *Status of Panchayati Raj in the States of India, 1994*. New Delhi: Institute of Social Sciences.
Mbembe, A. 1992. 'Provisional Notes on the Postcolony', *Africa: Journal of the International African Institute*, 62 (1): 3–37.
Nugent, David. 2008. 'Democracy Otherwise: Struggles over Popular Rule in the Northern Peruvian Andes', in J. Paley (ed.), *Democracy: Anthropological Approaches*, pp. 21–62. Santa Fe, New Mexico: School of Advanced Research.
Tambiah, S. J. 1992. *Buddhism Betrayed? Religion, Politics, and Violence in Sri Lanka*. Chicago: The University of Chicago Press.
Varshney, A. 2000. 'Is India Becoming More Democratic?', *Journal of Asian Studies*, 59 (1): 3–25.
West, H. G. 2008. '"Govern Yourselves!" Democracy and Carnage in Northern Mozambique', in J. Paley (ed.), *Democracy: Anthropological Approaches*, pp. 97–122. Santa Fe, New Mexico: School of Advanced Research.

5 'Pure democracy' in 'new Nepal'
Conceptions, practices, and anxieties[1]

Amanda Snellinger

Since the 1940s, Nepali politics has been defined by its struggle for multi-party democracy. After an unsuccessful democratic period in the 1960s, pro-democratic activists were pushed underground by the monarchy and its panchayat government. The 1990 People's Movement finally re-established multi-party democracy, but by 1996, it became apparent that democracy had not fulfilled the expectations and aspirations of all Nepali citizens. The Maoists' People's War (1996–2006) elevated the debate over what type of political system was appropriate for Nepal and, in doing so, produced a death toll of over 17,000. From 2002 through 2006, people from all different political ideologies collaborated to reinstate democracy in response to the king's dismissal of the democratically elected government. After a mass movement dethroned the king in 2006, an interim democratic government was established and the Constituent Assembly (CA) elections were held in 2008 (Thapa and Sijapati 2005). This period was popularly referred to as making of 'new Nepal'.

For almost a decade, political activists of all ideological backgrounds used the multi-party system to create consensus in the constitutional, administrative, and economic restructuring of the state. Reaching consensus, however, proved difficult, and the first CA shifted into the oppositional politics that threatened past democratic governments, particularly in 1960 and 2001 (see Baral 2006; Snellinger 2015). The first CA expired on 27 May 2012 when the deadline to promulgate a constitution expired because CA failed to reach consensus on a federal state structure. The prime minister was forced to call for new elections after the Supreme Court refused a fifth extension. New CA elections were finally held in November 2013 despite an intense boycott from a Maoist splinter group and a number of other parties from the thirty-three-party alliance. The results yielded a significant swing to the right, with the Nepali Congress (NC) securing the highest number of seats, a royalist party gaining several seats, and CA being overall less diverse. On 20 September 2015, Nepal promulgated its seventh constitution after a series of devastating earthquakes.[2] The top three parties, NC, Communist Party of Nepal (Unified Marxist–Leninist) (CPN-UML), and United Communist Party of Nepal (Maoist) (UCPN [M]), fast-tracked promulgation through majority vote despite deep opposition from women's groups and southern-based regional parties over citizenship, state demarcation, and political representation.

The turmoil during state restructuring is not an anomaly, but it is part of a pendulum-like trend wherein activists shift from opposing the state to running the state (Snellinger 2016). The country's on-going political struggle has engendered ideologies ranging from radical to conservative; nevertheless, multi-party democracy has always figured centrally. It became even more deeply engrained in political imaginary when the Maoist decided to join forces with the agitating political parties against the king in 2005 and then the public joined them en masse in the 2006 People's Movement. Nevertheless, By the time the multi-party democratic republic was realised in 2006, however, different political parties had instituted their own political rhetoric, practices, processes, and traditions that were not necessarily informed by liberal democratic values (Joshi and Rose 2004; Krämer 2002; Lawoti 2005; Panday 2000; Shah 2004; Upadhya 2002).

It is from this vantage that I explore different conceptions of democratic process in Nepali political practice. What democracy entails for political actors across the political spectrum is by no means consistent. I argue that democratic principles in Nepal have been rhetorically cultivated in conversation with other forms of power in a specific historical and cultural context. In this chapter, I examine ethnographic case studies[3] of Nepali student organisations' internal processes, specifically during their campus, district, and national conventions, to demonstrate the range of political attitudes towards democratic processes in Nepal.[4]

I have chosen to focus on the Nepali student organisations' practices because they serve as useful heuristic to understand democratic practices in Nepal. I suggest that as subsidiary organisations (sister organisations) to the mainstream political parties (mother organisations), student organisations are inherent to and an inescapable part of Nepali politics. Historically, the student organisations have been the political parties' foot soldiers, mobilising in street opposition, revolution, and electoral campaigns (Snellinger 2005, 2016). Their centrality was established during the panchayat era when political parties were banned and Free Student Union elections became the proxy for multi-party democracy (Snellinger 2010). Since democracy was re-established in 1990, a majority of political leaders emerged from their party's student organisation where they received their initial training and indoctrination into Nepali party politics. Therefore, analysis of the student organisations' processes and political attitudes demonstrates more pervasive conceptions of democracy. Furthermore, the analysis presented in this chapter demonstrates the integral role political party leadership plays in the political outcomes of student organisations. The actions of both student activists and party leaders reflect general anxieties regarding democracy in practice as well as what is to come in Nepal's political future (Snellinger 2016).

In my analysis I conceive of the student organisations as a 'mini-public' that provides insight into how deliberative processes and political culture play out in larger forums (Fung 2003). Nevertheless, I do not assume the mini-public is designed to foster deliberative democratic ideals; instead, I frame student politics as a mini-public that informs us of what democratic practice looks like.[5] I focus on the performative dimensions of elections to demonstrate how the students' and party leaders' self-conscious actions are attempts to control the agonistic nature of electoral politics (Spencer 2007). In the first section, I analyse different actors' perspective on deliberation and its place in political practice. I then outline the different forms that elections have historically taken in Nepali politics in order to highlight the issues that people confront when they pursue electoral politics. In the second and third sections I analyse consensus as a traditionally desired approach in the electoral process. I provide ethnographic examples of the way consensus unfolds to explain the preference for consensus and the anxiety around achieving anything less than 'pure consensus'. My analysis reveals how people's anxieties regarding electoral processes open up an interpretive space that J. Spencer calls a carnivalesque space that is full of possibility and license, 'license to argue, and license to joke, and license to experiment with challenges to the order of things' (ibid.: 94).

Deliberation: the basis for liberal democracy?

I begin this chapter by analysing different Nepali conceptions of the democratic practice by focusing on the topic of deliberation because it elucidates some contentious aspects of Nepali politics: inclusion, organisational unity, forms of competition, democratic claims, and dictatorial processes.

The academic debate surrounding deliberation reveals the inherent stakes that are present for Nepali political actors themselves. Political theory considers deliberation to be one of the central components of the liberal democratic political process as well as a main aspect of any form of societal maintenance that is not dictatorial in form. Political philosophers and social scientists often define deliberation according to the Kantian argument, claiming that reason, inclusion, and justice are the underpinning components of deliberation (Bohman 1996; Gutmann and Thompson 1996, 2004; Little 2007; Mouffe 2000; Schneiderhan and Khan 2008; Steiner *et al.* 2004; Sunstein 2003). Deliberation is enacted through the process of reasoned argument, or what Jürgen Habermas calls 'communicative action' (1984, 1990), which ideally includes the voices and perspectives of all those who are participating in the process. For this reason, deliberation is cited as central to democratic legitimacy. The assumption in a democratic state is that all citizens have a right to be included in the democratic process and, therefore, have access to deliberation.[6]

Habermas's work on deliberation has been central to the academic debate. He describes deliberation as an organic phenomenon that unfolds within the specific social process or context (1990: 66). Yet what E. Schneiderhan and S. Khan (2008: 2, 9) discovered in their study that imposed exogenous controls on the process of deliberation is that the more inclusive the deliberation process is, the more robustly group engages deliberation. Their conclusion may be accurate from the presumed premise of an inclusive group dynamic, but I warn against extrapolating beyond that. From what I have observed, political participation comprises either a partial inclusion or a semblance of inclusion (see Lawoti 2005; Malagodi 2013). Nonetheless, their study provides another useful observation about the nature of deliberation. It demonstrates that there are ways to affect the pace of deliberation; it is not an organic phenomenon the way Habermas conjectured. In this regard, B. Davies, Blackstock and Rauschmayer have questioned if deliberation has inherent value, premised on reason, inclusion, and justice, by querying the underlying assumption that deliberation naturally unfolds. They argue that there are 'recursive loops in which some form of deliberation is needed before determining how deliberation should proceed; but the question of how the earlier round of deliberations can commence without confronting the same selection problem is left unanswered' (2005: 605).[7] I. Pellizzoni (2003) further warns that we must consider the role of power relations in discursive interactions because discourse and social prestige can be deployed in order to marginalise alternative viewpoints. Therefore, one must consider the specific social and cultural dynamic in order to understand the parameters of deliberation before the value of deliberation can be understood.

The academic debate around deliberation runs parallel to the political debate regarding how to establish inclusion in Nepal. Inclusion (*samabesh*) was one of the main demands made to address the histories of marginalisation that fuelled People's War, the Second People's Movement, and the Madheshi Movements of 2007 and 2008. In order to foster more inclusion in politics, government, bureaucracy, and military, the interim and promulgated constitutions instituted a proportional election system and affirmative action quota system (Jha 2014; Shah and Shneiderman 2013). The idea of inclusion has captured public imagination wherein all institutional sectors are being assessed on the basis of how inclusive they are.

In its attempts to bring more diverse voices into the political fold, the UCPN (M) earned political capital among a number of marginalised groups. This strategy won it the majority of both the first-past-the-post and proportional votes in the 2008 CA elections. However, since then the UCPN (M) political record has demonstrated inclusion of diverse groups in the party, which does not necessarily ensure that internal policies promote active inclusion of various voices.[8] When I asked All Nepal National Independent Student Union (Revolutionary) (ANNISU [R]) students about this, they explained that the Maoists' main attempt at inclusion on an internal level is through deliberation. This struck me as a curious claim because many people mistrust the Maoists' democratic intentions. The Maoist leadership itself has justified coming into the political mainstream since 2006 – making a coalition government with the democratic parties and contesting in the CA elections – as the necessary step that the revolution must take to reach its ultimate end, a Maoist People's Republic. They argue that they must become a central part of the system in order to restructure the system (see Hachhethu 2009).

Nonetheless, ANNISU (R) leaders cited deliberation as a key component to their internal election process in response to my inquiries on how they choose their leaders during their campus, district, and national conventions. What I found is that they give more priority to deliberation than casting ballots, campaigning, or representational voting. A central committee leader explained it to me in this way:

> During our convention we elected our leaders. But our method of election is different. What the bourgeoisie do is, they use the ballot paper and cast their votes; they spend a lot of money to buy the votes and use knives, swords, and sticks to assault the opposition that is within their organisation. You might have seen the Nepal Student Union conferences in Chitwan and Nepalganj. They call it democratic norms. We are against that. Rather, we hold discussions until we reach a consensus. Therefore, the election procedure adopted by bourgeoisie is for mere show, a performance for the outsiders that elections took place. We don't agree with this process since it is full of conspiracies and tricks. . . . We prioritise internal discussion on our political agenda and road map. Only once we have established our political agenda do we engage in elections. Choosing our leadership is secondary to jointly organising our group. We feel that if an election is held without becoming clear on the organisation's ideology and programs then the organisation cannot lead the political movement in any real sense. These are our norms and values. Here lies the difference between other organisations and ours.[9]

It may seem odd that a Maoist student leader is embracing a political form that assumes the liberal ethic of individual rights and freedom of speech as its basis, values that seem counter to radical socialist views.[10] Yet it is important to take note of what he sets up as its juxtaposition, casting ballots. He argues that casting ballots is a bourgeoisie political form that promotes the thumbprint of each individual, but beyond that it is useless. In Nepal's history, the individuating process of casting ballots has often been manipulated or usurped in order to safeguard traditional, elite political rule. Deliberation, on the other hand, allows people a voice and an active social role in the process (Miller 1990). For the Maoists, individual right is not the primary focus of deliberation but a means to an end. Rather, deliberation is a communal process of consensus; it promotes sociality by establishing a group agenda.

The distinction between casting ballots and deliberation that the Maoist student leader makes is what A. Fung and E. O. Wright describe as the difference between 'real-world deliberation' and 'genuine deliberation' (2002: 17). They claim that the real-world deliberation involves heated conflict where there are winners and losers, whereas genuine deliberation is not necessarily about being fully convinced of the collective agreement, but through reasoned argument all participants are persuaded to endorse it because it is what is most advantageous for the group. If we were to extrapolate this ANNISU (R) student leader's logic and apply it to Fung and Wright's paradigm, then casting ballots would be real-world deliberation, and the Maoist internal consensus would be genuine deliberation. But, in order to further parse this out, there is another aspect that must be considered, one that Fung and Wright do not address in their analysis, which is the emphasis on solidarity in the deliberative process. Not everyone has his or her own agenda; therefore, it may be enough to provide people with a sense of ownership in the process in order for them to agree with the party in a consensual way. The degree to which one values the group's agenda over one's personal agenda reflects one's willingness to oblige genuine deliberation over a real-world deliberation situation. This is particularly relevant in the ANNISU (R), where students are ideologically well trained and disciplined in their shared political agenda. Their training is meant to put the students on the same ideological footing in the communicative process of deliberation.

The shared conviction to prioritise the group over the individual allows the ANNISU (R) conventions to have a focus other than the electoral process. Rather than encouraging people to exert their own opinions and leadership ambitions, it is about encouraging them to abide by the agenda that is best for their group. This not only allows them to become a part of the group, but it also reconfirms the social reality of the group. It is not group formation by popular mandate but group formation through the social process of 'genuine consensus'. Alexei Yurchak (2006: 117–19) describes this priority in his ethnography on the last Soviet generation within the cultural value of *svoi* or a sociality that produces a public. He documents the distracted, haphazard process by which *Komsomol* cadres vote for motions. These university students understand that it does not matter what the motions are that they raise their hands in favour of, but rather what matters is the act of supporting the motion. The multiplicity of raised hands confirms the sociality of the event, one that reconfirms the identity of their organisation in a public forum and further entrenches the dominance of the Communist Party. Similarly, the ANNISU (R) students do not proceed with elections until they are organised as a group; creating a shared political agenda is what creates social cohesion for them; only then are they able to choose a leader.

A Maoist central committee leader gave me an interesting explanation for the Maoists' resistance to the parliamentary system, which broadens the distinction between different forms of political participation. His explanation further distinguishes between real-world and genuine deliberation. He said that, at one time, the parliamentary system was progressive but that the Maoists no longer supported what it was in the 1990s because it had become a reactionary system, a guise to support the monarchy while providing a façade of democracy. He said, 'We believe in multi-party democracy if it implies creating consensus among the political parties in order to make Nepal a prosperous and developed country for the betterment and equality of its citizens.'[11] Ultimately, both systems claim to have the same end; yet he invoked Lenin to assert that the process of consensus insured equality and class struggle in a way that the parliamentary system precluded. He also added that consensus combats unhealthy competition. He felt competition stifled the system since it kept people from dedicating themselves to the larger aims of justice by prioritising their own victory. In other words, competition distracts people with the mere struggle to maintain their presence and to progress within the political system.

This tension between voting and consensus ultimately comes down to what people believe is the best way to balance the liberal individual right of representation or a socialist approach that prioritises the betterment of the group. In Nepal, this tension is informed by the historically proven suspicion that democratic governments are manipulated for spurious ends. Voting and the parliamentary system can encourage unhealthy competition that factionalises the larger governmental institution in overt ways, whereas consensus, in its ideal form, potentially reaffirms the solidarity of the group (or state) (Miller 1990). Yet those in favour of the democratic process present the counterclaim that dictatorial attempts are made in the name of consensus, which ultimately undermines the solidarity of the organisation. This too is a reasonable worry considering Nepal's political history of entrenched party and state patronage. Furthermore, some Nepali politicians have warily contended that consensus is not democratic because, in Nepali political history, the claims of consensus-building deliberation have been predicated upon the exclusion of at least one other political faction or social group (Lawoti 2005; Malagodi 2013).

In many ways, the preference for real-world deliberation or genuine deliberation falls along party fault lines in Nepal. On the internal level, the predilection for consensus is influenced by the degree to which organisations prioritise their organisational stability, solidarity, and unity, whereas intra-party interaction is more straightforward regarding real-world deliberation. The other factor that informs this preference is rank. Those who are in positions of power tend to endorse consensus because they are able to affect outcomes, while those who have more to risk and depend on possibility are willing to support the electoral process.

When I asked a seasoned CPN (UML) party activist about the differences between voting and consensus, his explanation was very insightful. It outlined how leadership has been traditionally chosen in Nepal's political organisations. He said,

> In Nepali political history there were three types of election systems. One was consensus-based election system; the other was the election system based on patron-client relationship; and the last one was the direct election system. The middle one, that is, patron-client relationship, is a defective one. The consensus-based system is fine since there is no need to go to the election if a consensus can be reached as to whom is the most qualified. Moreover, it is natural that the voices are raised against the person who is not popular and dynamic. For this reason, if consensus cannot be reached then a direct election system should be the alternative and there should not be influence from outside. This is the only way to declare a victor; he proves to be the most qualified, popular and possess the qualities that the voters desire. Our protest and critique is directed at the system that, in the name of consensus, comes from the basis of patron-client relationship. . . . We are trying to abolish the system of the patron inserting his client.[12]

During the process of the student organisations' conventions, I observed all these types of elections, but the process of consensus and the one of patron–client were the most common. All the student organisations, despite their claims that they are operatively democratic, would prefer the scenario of clear-cut consensus. As I will demonstrate, consensus and the electoral

'Pure democracy' in 'new Nepal' 143

process are not considered mutually exclusive when political actors access how democratic Nepali political processes are, particularly in organisationally internal processes. Consensus provides a sense of communalism that people regard as more cohesive than the voting process because it avoids the antagonism that electoral competition engenders (Mouffe 2000), and the risk of endangering organisational harmony. Yet, as I will also show, the desire for consensus allows the term to be rhetorically manipulated in order to mask processes that are seemingly less democratic, which can ultimately undermine the solidarity of the organisation.

I will now turn my focus to the types of elections for which different student organisations strive. Through case studies of these various types of elections, I will assess what the students perceive as the appropriate balance between competition, consensus, and mother-party interference in order to maintain a healthy political order.

The gap between 'arranging things' and 'full consensus'

The first district convention that I observed was a prime example of the patron–client election process, as described by the CPN (UML) leader in the previous quote. The participants, however, deemed it consensus. This event made me notice the flexibility in people's verbal patterns and dialogue, which allowed them to accommodate their sense of ideal political process. During the convention, people would say things 'were being arranged' and, once a final decision was made, they would say there was a full consensus. The following ethnographic analysis demonstrates the flexibility of the term 'consensus', and how it allows political actors to maintain the integrity of their democratic ideals.

I had arrived the day before the district convention elections with the female Nepal Student Union (Koirala) (NSU [K]) vice-president, Risha. Since Risha was running for president in the national convention, she was keen to attend district conventions, especially districts where she had established influence. This was obviously one of them. This district was the district of a female NSU (K) central committee member, Tanuja, whom Risha was openly promoting. As we arrived, we went directly to the NC party office. I was introduced to everyone and we had tea. Soon after receiving tea, the students and the NC district leaders made us aware that they had not yet been able to 'arrange things' for the convention the next day. The NC-appointed election committee excused themselves to have another meeting with all the possible candidates so they could agree upon a solution. They asked if Risha would like to attend. She declined, saying it was not her intention to interfere; she had come to be supportive of everyone.

Tanuja excused herself, saying she should probably participate to see if she could help broker an amicable agreement. As we departed, Tanuja whispered to Risha, 'I'll represent us.'

At about 10 p.m. that evening, Tanuja arrived at our hotel room very stressed. She said that they still had not reached an agreement and that the NC district leaders were at an impasse with some of the younger students because the leaders felt these students did not have the experience to take such key leadership positions. The NC leadership preferred to endorse the current president for re-election; with the impending CA election, they needed reliable leadership. She expressed disgust with the NC leaders' heavy-handedness in this matter and their sense of impunity. She felt they were using the election-committee responsibility to ensure that the process ran smoothly as an excuse to interfere. She had sympathy for some of the students who had aspirations to compete in the elections. She said,

> They fought so hard for the party during the 2nd People's Movement and were active all through the Movement Against Regression. They spent time in jail and were injured. They feel empowered to serve central roles in this party after all they have contributed. This is how they are compensated, with doubt over their leadership abilities?[13]

Both of these women felt frustrated by the interference, even though they were both appointed to their leadership positions by the NC central leadership. Their frustration and the positions they held revealed how little autonomy their organisation has and the extent to which they are beholden to the NC party leaders.

The next morning, the meeting began early in order to reach an agreement before the delegates came. The convention was supposed to begin at 9 a.m.; by 11 a.m. the meeting with the election commission was ongoing. Delegates had come from all over the district, some travelling over five hours to reach there by 9 a.m. At the time when everyone was getting hungry, Risha barged into the office and started lecturing the NC leaders. She said that, if nobody was willing to relent in order for an agreement to be reached, then they should hold elections and let the students decide. She berated them, saying that their behaviour showed they had little faith in the students of their organisation. Within fifteen minutes all the students were called into the convention hall to begin the inauguration. At the last minute it was announced that they would serve lunch first and then begin. This bought the party leaders another hour to push their agenda. By the time the inauguration ceremony began, the NC leaders were relieved and the candidates were distressed. An agreement had been enforced.

During her speech, Risha told the students what had been going on. She emphasised her point, saying,

> You have been called here to participate in this democratic process, just as you had been called on to fight to protect our democracy. Now you sit here and wait, wait for the leaders to decide for you. Is this how we should be democratically running things?[14]

When the NC district vice-president,[15] who was serving as the election committee chair, came up to give his speech, he acknowledged Risha's critique but claimed that they had reached full consensus among all the candidates for the good of the NSU (K)'s district committee. He said,

> You have a big responsibility to campaign for the constituent assembly elections. This is as important as the roles you have served in the past in your fight for democracy. You need strong leadership right now that has experience. All the candidates will get the opportunity to gain that experience during this administration.[16]

As we were leaving the party office, there was an air of discontent. A fight broke out between some of the students who were supporting a candidate who had been sidelined and students who supported the two-term victor. Party leaders rushed to break it up. I asked Risha why they had not let the matter go to a vote. She called the NC district vice-president over and said, 'Amanda asked why the students were not allowed to vote, please explain it to her, Sir [older brother].' He explained that many of these students were from plus-two colleges and were immature. If there was an election, it would have gotten ugly. 'See that tussle that we just suppressed? It's a good example of the risks that would've been involved in an election.' We talked for a while. The conversation was relatively good-natured because all the frustrations had been voiced. While I was waiting to get a copy of the district proposals and report, I overheard Risha say to the very same NC vice-president,

> Sir, you know we need thirty three per cent female representation not only at the country level but also in the party and NSU (K). I expect at least fifty per cent of the delegates you send to the national convention to be female. It is in your power; make sure it gets done.[17]

He agreed to do so. I was surprised that Risha had spurned him and the party's interference in the convention, but was willing to rely on it when it was to her advantage. She later explained to me that she is willing to deploy the traditional hierarchical network if it can be used to establish more equal representation in the party system.

As we were having our last cup of tea with the party leaders at the hotel before leaving, the NC vice-president seemed exhausted and a bit disheartened that things had not gone smoothly. He explained that things were not completely worked out and he would need to do some damage control in order to ensure that all the aspiring candidates would cooperate with the committee president. Throughout the next couple of days on our trip to other district conventions, I overheard Risha and Tanuja provide different versions of what happened depending on the listener: sometimes they said it went well and there was full consensus and at others they went into a tirade about the district committee's interference.

Another example of this sort of manipulation of the term 'consensus' was right after the 2005 NSU (K) national convention, which became known as the Pokhara scandal because it disintegrated into chaos and vandalism in response to widespread rumours of party leaders vote rigging to defeat a popular candidate who did not have the blessing of the NC president.[18] It became apparent that the NSU (K) was unable to conduct convention elections in this climate, so the NC constituted a selection committee to form an *ad hoc* NSU central committee to fill in before they could have the next national convention. This selection committee's responsibility was to work with all the student leaders and recently active ex-student leaders to form an NSU (K) central committee. Although everyone refers to the positions as appointed, NC made all the current and previous student leaders sign a document agreeing that the list of appointments was in the best interest of NSU (K). After receiving the signatures of all the key players, NC was able to claim that the NSU (K) central committee was consensually formed and played down party interference. I confirmed this with Akash, the key ex-student leader, whose experience of being sidelined by the party at this convention had sparked the riots and vandalism. He explained that this was NC's regular tactic when it dissolves and appoints NSU administrations. It must manufacture a consensus among the students since the NSU constitution explicitly states that NC will not appoint student leaders. The signed agreement is their loophole. He chuckled, saying, 'Yeah, I have signed two of those consensus agreements for their appointed leaderships, once when they dissolved my committee during my general secretary tenure and the second time after I tried to run for president.'[19]

The discrepancy in the students' language and the party's actions indicates how it rhetorically manipulates its claims to provide a democratic façade. I do not want to assert that this is a cynical practice; rather, it is a reaction to a political reality beyond its control. The paternalistic anxieties of the NC leaders reveal that they do not feel the students are ready to govern themselves. In response, the students have adopted cues that indicate democratic aspirations while masking their lack of autonomy. Nonetheless, this does impact the students' political behaviour, and how they will serve as politicians. They may not only transfer their leaders' wariness onto the next generation, but they are also developing sophisticated patterns of rhetoric that blur the boundary between intentionality and actuality.

The desired 'safe landing': 'pure consensus'

In order to better understand why people manipulate the word 'consensus' as an attempt to tag irregular political processes as democratically normative, it is important to highlight the anxiety around maintaining the image of a clean, healthy democratic process. It is this anxiety that compels people to be invested in a full consensus outcome. The example of what my informants refer to as pure consensus demonstrates the ability of consensus to strengthen organisational unity.

A particularly central fixation of the district conventions of the two Nepali Student Unions – NSU (K) and NSU (D [Deuba])[20] – was the concept of safe landing. The NSU (K)'s 2005 national convention was a scandal that not only was a black mark for NSU (K) and NC (K) but became an often-cited example of why student politics is a 'dirty game'. Therefore, it was necessary that all the 2007 conventions run smoothly. An urgent text I received from a Nepali friend during the NSU (K)'s national convention in Chitwan revealed how much was at stake in holding these conventions. He texted the morning after an extremely tense day to inquire if I was safe because he had just seen footage of the previous day's scuffle between the students and the police. The students had tried to storm the convention office after a rumour spread that the central committee was fixing the voter list. He lamented how bad the news coverage was. 'Do they not realise that the whole country's eyes are on Chitwan right now? Do they understand how bad this makes them look, let alone the enterprise of democratic politics?' he texted.[21] His worried message signalled an agreement among all political factions: the student conventions should not disintegrate into chaos; everyone must do whatever is in his or her power to ensure a safe landing. The students once again served as a proxy for democracy. But rather than representing what was not possible due to government suppression as was the case in the panchayat era, the students' elections were seen as a litmus test for the CA elections to come. All the political parties understood that the public was watching their student organisations' conventions to assess their ability to contest the upcoming CA elections in a free and fair manner. It was for this reason that there was so much party oversight of the student conventions.

A good example of a safe landing was the smooth consensus process that I observed at Padma Kanya, the all-female college in Kathmandu.[22] I was able to sit through the entire convention, including the closed session. Throughout the convention, things were pretty chaotic. The female central committee member, Risha, who was meant to observe the convention, actually oversaw many of the processes that should have been the campus leaders' responsibility, including writing the proposals for the convention report. What seemed like interference to me was not only tolerated but also appeared normal. In fact, nothing seemed to run in an official fashion. The whole process resembled family *puja*s (religious offering ceremonies) that I have observed wherein participants have their own ideas of how things should be conducted and simultaneously contribute their input, often bickering about it. The *puja* procedure is ultimately a combination of everyone's input, which the most experienced or respected of the family decides to incorporate as he or she sees fit. Risha, who was no longer a student at this campus, seemed to fill this role, coordinating with the most senior of the campus leaders, who served as the moderator.

When it finally came to nominating the candidates, two were nominated. After they registered and someone paid their dues for running, the moderator called a break in order to have a discussion with the two candidates.[23] This discussion happened outside the hall among the moderator, the candidates, the soon-to-be ex-president, and Risha. During the discussion, the female delegates were chanting the name of one of the candidates in unison. After about ten minutes, the team returned and declared consensus: the female candidate who seemed to have obvious support from the hall of chanting delegates had won, because the other candidate had withdrawn. The crowd enthusiastically cheered, and then the convention was over. The students crowded around to congratulate the victor and thank the other candidate for her respectable withdrawal.

The moderator told me that the discussion that was held among the student leaders and candidates was a bargaining process to establish the new campus administration. The candidate who had withdrawn would be appointed general secretary by the new president, since it is the president's prerogative to appoint her own cabinet. The female student who withdrew would be next in line for the presidency, just as the student who had won was in line for it from the previous election.

The campus convention culminated in all of us – delegates, former leaders, newly consented leaders, central committee members, and I – eating lunch together. The participants embraced the full consensus. It did not matter that they did not vote; everyone was happy with the procedure and the outcome. Yet, this time, Risha did not describe it to external party leaders as 'full consensus'. Rather, I overheard her on the phone reporting that the election was a 'pure consensus', which she said in English. Using the word 'pure' to describe an election process indicates how coded political processes are in the dirty game of politics. In this context, pure consensus represented a process in which everyone agreed. Pure consensus produces organisational harmony because it occurs from a united front whereby there are no vying interests and all participants unite in their aim of organisational betterment. In pure consensus, they are a socially constructed singular with no surplus identities (Rancière 1999: 124).

A conversation I had with a few NSU (D) central committee members shed light on this procedure of consensus and how people value it as part of democratic exercise. We were returning from the Nuwakot district convention. We had attended the inauguration but decided not to stay for the closed session. On the road back, one of the student leaders was receiving updates on the convention's progress by phone. I asked him how many candidates had been nominated; he said, at the moment, it was five or six; the nomination process was still occurring. I articulated my surprise that there would be so many candidates since I had heard that there would be no election. Another central committee member explained, 'The students come forward as candidates and state their intentions and then they talk it through. If they have the ambition to be president, then they'll be willing to serve another position if the delegates don't support them as president.' I commented that, as far as I had observed, during and before the closed sessions, this scenario is referred to as 'arranging things' and, after it was arranged, it is referred to as 'full consensus'. He responded, 'Well, what do you expect, us to compete with guns or throw rocks at one another?[24] We want to create leadership and teams to strengthen our organisation; that all our delegates will support.'[25] His response emphasises that organisational cohesion should not be jeopardised by democratic competition. As I have shown, choosing leadership is an anxiety-ridden process for all student organisations during which they cite other student organisations' blunders and failures to justify their own approach to establishing political leadership.

Conclusion: establishing mandate

I have revealed pervasive conceptions of democracy in Nepali political culture through my analysis of the Nepali student organisations' internal elections. As I have shown, choosing leadership is an anxiety-ridden process for all student organisations. They are caught in an echo chamber wherein they cite each other's blunders and failures as justification for their own particular political processes. It is a challenge for the student organisations and their mother parties to portray active competition within their organisations while ensuring that the process does not disintegrate into factionalism. The stakes of gaining or the risks of losing political influence in any sector are too high. The reality is that democratic competition often results in factionalism.[26] This is why appointing leadership has been a long-maintained tradition in these so-called democratic institutions; dictatorial decisions handed down often secure the integrity of a group that is willing to abide the leadership. The consistency in leadership also helps to shape and maintain the group's identity (Auyero 2001), but it can also cause organisational stagnation (Gellner and Karki 2008). The liberal democratic process, on the other hand, is about everyone's voice mattering; power is supposed to be shared by all, but in practice, it often results in grabbing by a few and the continual process of convincing others to follow.

After observing six national conventions and numerous campus and district conventions of the student organisations from 2006 through 2007, I constructed a series of questions for the students about the conventions, followed by questions about the FSU elections (campus-wide elections in which the different student organisations compete with each other for seats) and about student organisation alliances in order to understand how the students make meaning of the inter- and intra-organisational elections. A Maoist student leader reacted to my questions by saying,

> Holding the conferences and choosing the leadership of the unit committee or the central committee are different processes than FSU elections. . . . Our internal election procedure follows a different pattern. The election within our organisation is the competition of those having the same ideology, a common program, and they share norms and values. This is the competition of a bicycle with a bicycle, a motorbike with a motorbike, or car with a car. It is an organisational process to determine which bike will get us there in the best way. But the FSU elections are about how do you prefer to travel, bike, motorbike, or car? One should choose according to ideological preference. For this reason, we think that the two cannot be placed together and one cannot draw a conclusion on the basis of this comparison.[27]

Indeed, how democracy occurs internally is construed very differently than what people expect of the larger democratic political system. Nonetheless, the discrepancies between the two levels elucidate people's attitudes and ambivalent feelings about democratic practice as a societal form. This same student leader used this logic to argue in favour of a proportional system as opposed to the traditional first-past-the-post system used in the FSU elections. This was an issue that the Maoists fought for during the People's War and pushed in the CA election process. Their argument was that it should be a competition of ideologies, not personalities (or, as it is known in liberal democracy, individuals). Furthermore, the proportional system encourages all to work with one another rather than have individuals squabble over perceived mandates they received for their various positions. He argued that a proportional system 'will represent all. . . . The representation of all the student organisations means collective work; they would work together; the programs would be launched after the discussion held in the presence of all'.[28]

The Maoists chose to embrace the democratic process in the 2008 CA elections in order to restructure the constitution, the state, and the army. Many doubted their sincerity, and everyone underestimated their ability to contest successfully. The results were surprising; not even the Maoists predicted them. They gained over 40 per cent of the first-past-the-post seats and 30 per cent of the proportional positions. One activist told me that the Maoists won 'by hook or crook' (*sam, dam, dhanda, bhed*).[29] I retorted, 'As far as I observed, all the parties exacted their advantage to win; therefore, the Maoists' victory must be legitimate.' Another student responded, '*Sam, dam, dhanda, bhed* is the operative style of Nepali elections. So, I guess you are right, they played by the tradition that everyone follows.' He paused, cracked a smile, and continued, 'They just played it better.'[30] It is understandable why people take pause at the prospect of direct elections when a proverb such as this describes the operative style of politics. Nonetheless, there is a desire to achieve democratic process, which has been proven by the rhetorical resonance of the promise made by the parties to establish a 'pure democracy for new Nepal' after they regained power in 2006.

The Maoist government and subsequent governments have attempted to run their government in the consensus style that was used by the interim government. As my data has shown, this is the style with which most Nepali political organisations are most comfortable, at least internally. However, attaining consensus across ideological differences is much more complicated because it involves multiple ideological positions or surplus identities.[31] Yet, within Nepal's context, it provides a safety measure that direct democracy has not provided thus far. 'Democratic spontaneity encodes a measure of uncertainty and indeterminacy into the operative style of the politics' (Connolly 2001: 15). The consensual process, conversely, rules out that degree of uncertainty. Most Nepalese would agree that there has been far too much uncertainty since the establishment of democracy.

For this reason, there is logic in the political actors' reliance upon consensus (Snellinger 2015). In Nepal's case, parliamentary politics that attempts to restructure the state through consensus building has been favoured after the contentious politics of civil war and street protests during the first decade of the 21st century. Nevertheless, the consensual process of

152 *Amanda Snellinger*

state restructuring during the first CA has produced little and reaffirmed that consensus crystallises power relations; the promulgation of the 2015 constitution has amply demonstrated that consensus is an artefact that is produced by and produces hegemony (Mouffe 2000: 49). The political pendulum may very likely swing back into contentious action of *āndolan* (political movement), based on how exclusionist and regressive many feel the newly promulgated constitution is. People, namely women and Tharu and Madheshi communities, are again questioning the policing logic and distribution of the sensible that is attempting to restructure the Nepali state (Rancière 1999), for this has been Nepal's modern political history, a cycle tacking back and forth between direct political action and political restructuring.

Notes

1 This chapter is a revised and updated version of an article ('Democratic Form: Conceptions and Practices in the Making of "New Nepal"') published in *Sociological Bulletin*, 58 (1), January–April 2009. The Indian Sociological Society's permission to reproduce it here is gratefully acknowledged. The paper was revised as per the editor's and referee's suggestions.
2 The earthquakes struck in April and early May 2015, affecting 14 districts in central Nepal and leaving almost 9,000 dead and over 24,000 injured, and an estimated 50,000 buildings collapsed (http://reliefweb.int/report/nepal/humanitarian-bulletin-nepal-earthquake-issue-04-final-issue-1-30-september-2015).
3 This research was sponsored by a Fulbright IIE Research Grant (2003–4), Einaudi International Research Grant (2005), Fulbright Hays DDRA Grant (2006–7), and a Wenner Gren Dissertation Fieldwork Grant (2007–8), and ANHS Senior Research Fellowship (2011).
4 The ethnographic material presented in this article was collected in Nepal during 2006–8, after the People's Movement II that ousted King Gyanendra, and during the operation of the comprehensive peace treaty between the Maoists and the other major political parties through which they formed a joint interim government; this research ended soon after the CA elections of 2008. This research benefited from preliminary research I did with student organisations in 2003–4 during the Movement against Regression, and from February through August 2005 after King Gyanendra's royal takeover. My research was a top-down project. I worked at the political centre, Kathmandu, with the central committees of the student organisations and political parties, from which I followed student political activity on campuses and in districts throughout the country. I worked across party and student organisation lines with the major political parties and their student organisations (due to splits and mergers this number varied at different phases of my research). I was fortunate to have established rapport with the students during political protests in 2003–4, which provided me a first-hand view of their life as activists; on the streets; underground; and in the hospitals, courts, and jail. Tracking the students during this tumultuous

'Pure democracy' in 'new Nepal' 153

period allowed me access to their internal organisational processes as well as their inter-organisational collaborations and competitions, and students' interactions with their political parties. I was fortunate that all my political interlocutors wanted their student organisations and parties represented in my study.

5 My analysis is informed by political anthropological perspectives with a focus on political culture. As Lawrence Rosen (2006: 163–64) has argued in his article on the cultural components of Arab governance, it is not that the political science, political philosophy, international policy, or organisational theory studies about democracy lack merit, but they tend to 'exist in a partial cultural vacuum' that does not incorporate culture-specific factors such as patronage; networks of obligation; conception of self and group; the perceptions of context, dispute, and resolution; or how power is linked to notions of reciprocity, which very much inform people's notions of what democracy is and how it should fit into their society. I ground my ethnographic analysis in the belief that 'political ethnography allows the research to bring up the mundane details that can affect politics, providing "thick description" where one was missing' (Baiocchi and Connor 2008: 141). The mundane details of my case study elucidate the incongruity between democratic theory and practice in a way that pushes the theoretical bounds of democracy and reveals the terrain of politics in a specific cultural context.

6 Lakier (2007) borrows the phrase 'illiberal democracy' from F. Zakaria (1997) in her analysis of the role of public protest in Nepal in the democratic years of the 1990s. She argues that without access to liberal, legal forms of representations, people publicly protest to have a voice – or as I have shown, in the case of the political elites, to enforce their political views by usurping public space (Snellinger 2007). However, I must emphasise that the trend of public protest in Nepal is not seeking liberal ground that Lakier argues is lacking in Nepali democratic institutions. Rather, it is communicative action that demands the right to representation for groups, not a liberal-oriented stand for individual rights that the justice system is traditionally based on in established liberal democracies.

7 Fearon would argue that what Davies, Blackstock and Rauschmayer are referring to as the earlier round of deliberations is merely discussion: 'Although "mere communication" may not be deliberative, discussion is a necessary prerequisite of the deliberative process because, without discussion, there can be no deliberation' (1998: 404). Whether it is referred to as deliberation or discussion or it allows discussion to be a proxy for deliberation, it is true that the parameters a group deliberates within are often decided by a core group of elites, or leaders who are limited by particular political or social principles, none of which is inclusive of the larger group and or society.

8 Maoist party leader Mohan Baidya split from the UCPN (M) and formed the CPN-Maoist party because the party leadership was compromising Maoist party position on ethnic federalism in negotiations with status quo factions of the CA.

9 Translation of an interview with an ANNISU (R) central committee member on 11 December 2006.

10 C.K. Lal, a prominent Nepali journalist and political analyst, claimed in a public forum after the CA elections that the 'Maoists were not real Maoists'. He cited their willingness to participate in the CA elections, their

willingness to embrace private market economic policies as a transition into their own economic policies, and burgeoning diplomatic ties with conservative foreign powers as proof of their lack of political authenticity within the Maoist ideological orthodoxy (at Martin Chautari, Kathmandu, Nepal, 16 April 2008).

11 Translation of an interview with a CPN (Maoist) central committee member on 18 January 2007.
12 Translation of an interview with a CPN (UML) central committee member on 14 January 2007.
13 Transcription of a conversation with an NSU (K) central committee member on 9 February 2007.
14 Translation of a speech given by an NSU (K) central committee member on 10 February 2007.
15 The NC district vice-president is Tanuja's father.
16 Translation of a speech given by the NC (K) district vice-president on 10 February 2007.
17 Conversation with NSU (K) central committee member and NC (K) district vice-president on 10 February 2007.
18 During the NSU (K) national conference in 2005, the NSU (K) students clashed after some irregularities. The then-appointed president, who was a candidate, was blamed for manipulating the list of voting representatives with the support of NC leaders. The clashes resulted in serious injuries, vandalism of public property, and the torching of the convention hall, causing damages costing over eight million Nepali rupees. The NC had to cancel the national convention and appoint a new NSU panel, again postponing the national convention that had been overdue since 2004. During the 2006 Free Student Union elections – a nationwide campus competition that takes place among all the student organisations – NSU lost many of its campus strongholds due to the fact that the central committee was ineffective and did not represent the sentiment of the NSU students.
19 Interaction with an ex-NSU (K) central committee member on 5 March 2007.
20 During my research (2003–7) the Nepal Student Union split into two factions mirroring the NC parties that had split over a high-level party dispute between party president G. P. Koirala and then prime minister Deuba in the early 2000s. The two reunited in 2007 in order to contest the CA elections together. But, before doing so, both the Nepali Student Unions had their national conventions to stake their positions on the united central committee.
21 Translation of a text interaction on 24 May 2007.
22 The girls from this campus are known to be some of the most active members of all the student political organisations, particularly during the political agitation of the past few years. This campus was one of the main protest zones during the political movement from 2003 to 2006.
23 As far as I have observed at the closed sessions that I have attended, all the candidates were sponsored. Their supporters contributed a fixed amount to that wing of the organisation (district or campus). Often, the central committee members (who technically are there only as external representatives) solely contributed the money for a specific candidate, which was not regarded as conflict of interest by the participants.
24 He was insinuating that, as an organisation, NSU (D) is not violent like the Maoists or as cutthroat as NSU (K).

25 Conversation with an NSU (D) central committee member on 18 March 2007.
26 Punnett has argued that 'other than when a natural vacancy occurs, leadership contests should be avoided because they can threaten party unity, provide comfort to the enemy, and distract the party from its tasks in government and opposition' (1992: 173). Davies, Blackstock and Rauschmayer have referred to this challenge as a 'we rather than me in decision-making issue of ancient-modern controversy over whether a public-centered perspective can itself be meaningfully separate from a private interest' (2005: 607).
27 Translation of an interview with an ANNISU (R) central committee member on 12 November 2006.
28 Translation of an interview with an ANNISU (R) central committee member on 12 November 2006.
29 '*Sam* (persuasion), *dam* (economic incentive), *danda* (coercion), *bhed* (divisiveness)' is a political proverb that is equivalent to 'by hook or crook', meaning to exhaust all measures for a favourable outcome. It has a negative connotation.
30 A conversation I had with students of various student organisations about the election results at a farewell tea party I hosted on 15 April 2008.
31 Rancière posits that the potential for disagreement lies in the fact that consensus is never seeing of eye to eye. The surplus identities inevitably result in

> a determined kind of speech situation: one in which one of the interlocutors at once understand and does not understand what the other is saying. (It is the conflict of one who says white and another who says white but does not understand the same thing in the name of whiteness.)
> (1999: x)

References

Auyero, J. 2001. *Poor People's Politics: Peronist Survival Networks and the Legacy of Evita*. Durham, NC: Duke University Press.

Baiocchi, G. and B. T. Connor. 2008. 'The Ethnos in the Polis: Political Ethnography as a Mode of Inquiry', *Sociology Compass*, 2 (1): 138–55.

Baral, L. B. 2006. *Oppositional Politics in Nepal*. Kathmandu: Himal Books.

Bohman, J. 1996. *Public Deliberation: Pluralism, Complexity, and Democracy*. Cambridge, MA: MIT Press.

Connolly, W. 2001. 'Politics and Vision', in A. Botwinick and W. Connolly (eds.), *Democracy and Vision*, pp. 3–24. Princeton, NJ: Princeton University Press.

Davies, B., K. Blackstock and F. Rauschmayer. 2005. '"Recruitment", "Composition", and "Mandate" Issues in Deliberative Processes: Should We Focus on Arguments Rather Than Individuals?', *Government and Policy*, 23 (4): 599–615.

Fearon, J. D. 1998. *Deliberation as Discussion: New Directions for Democratic Reform*. New Haven, CT: Yale University Press.

Fung, A. 2003. 'Survey Article: Recipe for Public Spheres – Eight Institutional Design Choices and Their Consequences', *Journal of Political Philosophy*, 11 (3): 338–67.

Fung, A. and E. O. Wright. 2002. 'Thinking about Empowered Participatory Governance', in A. Fung and E. O. Wright (eds.), *Deepening Democracy: Institutional Innovations in Empowered Participatory Governance*, pp. 3–42. London: Verso.

Gellner, D. and M. B. Karki. 2008. 'Democracy and Ethnic Groups', in D. Gellner and K. Hachhethu (eds.), *Local Democracy in South Asia*, pp. 105–27. London: Sage Publications.

Gutmann, A. and D. Thompson. 1996. *Democracy and Disagreement*. Cambridge, MA: Belknap.

———. 2004. *Why Deliberative Democracy?* Princeton, NJ: Princeton University Press.

Habermas, J. 1984. *Theory of Communicative Action*. Boston, MA: Beacon Press.

———. 1990. *Moral Consciousness and Communicative Action*. Cambridge, MA: MIT Press.

Hachhethu, K. 2009. 'The Community Party of Nepal (Maoist): Transformation from an Insurgency Group to a Competitive Political Party', *European Bulletin of Himalayan Research*, 33–34: 39–71.

Jha, P. 2014. *Battles for the New Republic: A Contemporary History of Nepal*. Delhi: Aleph Press.

Joshi, B. L. and L. E. Rose. 2004/1966. *Democratic Innovations in Nepal: A Case Study of Political Acculturation*. Kathmandu: Mandala Press.

Krämer, Karl-Heinz. 2002. 'How Representative Is the Nepali State?', in D. Gellner (ed.), *Resistance and the State: Nepalese Experience*, pp. 179–98. New Delhi: Social Science Press.

Lakier, G. 2007. 'Illiberal Democracy and the Problem of Law', in M. Lawoti (ed.), *Contentious Politics and Democratization in Nepal*, pp. 251–72. New Delhi: Sage Publications.

Lawoti, M. 2005. *Towards a Democratic Nepal: Inclusive Political Institutions for Multicultural Society*. New Delhi: Sage Publications.

Little, A. 2007. 'Between Disagreement and Consensus: Unravelling the Democratic Paradox', *Australian Journal of Political Science*, 42 (1): 143–59.

Malagodi, M. 2013. *Constitutional Nationalism and Legal Exclusion: Equality, Identity Politics, and Democracy in Nepal*. Oxford: Oxford University Press.

Miller, C. 1990. *Decision-Making in Village Nepal*. Kathmandu: Pilgrims Press.

Mouffe, C. 2000. *The Democratic Paradox*. London: Verso.

Panday, D. R. 2000. *Nepal's Failed Development: Reflections on the Mission and the Maladies*. Kathmandu: Nepal South Asia Centre.

Pellizzoni, L. 2003. 'Legitimacy Problems in Deliberative Democracy', *Political Studies*, 51 (1): 180–96.

Punnett, R. 1992. *Selecting the Party Leader: Britain in Comparative Perspective*. London: Wheatsheaf Press.

Rancière, J. 1999. *Disagreement: Politics and Philosophy*. London: University of Minnesota Press.

Rosen, L. 2006. 'Expecting the Unexpected: Cultural Components of Arab Governance', *ANNALS – American Academy of Political and Social Science*, 603: 163–78.

Schneiderhan, E. and S. Khan. 2008. 'Reasons and Inclusion: The Foundation of Deliberation', *Sociological Theory*, 26 (1): 1–24.
Shah, A. and S. Shneiderman. 2013. 'The Practices, Policies, and Politics of Transforming Inequality in South Asia: Ethnographies of Affirmative Action', *Focaal – Journal of Global and Historical Anthropology*, 65: 3–12.
Shah, S. 2004. 'A Himalayan Red Herring? Maoist Revolution in the Shadow of the Legacy Raj', in M. Hutt (ed.), *Himalayan People's War: Nepal's Maoist Rebellion*, pp. 192–225. Bloomington, IN: Indiana University Press.
Snellinger, A. 2005. 'A Crisis in Nepali Student Politics?: Analyzing the Gap between Politically Active and Non-active Students', *Peace and Democracy in South Asia Journal*, 1 (2): 18–43.
———. 2007. 'Student Movements in Nepal: Their Parameters and Their Idealised Forms', in M. Lawoti (ed.), *Contentious Politics and Democratisation in Nepal*, pp. 273–98. New Delhi: Sage Publications.
———. 2010. 'Maoist Student Organisation's Notion of Scientific Organisation', in M. Lawoti and A. Mahara (eds.), *The Maoist Insurgency in Nepal: Dynamics and Growth in the Twenty-first Century*, pp. 73–91. New York: Routledge Publications.
———. 2015. 'The Production of Possibility through an Impossible Ideal: Consensus as a Political Value on Nepal's Constituent Assembly', *Constellations*, 22 (2): 233–45.
———. 2016. '"Let's See What Happens": Hope, Contingency, and Speculation in Nepali Student Activism', *Critical Asian Studies*.
Spencer, J. 2007. *Anthropology, Politics, and the State: Democracy and Violence in South Asia*. Cambridge: Cambridge University Press.
Steiner, J., A. Bachtiger, M. Sporndli and M. R. Steenbergen. 2004. *Deliberative Politics in Action*. Cambridge: Cambridge University Press.
Sunstein, C. 2003. *Why Societies Need Dissent*. Cambridge, MA: Harvard University Press.
Thapa, D. and B. Sijapati. 2005. *A Kingdom under Siege: Nepal's Maoist Insurgency, 1996 to 2004*. London: Zed Books.
Upadhya, S. 2002. 'A Dozen Years of Democracy: The Games That Parties Play', in K. M. Dixit and S. Ramachandran (eds.), *State of Nepal*, pp. 62–76. Kathmandu: Himal Books.
Yurchak, A. 2006. *Everything Was Forever, until It Was No More: The Last Soviet Generation*. Princeton, NJ: Princeton University Press.
Zakaria, F. 1997. "The Rise of Illiberal Democracy." *Foreign Affairs* 76(6): 22–43.
Zakaria, F. 2007. *The Future of Freedom: Illiberal Democracy at Home and Abroad*. New York: WW Norton & Company.

Part III
Territorial conflict and after

6 Demand for Kukiland and Kuki ethnic nationalism[1]

Vibha Arora and Ngamjahao Kipgen

Insurgents and political elites often posit the existence of their nationality in history and embedded in specific locality in order to legitimise separatist demands for ethnic homelands. A review of relevant literature on Northeast India reveals that ethnic subjectivities and nationalist sentiments are intimately connected with territory, and increasingly many tribes and minority groups are demanding exclusive homelands for ensuring adequate political representation and safeguarding their economic development. Given the overlap in territorial habitation and the on-going fluidity in ethnic identity between the Kuki and the Naga groups, it is nearly impossible to analyse Kuki ethnic nationalism in isolation. Currently, nationalist aspirations among both Kukis and the Nagas focus on uniting Kuki and Naga settlements into a state within India or as an independent nation. Given the spatial distribution and the prevailing settlement pattern, this demand for exclusive ethnic territories is unsustainable and impossible to achieve for either the Naga or the Kuki. It is this desire to transform multi-ethnic areas into singular ethnic settlements that has exacerbated clashes and unleashed violence and ethnic cleansing in the rural areas of the contemporary state of Manipur. Ethnic conflicts aim at altering the settlement pattern and establishing ethnically homogenous and contiguous areas. Furthermore, the Naga–Kuki conflict and their respective nationalist aspirations have a strong transnational basis, since a sizeable number of Nagas and Kukis reside in Myanmar. In fact, many of the militant leaders of the insurgents and ethnic militia operate from neighbouring Myanmar (refer to Das, in this volume).

This chapter explains the historic rise of Kuki ethnic nationalism in Northeast India, particularly in Manipur, and the emergent demand for an exclusive Kuki homeland. It focuses on key events both in history and in the contemporary period, especially the ethnic violence of the 1990s, which have challenged the pace of democratic development in the state. It highlights the role of chiefs and Kuki political elite and their organisations in mobilising support for their ethnically specific cause.[2] In doing so, we are broadly engaging with the following issues. How does the politics of identity shape the nationalist aspirations of ethnic groups? How are territorial aspirations and ethnic competition over resources interlinked in contemporary Manipur? What is the correlation between ethnicity and nationalism among the Kukis (and their opponents, Nagas) living in Northeast India? What explains the escalation of ethnic violence and rise of militancy among the Kukis? How are the political elites organising their separatist and nationalist aspirations and engaging with structures of democracy in post-colonial India? Are they inclusive or exclusive in their orientation? We briefly analyse the complexity of the Kuki quest for identity and homeland and, in doing so, factor in Naga nationalism and the demand for Greater Nagaland. Both reflect challenges to sustaining an effective democratic order.

Manipur is a state located in Northeast India adjoining Myanmar, and it formally joined the Indian Union in 1949 after the Meitei Maharajah signed a merger agreement. Historically, Manipur is an erstwhile independent kingdom that was subjugated by the British in 1891. Geographically, Manipur has a total area of 22,356 sq. km; ecologically, it is divided into the valley (2,040 sq. km) and hill areas (20,316 sq. km). The Nagas and the Kukis inhabit the hill areas of the state. According to the 2001 Census, the population of Manipur was 2,293,896 persons, of which the tribal population constituted 741,141 persons (or 32.31 per cent). The population of the state was reported to be 2.76 million by the 2011 Census. It is a multi-ethnic state where the main groups are the Meitei (Hindus and Muslims, who are called Pangals), the Naga, and the Kuki. Ethnically and geographically, the hills indicate some exclusive habitation by the tribal groups although Naga and Kuki villages are not entirely congruous but intersperse each other, while the valley area is nearly exclusively inhabited by the non-tribal population.

There is much debate in colonial records and ethnographic literature on the similarities and differences between the Nagas and the Kukis and how the Meitei are a hybrid group arising from the intermixture of the Nagas and the Kukis (Elwin 1969: 451; Hodson 1901: 11; McCulloch 1859: 4; Sanajaoba 1995: 11). G. Kabui (1995: 21) contends that, over time, the Nagas and the Kukis clearly established their distinct identities, and these have been much politicised recently. Linguistically, G. A. Grierson (1904) places all three ethnic groups in the Tibeto-Burman category. After the 2001 Census, the number of scheduled tribes has increased from twenty-nine to thirty-three, with the inclusion of the Pouami Naga, Tarao, Kharam, and Any Kuki tribes.[3] Both the Nagas and the Kukis are a conglomeration of different groups and not a homogenous group. The Meitei are the dominant ethnic group controlling the political economy of the state, and they reside in the valley areas (four districts of Imphal East, Imphal West,

Thoubal, and Bishnupur). The hill areas (five districts of Churachandpur, Chandel, Senapati, Tamenglong, and Ukhrul) are backward and underdeveloped and inhabited by different tribes that are affiliated to either the Naga or the Kuki groups.

The Kukis belong to the Kuki-Chin group comprising several tribes who are cognate clans tracing descent to a common ancestor. According to mythology, the Kuki-Chin emerged from a cave called Sinlung or a rock called Chinlung or from a *khul* (fortress) (Dena 2008: 12; Gangte 1993: 14–16; Kabui 1995: 41; Shakespear 1912: 91; Shaw 1929: 24–26). All Kuki-Chin groups (tribes) trace their origin to a common location and are descendants of the great patriarch Chongthu. These clans share a common past, culture, customs, and traditions and reside in the hills (Gangte 1993; Shakespear 1912; Shaw 1929). Elsewhere (see Arora and Kipgen 2012) we have detailed the ethno-genesis and ethnic competition defining Kuki identity in Northeast India. Hence, here we will only briefly mention the historic understanding of the Kuki group in colonial ethnography and administrative classification.

According to Grierson (1904: 126), the words 'Kuki' and 'Chin' are synonymous and primarily used for the hill tribes. Locality and territorial affinity have defined who are located in the Kuki-Chin conglomeration. According to the definition given in the *Encyclopaedia Britannica*, 'Kuki is the name given to a group of tribes inhabiting both sides of the mountains dividing Assam and Bengal from Burma, south of Namtaleik river' (1962: Vol. 13: 15). E. T. Dalton defined them as hills men occupying a territory extending from 'the valley of Koladyne, where they touch on the Khumis to Northern Kachar and Manipur' (1872: 44).

The following sections highlight the relation between existing theories of ethnicity and nationalism and their application to Manipur and the Kukis and correlate the importance between land and identity, resource conflict, and desire for homelands that is being raised since 1947.

Ethnic competition, nationalism, and demand for homeland

Analysing the reigning theories on ethnic identity (Barth 1969; Brass 1991; Cohen 1985), we follow that, nearly in all cases, ethnic identity is an assertion of a difference between ethnic groups based on certain ethnic markers (religion, language, customs, etc.); due to space constraints we are unable to differentiate between variants and differences in these ethnic-nationalist theories. There are both objective differences between groups, along with an emphasis on the subjective process of identification; and various strategies are used by groups to define and maintain boundaries (Barth 1969;

Brass 1991; Cohen 1985; de Vos 1975). Ethnic identity is continually dependent on an assertion of difference(s) from others, and it is, therefore, relational, contextual, and contingent in specific ethnographic contexts (for details, refer to Arora 2007).

Ethnic conflict is not necessarily rooted in any objective factor or in difference; sometimes it is due to groups engaging in competition (Horowitz 1985: 73). This explains why many thinkers emphasise the symbolic and subjective use of ethnic identity by groups to differentiate and organise themselves into interest groups. Fredrick Barth (1969) has emphasised how inequality in access to and control over resources perpetuates ethnic stratification and accentuates ethnic boundaries. Similarly, Paul Brass (1991: 47) also recognises the potential value of ethnic stratification of resources, and how the domination of one group over others in control over them fosters ethnic nationalism. Conflict of interest and acute ethnic competition over resources can result in ethnic conflict and escalate violence (Weiner 1975). Such a situation prevails in multi-ethnic Manipur, which is inhabited primarily by the Meitei in the valley areas, while the Kuki and the Naga groups reside in the hill districts. Differential use and control over land has shaped and defined ethnic identities, with the Nagas and the Kukis practising shifting cultivation, while the Meiteis have settled terraced cultivation. Due to clash of interests and overlapping demands, Manipur has been rapidly transformed into an ethnic cauldron wherein ethnic mobilisation has fuelled counter-mobilisation of group demands, thereby diminishing effective functioning of democratic structures and undermining the process of development. Recent mobilisations have widened the gap, furthered distrust, and fostered animosity between the inter-tribal and the intra-tribal groups.

Ethnically, there are contiguities and affinities and also perceptible differences between the Naga and Kuki groups. Ethnic identity gets politicised when political coalitions are organised along ethnic lines or when access to political or economic benefits depends on their recognition. J. Friedman (1994: 233) emphasises how cultural identities are a profoundly existential phenomenon, and for those involved, it is a matter of social survival. This explains the fluidity of identity, and the conversion of some Kuki tribes such as the Anal, Chothe, and Lamkang into Nagas is now conceptualised by Dena (2008: 179–80) as 'Nagaisation'.[4] This is explicit from the case discussed here and also in the case of Hmar identity (see Arora and Kipgen 2012). Guided by macro-theorisation of identity assertion, we seek to explain the interplay of ethnic identity, ethnic assertion, tribal conflict, and demands for territorial autonomy with structures and institutions of democratic development in the contemporary state of Manipur.

Manipur is primarily an agrarian economy. Unemployment is quite high due to lack of industrial development and expansion of the tertiary sector despite significant efforts of the government. The hills make up nine-tenths of the total geographical area of Manipur and are exclusively inhabited by tribal population constituting 37 per cent of its total population. In popular perception and in allocation of resources for economic development, the hill areas continue to be backward and underdeveloped and far behind the valley areas inhabited by the Meitei community. Furthermore, even within the hill areas, intense ethnic competition persists between the Naga and the Kuki groups, although the Indian constitution grants them specific resources for tribal development and recognises their constituents as scheduled tribes. Over time, preferential allocation to ethnic groups can aggravate competition over shared scarce resources, including land, and promote conflict between them. Such claims and subjective resentment often get interwoven into ethnic politics and political identity of groups (Crawford and Lipschutz 1998: 32), and Manipur indicates these explicitly. Recognising such situations, Rodolfo Stavenhagen states:

> Ethnic conflicts generally involve a clash of interests or a struggle over rights that is rights to land, to education, to the use of language, to political representation, to freedom of religion, to the preservation of ethnic identity, to autonomy or self-determination and so forth.
>
> (1995: 509–10)

The main theories of nationalism recognise the importance of the link between ethnicity and nationalism. Both are social constructions and constantly reconstructed over time. Benedict Anderson (1991: 6) postulated and has popularised the idea of nation being an 'imagined community' – imagined as both inherently limited and sovereign. Nationalism is invented, and nations do not awaken to self-consciousness suddenly (Gellner 1964: 169). For Ernest Gellner, nationalism is a theory of political legitimacy where there is a close connection between ethnicity and nationalism whereby cultural communities are created and maintained. Nationalism requires that 'political boundaries should not cross cut political ones' (1983: 1). Paul Brass (1991: 42–43) has explained that the objective existence and subjective perception of inequality are indispensable to justify and ground nationalism. The consequent feelings of frustration and relative deprivation in control over resources do precipitate ethnic nationalism. On the other hand, pre-existing ethnicity has often been rhetorically used or sometimes even been invented in order to legitimise nationalist claims, and justify various political actions and demands (Calhoun 1993). Nationalism often instrumentally uses diverse cultural symbols and rituals, and reinvents history and traditions to give meaning to political claims and justify them to the self and to the others (Guibernau 1999). We attempt to indicate the interplay of these in a specific context of clash of ethnic-national interest of two tribes inhabiting large tracts of contemporary Northeast India, although our analysis is limited to the boundary of Manipur State. Herein ethnic interests are shaping and influencing the contours of democratic institutions and procedures, while challenging or undermining them with escalation of conflict and sometimes violence.

We show how it is not merely history and ideologies but instrumental orientation and aspirations of controlling territory and gaining access to political power and material benefits that are fuelling ethnic conflict in contemporary Manipur. The impact of ethnicity on political representation is explicit in that forty members of the State Legislative Assembly are elected from the valley area, while only twenty members are elected from the hill areas. Within the hills, the Tangkhul Nagas represent Ukhrul district (which has three seats), the Zeliangrong Nagas dominate the Tamenglong district, while the Kukis (Thadou, Paite, and Hmar) represent Churachandpur district. The Nagas and the Kukis share seats in Senapati and Chandel districts.

Nathan Glazer and Daniel P. Moynihan (1975: 12–24) argue that ethnicity gets politicised when status inequalities are untenable between the dominant and non-dominant groups. This gets accentuated when there is no single dominant group and competition gets intensified. In Manipur, the state government is constantly accused of being biased in favour of the Meitei in the allocation of facilities and funds for development. Tribal leaders continually complain and point towards the lack of infrastructural development, the poor condition of the educational and health services, endemic poverty, lack of employment opportunities, and lack of access to resources for their development. A survey of budget allocation for the hill districts in 2004–5 is indicative this situation (Government of Manipur 2004): in education, only 26 per cent was allocated to the hill districts, while this was 25 per cent in health and 22 per cent in the public works department. Four out of five hill districts figure at the bottom of the heap on the human development index (Government of Manipur 2003). These districts also have a larger proportion of the poor than the valley areas.

As a Kuki villager lamented, 'Above all, we [Kukis] are deprived of government development funds and have become strangers in the land of our ancestors.' The tribal communities inhabiting Manipur have often complained of their poor representation in government jobs and of the paucity of personnel and poor functioning of public offices in the hills. While it is mandatory to have at least 31 per cent tribal employees in all government departments,[5] few departments have been able to meet this target, sometimes due to a shortage of adequately qualified candidates, but mostly on account of a lack of political and bureaucratic commitment.

Tribal leaders attribute these problems to the concentration of power and resources in Meitei hands. The head of Sipuikawn village (Churachandpur district) lamented, 'Inadequate access to government and private jobs, poor functioning of local government in the hills, and reluctance of state government to devolve power to tribal representatives, have directly resulted in feelings of alienation and lack of democratic accountability.' The Kuki chief of Gelnel village (Senapati district) remarked, 'Most departments are centralised with almost all development schemes being formulated and implemented from Imphal and they neglect our needs.' The village authorities set up as per the Manipur Village Authorities (in the Hill Areas) Act, 1956, along the lines of traditional village councils, have limited powers to implement development projects and are generally sidelined by the state bureaucratic machinery. Autonomous District Councils (ADCs) were established under the Sixth Schedule in 1973, but these have limited political autonomy and have not empowered the tribal villagers. This justifies their demand for ADCs under the Sixth Schedule that provides greater economic control over land and forests, gives widespread executive and legislative powers, and secures greater access to frame and implement development plans. The solution proposed in the form of a separate Autonomous Hill District, or political autonomy, in the federal frame under the Sixth Schedule, is continually peddled at the time of elections. Meitei civil society organisations and elite understandably oppose these demands and any division of the state (see *The Sangai Express*, Imphal, 31 October 2002, and *The Imphal Free Press*, Imphal, 2 November 2002). The Meitei leaders want to abolish chiefship and constantly argue that the existing provisions for the tribal people are sufficient for their protection and development. The Meitei have been resentful of reservations for tribal communities in jobs within the central public sector, claiming that opportunities for educated Meitei youth are limited and are demanding implementation of Manipur Land Revenue and Land Reforms Act, 1960 (it was amended in 1989), in the hill areas.

Land has become scarce in the valley areas, while the lack of land reforms in the hill areas has ensured that tribal lands are inalienable. Hence, it is not surprising to find land becoming the central focus of ethnic competition over resources and the justification of indigeneity in Manipur, as in other parts of Northeast India (Baruah 2003; Bhaumik 2009: 23; Sivaramakrishnan and Cederlof 2005: 2). Land is not merely a material resource but simultaneously a landscape. The landscape is theorised as text and a scape of history (Stewart and Strathern 2003). The naming of villages, rivers, and mountains has a tremendous symbolic power, as in humanising the landscape groups stamp their identity and inscribe it with their life stories (Sahlins 1992; Strang 1997). Veronica Strang (1997: 84) highlights how land is a central medium of mediating all aspects of history, economy, and society, and economic considerations are a small part of an immediate, intimate, and fundamentally holistic relationship that the indigenous have with land. Our research confirms the broader postulate that people seek in land not just material resource of satisfaction of needs; it is the source and locus of power, wealth, and meaning. This explains why land rouses deep passions among individuals and communities (Arora 2009).

What other factors explain this inordinate concern with territorial control and the popularity of demand for ethnic homelands? The idea of a historic land and the metaphor of an ancestral homeland has been a powerful one that has excited the imagination and justified various actions (including violence) of political activists and ethnic associations associated with this struggle in order to realise it. We follow A. D. Smith in understanding this desire for 'the land of their putative ancestors and the sacred places where their heroes and sages walked, fought and taught' (1991: 63). What excite intense passions and legitimise violence are ideas of historic exclusivity, 'one which they believe to be exclusively "theirs" by virtue of links with events and personages of earlier generations of "their" people' (ibid.). Smith has shown how the homeland's resources are considered to be 'exclusive' to the people; they are not for 'alien' use and exploitation (1991: 9).

Our research on the Kukis affirms the presence of sacred sites where remnants of their legendary hero Gaalngam are available in the hills of Manipur. Traditionally, for the Kuki community, land was the scape and locus of their inter-relationship with the Supreme Being (Pathien) whose blessings and actions were indicated in it. A Haokip chief of Champai village elaborated, 'Land to us means identity. Land refers to our culture, our heritage and our unique identity. It is part of our social fabric and selves, as indicated and interwoven by kinship.' Ethnic identification among tribes of Northeast India has centred on territorial affiliation and claims over them based on mythology and historical habitation. This explains the ethnic politics of separatism and nativism miring Northeast India (Bhaumik 2009; Chaube 1973; Phukon 2003). Historian G. Kamei (2006: 101) forcefully argues how for the tribals, issues of identity, ethnicity, and landownership are integral to their idea of self and bounded-ness as a political community within Manipur. Landownership bestows identity, simultaneously affords sustenance and a livelihood, and confers a sense of power in an area. This shapes their notions of belonging, experience of shared history, and ethnic unity. For the Kuki groups like the Nagas (see Das, in this volume), cultural heritage, control of land, and sense of identity are closely interlaced. The empirical case study highlights the complexity of this relationship and the challenges to the same with a transition in polity and governance mechanisms.

Demand for Kukiland and Kuki ethnic nationalism 169

As effectively theorised in literature, history and mythology are effectively used to demarcate homelands. The nationalist idea of an original territory inhabited by specific communities and the separatist demand for exclusive ethnic homelands are premised not on an imagination but in demonstrated kinship.[6] Nationalism is a form of metaphoric kinship (Anderson 1991), and the strong presence of kinship connections can facilitate the powerful development of ethnic nationalism. Most Kuki villages are inhabited by kin members belonging to a specific patrilineage and clans. Hence, members inhabiting any village are connected through either descent or marriage. The contiguous settlement of Kuki clans in specific territories such as villages underlies their ethnic-nationalist desire for a homeland. In the pre-colonial period, the Kukis did not have a state but nonetheless constituted a nation. The Kukis were subdivided into settlements in Northeast India and in neighbouring Myanmar. Over time, a national identity was transformed into an ethnic one. Zalen'-gam aimed to unite the erstwhile ancestral domain of the Kukis prior to the advent of the British. This was the sentiment reiterated by P. S. Haokip (2010) on 24 February 2010 as part of the twenty-third KNO Raising Day address.

Kuki ethnic nationalism (1917–80s) and Kukiland

Territorial independence and affinity with land have been historically strong among the Kukis despite the historic absence of their organisation into a state or a distinct nation. The Kuki chiefs were politically independent in the past but nonetheless recognised themselves as related by descent from a common ancestor. Ethnic distinctiveness and a sense of belonging to a nationality effectively propelled their nationalist aspirations and 'justified' their demands in the present. Hence, the Kuki nation is not an imagined community but comprises kinsmen who speak a common language, follow distinct customs and cultural traditions, inhabit a specific territory, and have a shared history. Nonetheless, the demand for a Kuki nation is a product of their aspiration to control their political economy and preserve their cultural integrity; it definitely is a product of their active imagination and construction.

Kuki historians such as Gangte (1993: 10) argue that Kuki polity comprised of village republics under various chiefs and they were largely a loose federation until the British interfered in the region and tried to subjugate them. There is explicit documentation of Kuki attacks on the British, their invasion of Tripura, and the launch of several British expeditions to subjugate and control them (Chakravorty 1964: 53; Elly 1978: 8; Reid 1997/1942: 1; Shakespear 1909: 371). However, the Kuki chiefs politically united during the momentous offensive against the British during what is popularly referred to as the Kuki Rebellion of 1917–19. The principal causes fuelling rebellion were general hostility towards the alien British; resistance to British presence as it threatened their independence; and the British imposition of land revenue and house tax and practice of forced labour (*pothang* in the Meitei language), which contradicted Kuki customary practices and laws. Nonetheless, the immediate trigger for this armed uprising was the recruitment of Kuki villagers as labour corps and their deportation to France (Chishti 2004; Gangte 1993; Haokip 2003; Palit 1984).

According to archival sources, Chengjapao (the clan chief of Doungel) convened a meeting of various Kuki chiefs, and a *shajam lha*[7] was performed in early March 1917 and later in various Kuki enclaves in many parts of Northeast India. To declare their political resolve to resist imperial rule and to announce the Kuki rebellion, king-sized red chillies wrapped on smouldering firewood (*thingkho le malchapom* in Thadou Kuki language) were passed through Kuki villages. According to a letter written by Higgins in 1917, the Kukis rebelled in order to preserve their political independence and protect their land and culture.[8] The British suppressed it with great difficulty. According to an archival note, there were, '23 principals involved, 13 in Manipur under Assam, 10 in the Somra Tract under Burma'.[9]

The Kuki villagers were united into a nation when their chiefs decided to launch an armed rebellion during 1917–19. An elderly man who is also a village council member at Gelnel village explained how the Kuki's became a nation:

> The Kukis were customarily dictated by culture and tradition to obey their chiefs. Therefore, fighting or defending their [village] land and independence is an expression of loyalty and solidarity. Every villager is bound by this unwritten rule and abides by every member.

The Kuki rebellion effectively crystallised the political unity of the Kuki community and served as the foundation of their ethnic nationalism (Chishti 2004; Gangte 1993; Haokip 2003; Palit 1984); this is quite contrary to others (e.g. Naga scholars), who often emphasise the post-colonial emergence of ethnic nationalism. During group discussions conducted in Manipur in 2009–10, many chiefs and politicians referred to the Kuki uprisings of 1917–19 as the turning point of Kuki political history, attesting to its extended significance and its memory as a reminder of their spirit of oneness and their political unity as a distinct and historic nationality.

The setbacks in the Kuki rebellion of 1917–19 did not dampen the spirit of Kuki nationalism. During the First World War, many Kukis joined the Indian National Army and aligned themselves with the Japanese forces in Northeast India to counter the British Indian army. However, the defeat of the Axis group dashed their hopes of restoration of their political independence and control over their territory and demoralised them. To foster political unity and forge an ethnic identity, in 1936, many Kuki chiefs came together under a Kuki Chiefs' Association, and this was their first political organisation. The Kuki Chiefs' Association later led to the formation of the Kuki National Assembly (KNA) on 24 October 1946 in order to make concerted efforts to preserve their territorial integrity. The assembly included all chiefs as representatives automatically. The constituent tribes were Thadou, Paite, Vaiphei, Gangte, Simte, Zou, Anal, Kom, Hmar, Guite, Chiru, Monsang, and Koireng (comprising both the old and new Kuki groups) (Nabakumar 2004: 29–32). The assembly planned to establish another pan-Kuki platform for the Kuki-Chin kindred groups of Manipur. They were hopeful that they would regain political independence after the British left India in 1947. In 1947, the Kukis made a political pact with the Nagas to resolve some problems common to both the communities. They also made a pact with the Lushai/Mizo to unite for specific ends, which led to their inclusion in the Mizo National Front in 1964. In its working committee meeting held on 11 August 1947, the chiefs announced their three-point objective to unite Kuki groups, achieve better understanding with the Nagas, and peacefully cooperate with the Meitei residing in the valleys of Manipur.

The Nagas declared their political independence in August 1947 and, if necessary, to follow an armed path to achieve a separate nation. Meanwhile, the Kuki chiefs collectively tried to dissuade the Meitei Maharaja from signing the political agreement for merger of Manipur into India but were finally unsuccessful (Thomson 1971: 80). The Kuki chiefs were quite disheartened when Manipur joined the Indian Union in September 1949. They proclaimed that they never had been part of India until the British annexed them and hence saw no reason to be part of India after the British left. A seventeen-point election manifesto was drafted by the KNA to fight the elections in 1952 wherein they declared their opposition to the merger of Manipur into Assam and stressed their distinctive political status and identity. Dominated by the chiefs, KNA held a general meeting at Thingkangphai village in Churachandpur district during 19–22 January 1960 and prepared a memorandum and resolved to submit it to the Government of India to assert their political freedom and autonomy, and demand a separate Kuki state. United under the banner of the KNA, the leaders asserted, 'The hills had never been part of India prior to the British annexation of the region' (Letter of the KNA President, Kohima, 15 August 1947).

Nonetheless, the Kuki chiefs largely followed a restricted but democratic style in presenting their case to the Government of India and remained largely peaceful. They entered into strategic alliances with the Mizo National Front to press for the formation of a Greater Mizoram, which would integrate the different Kuki-Chin-Mizo inhabitants of the region. During 15–18 January 1965, a convention of various Kuki-Chin ethnic groups took place at Kawnpui in Churachandpur.[10] However, the Kuki hopes were belied with the signing of the Mizo peace accord between the Government of India and the Mizo National Front led by Laldenga, which resulted in the formation of Mizoram State in 1986. The Mizo accord completely sidelined and ignored the Kuki demands (Bhaumik 2007: 14; Haokip 2006: 10–15).

The Kukis realised over time that their aspirations for self-determination were being ignored by the state and the state and the national governments. The Kuki's feeling of relative deprivation, frustration, and alienation, on the one hand, and territorial acquisitiveness and hegemonic policies of the Meiteis and the Nagas, on the other, have directly contributed to the formation of ethnic militia and emergence of militant organisations resorting to violence.[11] The formations of militia are guided by an aspiration for political autonomy and self-governance. On 18 May 1987, the Kuki National Front (KNF) was formed under the leadership of the late Pu Nehkholun Kipgen[12] at Molnoi village (Myanmar) to secure a separate 'Kuki state' within the Indian Union by integrating all Kuki-inhabited areas of Ukhrul, Tamenglong, Chandel, and Churachandpur districts and Sadar Hills sub-divisions of Senapati district of Manipur (*The Shillong Times*, Shillong, 1 October 1993). KNF was established to accelerate the demand earlier raised by KNA in the 1960s for creating a Kuki state (Gangte 2007: 7). Kuki youth influenced by the rousing speeches of Pu Nehkholun Kipgen in mass meetings held in Kuki villages pledged their life and were sent to Kachin (Myanmar) to train in guerrilla warfare. After their training, they infiltrated Kuki villages and initiated boycott of national celebrations, such as Independence Day and Republic Day; they called for strikes and started economic blockades on the highway to press their demand for a separate Kukiland. They even started attacking security forces guarding the highway in order to exert control over the region. The untimely demise of the KNF leader, the charismatic Nehkholun Kipgen on 12 October 1993 at the hands of Indian security forces, was a major setback. Many Kuki youth inspired by Nehkholun Kipgen's speeches sacrificed their life for the cause during the 1980s. What is important to remember as part of Nehkholun Kipgen's unfilled legacy is how he wanted to carve a separate state for the Kukis within India (Kipgen 1993) and not outside it, unlike the other Kuki militants and revolutionaries.

The formation of armed militia among the Kukis is not simply an emergent response to domination of other groups in Manipur, as they have legitimised their claims by linking to pre-colonial geographies of affective belonging and power. The strong desire to carve out a separate homeland for the Kukis led to the formation of another armed group, namely the Kuki

Demand for Kukiland and Kuki ethnic nationalism 173

Figure 6.1 Kuki National Front (KNF) armed cadres
Source: Copyright Kipgen.

National Army, in 1988 under the leadership of Pu Thangkholun Haokip.[13] These militants aimed to unite the Kuki populated areas of Myanmar with portions of Kuki-inhabited areas in Thoubal, Ukhrul, and Chandel districts in Manipur (Phanjoubam 2004: 171). P. S. Haokip,[14] who is the president of the Kuki National Organisation (KNO), propounded this idea of Zale'n-gam, which means 'freedom of the people in their land'. His vision for the Kuki people and his ideology were published in 2008 in the form of a booklet entitled *Zalen'-gam: The Kuki Nation* (KNO Publication, Private Circulation). The Kukis vehemently opposed the Nationalist Socialist Council of Nagaland (Isak and Muivah) (NSCN [IM])'s ethnic cleansing policy and communal war to create a Greater Nagaland.[15] More recently, some other parts of Kuki-inhabited areas in Northeastern India have been included in the map of Zale'n-gam; this expansionist aspiration may also be a reaction to the ambitions of a Nagalim/Greater Nagaland, and it aims to unite all Kuki-Chin-inhabited areas into a single state.

Politics of contiguous homeland and the Kuki–Naga clashes (the 1990s)

The practical and political difficulties in demarcating ethnic homelands lie at the core of ethnic discord and violence among competing groups in Manipur. The territorial claims are quite unfeasible given the settlement pattern in the hill areas, while each ethnic group with its militia tries to further exclusive control over territory and mobilises resources for furthering these claims. These only exacerbate conditions of further conflict and ethnic violence. The territorial claims of the Kukis pursued by the KNF and Kuki National Army overlap the territorial demands of the Nagas (NSCN [IM]) in Manipur. As much as KNA (presently by KNF and Kuki National Army) claimed a Kuki homeland, the Nagas claimed large parts of Manipur as Naga territory; overlapping settlements render the desire for exclusive homelands to be impossible, and Kuki or Naga areas may transcend contemporary administrative and state boundaries. According to the Kuki Inpi Manipur[16] the Kuki–Naga conflict started in post-independent India.[17] The Kuki Inpi Manipur elaborated that the Kukis accepted the Indian government as the legitimate successor to the British, while the Nagas proclaimed their independence on 14 August 1947.

Established in 1980, the NSCN (a Naga insurgent group) wanted to bring the Nagas under one nation. Led by Isak Chisi Swu and Th. Muivah, it rejected the Shillong Accord signed between the Government of India and the Naga National Council on 11 November 1975. The manifesto of the NSCN since its inception in January 1980 stated: 'We stand for the unquestionable sovereign right of Nagaland people over every inch of Nagaland whatever it may be and admit of no other existence whatever' (Koireng 2006: 77). The Nagas perceive the Kukis to be an obstacle to their long-cherished goal of unifying the Naga-inhabited areas.

Ethnic-nationalist claims and assertions have become a contestable complex discourse wherein history and contemporary interlace each other. If we analyse the settlement pattern, then we discern that Kukis are a majority only in Churachandpur and Chandel, while the Nagas are a dominant majority in Tamenglong and Ukhrul, and both have an equal representation in Senapati district. The Kuki demand for the division of the Kuki-dominated area of Senapati district in 1973 and creation of a Sadar Hills district is perceived to be a grave threat by the NSCN (IM) insurgents who have their political agenda to further Nagalim. The political quest for regaining control over ancestral lands has galvanised and energised the ethnic leaders and furthered ethnic conflict and undermined development.

The Indo-Naga ceasefire of 1964 was extended to Ukhrul, Mao-Maram, and Tamenglong sub-divisions of Manipur (ibid.: 75). This engendered a fear among the people of Manipur that Ukhrul, Mao-Maram, and Tamenglong would be made part of an independent Nagalim. Concerned over this development, the All Manipur People's Convention, Imphal, perceived that it would have serious effects on the well-being of the Kuki-Chin tribes inhabiting the same territory with the Nagas. The convention submitted a

Demand for Kukiland and Kuki ethnic nationalism 175

memorandum to the Government of India in protest against the inclusion of Ukhrul, Mao-Maram, and Tamenglong sub-division of Manipur in the ceasefire as agreed upon by the Government of India, on the one hand, and the Government of Nagaland, on the other.[18]

The Naga militants have justified and pursued a policy of ethnic cleansing against the Kukis and engaged in violent clashes with them during the 1990s. Despite claims, none of the hill districts in Manipur are exclusively inhabited by the Nagas. Therefore, in such a situation, it would be extremely difficult to presume absolute majority of one tribe over the other. The overlapping of landholdings explains how the Kukis emerged as a stumbling block in the NSCN (IM)'s on-going effort in achieving a Nagalim. Ethnic cleansing has not taken place in Churachandpur district where there is no Naga settlement. On 27 June 2001 a memorandum was submitted by the Delhi-based Kuki Students' Organisation to the prime minister of India, documenting the landholding pattern in the hill districts of Manipur (see Table 6.1).

Violent ethnic clashes have been reported after the communalisation of the demand for ethnic homelands, and the 1990s are considered a dark period in Manipur's social history. The Kukis have been enraged by the series of massacres organised by the NSCN (IM) (see Table 6.2). Attacks have provoked counter-attacks transforming Manipur into an ethnic cauldron while the state government has repeatedly failed to protect the innocent villagers.

Haokip (2008/2003: 331) has argued that the Kukis retaliated in self-defence, and, unfortunately, these have been reported by the mass media as events of ethnic conflict. From data presented in Table 6.2, we can observe how seven out of nine cases of massacres had been perpetrated by the Nagas. The Naga insurgents have indiscriminately killed innocent villagers and forced migration of thousands in the Manipur hills.

The number of Kukis killed by the NSCN (IM) is reported to be more than 900, while more than 350 villages have been uprooted and 50,000 Kukis have been displaced (Haokip 2008/2003: 346–73). According to

Table 6.1 Landholding pattern of Nagas and Kukis in Manipur's hill districts

Name of district	Kuki (%)	Naga (%)
Chandel	75	25
Senapati	50	50
Tamenglong	35	65
Ukhrul	70	30

Source: Adapted from Gangte (2007: 96).

Table 6.2 List of major Naga and Kuki massacres reported in Manipur

Date	Location and details	Perpetrator
8 October 1992	Massacre of Kukis at Moultuh in Chandel district. Here three women were murdered after being raped, and a two-month-old female baby and two men were killed[a]	Naga
8 August 1993	Massacre of Kuki villagers living at Khallongching near Nongmaijing in Senapati district. The Naga militants killed thirteen villagers, which included ten women, an infant, and two men including the chief of the village (Gangte 2002: 4)	Naga
13 September 1993	Massacre of Kukis in Gelnel village: seventeen were killed and seven injured; 80 of the 100 houses were completely gutted. In the attack, three NSCN (IM) cadres, including one commander, were also killed (Haokip 2008/2003: 345)	Naga
13 September 1993	Massacre in Joupi village located near Tamei in Tamenglong district. The Nagalim Guard and the Naga Students Volunteer Organisation (see Koireng 2006: 96) served villagers of Joupi a notice to vacate their land/village on or before 15 September 1993. When they did not do so, about eighty persons including women were killed and many were fatally injured	Naga
19 September 1993	Massacre of Kukis in Taloulong village in Tamenglong district. NSCN (IM) activists swooped down upon innocent villagers, forcing the adults to flee leaving behind small children under ten years of age. Thereafter, NSCN (IM) activists hacked to death thirteen minors, including a girl child. They were served a quit notice by the United Naga Council and Nagalim Guard earlier. All the houses were also completely burnt down (Gangte 2002: 13–16)	Naga
29 September 1993	Kuki militants attacked Ngariyan Kabui village of Churachandpur district. All the sixty houses were completely burnt down, and four villagers were killed (Koireng 2006: 99)	Kuki

Date	Location and details	Perpetrator
1 December 1993	Nagas attacked Kaihao Tangkhul village under Saikul sub-division of Senapati district. Three male adults were killed, and sixty-five houses were also burnt down (Koireng 2006: 99)	Kuki
16 December 1993	Kuki army attacked Khongbal Tangkhul village, which is about 25 km northeast of Imphal. Eight persons of the village were killed, and five others sustained fatal injuries (Phanjoubam 2007/2004: 196–99)	Naga
19 November 1994	Massacre of Kuki villagers in Thingsan village in Chandel district. NSCN (IM) cadre dressed in Indian Security Forces' uniform killed twenty-five Kuki men	Naga

Cited in *Memorandum* submitted to Dr Kofi Anan, Secretary-General, United Nations Organisation, by P. S. Haokip, President, KNO, dated 21 May 2005.

data compiled by Phanjoubam (2007: 200) for 1993–95, about 534 persons (391 Kukis and 143 Nagas) were killed and 4,900 houses burnt down (2,649 belonging to the Kukis and 2,251 to the Nagas). Furthermore, during 1992–99, more than 900 people, including 534 Kukis and 266 Nagas, were killed, while others (257 Kukis and 223 Nagas) sustained injuries, and 5,724 houses (3,110 belonging to Kukis and 2,614, to Nagas) were set ablaze.

During interviews conducted in Manipur in 2010, some Kuki militia mentioned that they were forced to raid Naga villages and kill innocent Nagas, as they did not want others to perceive them as weak and ineffective. Every year, 13 September is observed as 'Black September' by the Kukis in commemoration of the Kukis killed during the Joupi massacre. There has been both inter- and intra-district-level transfer of the tribal population due to ethnic conflict. The majority of the displaced Kukis have been resettled in the Sadar Hills area of Senapati district and Churachandpur district of Manipur. Many new Naga villages have come up at the site of abandoned Kuki villages. Likewise, the Kukis also have established new ones at the site of erstwhile Naga villages. For example, Nungka, an erstwhile Kuki village of Ukhrul district, was resettled at Saikul sub-division of Senapati district in 1995. Likewise, another Kuki village, Bollen, was shifted to a site near Sapermeina of Kangpokpi sub-division of Senapati district; Molsang, a Kuki village of Tamenglong district, is today established in Senapati district.

Most Kuki leaders remember and keep the memory of the 13 September 1993 massacre alive by continually referring to it in their speeches and commemorating it as a black day in their history (*The Hindu*, Chennai, 13 September 2013). As long as these tragic incidents are relived, wounds will not heal. The Naga–Kuki clashes have shown how conflicting homeland demands can lead to ethnic cleansing in pursuit of 'pure ethnic states' (Bhaumik 2004: 231). These ethnic clashes have led to the sidelining of social problems and tribal development issues. Violence begets violence, and there is no justification for it. However, the truth is that democratic strategies have not been as successful in getting the attention of the Government of India.

We agree with Bhaumik's (2009: 23) observation that pure ethnic homelands have proved to be a costly mirage for these battling ethnicities in Northeast India. In conclusion, the failure of the central and state governments to acknowledge the peaceful demand of the Kukis for a separate state in the 1960s, the betrayal of Mizo National Front in the 1980s, and the territorial acquisitiveness and hegemonic policies of the Meitei and the Naga insurgents in the past few decades have led to the emergence of the Kuki revolutionary movement. There has been some change in the past few years after the 'Suspension of Operations' (Ceasefire) signed on 10 August 2005 between the Indian army and the KNO. This was supplemented by signing of the Suspension of Operations on 22 August 2008 between the Government of India, KNO, and the state Government of Manipur.[19]

Time and again KNO has pressed its demands and submitted its needs to the national government, and complained that its delegations have been ignored and not given an audience – even in November 2011 when the home minister visited Manipur (*The Sangai Express*, Imphal, 3 August 2012). Other Kuki organisations assert a similar narrative of not being heard and being sidelined. Some are optimistic that the present ceasefire would find a lasting solution, while other sections of the Kuki community are sceptical and getting restless. At a meeting held in Monpi village in Chandel district on 16 October 2012, the representatives of numerous Kuki organisations indicated their restlessness that the peaceful negotiations after the ceasefire that has been operative for five years have not yielded any outcome (*The Sangai Express*, Imphal, 18 October 2012). In an earlier press conference, the KNO president had equally asserted the necessity of finding a timely solution and recognition of their fifty-year-old demands, and how the armed insurgents were committed to sacrificing their lives for this cause rather than allow the Nagas to dominate them and usurp their demands for a homeland. A memorandum submitted by Kuki State Demand Committee to the former prime minister Manmohan Singh on 10 May 2012 reiterated that, despite having a history of self-rule and autonomy, the Kuki nation opted to be loyal and join the Indian Union, and feels their loyalty has neither been adequately recognised nor been rewarded. The memorandum highlights the partiality shown by the Government of India to the Naga insurgents.

In July 2011 and May 2012, the Kuki State Demand Committee organised blockades that paralysed the economy and caused severe hardship to the residents of the area, and the Nagas retaliated by organising blockades soon thereafter. The Kuki Inpi continually blames the national government for not heeding to its legitimate demands and excluding it from talks held with the insurgent Nagas; it insists on a tripartite settlement (*The Sangai Express*, Imphal, 20 October 2012). In October 2012, after being re-elected as president of Kuki Inpi Manipur, Thangkhosei Haokip declared that 'justice has to be delivered to the Kukis before any settlement is arrived at between the NSCN-IM and the Government of India' (*The Times of India*, Guwahati, 21 October 2012). T. Haokip further explained that they were opposing the NSCN (IM) policy of ethnic cleansing carried out in the 1990s because of which there had been mass displacement and more than 1,000 Kukis were killed. Hence, he was not opposed to a political faction leading the Nagas and was not against the other Naga groups in general (ibid.). Such press statements and attempts to redraw the boundaries of Senapati district by the Kuki State Demand Committee resulted in hostile responses from not merely the Nagas but also the Meitei, escalating further tension in the region (see *The Sangai Express*, Imphal, 30 November 2012 and 3 December 2012).

The Kuki militants are getting increasingly restless and have threatened to resume militancy if their demand for Kukiland is not redressed immediately (*Imphal Free Press*, Imphal, 15 July 2013). In an interview posted online, Seilen Haokip, the KNO leader, asserted that they found it discriminatory to be ruled by other groups and wanted security (see Haokip 2014). He explained, 'Zale'n-gam is essential for equitable socio-economic-politico development, which has not been the case in post-independent India' (ibid.). Geographically, a Kuki state comprising 'Chandel, Churachandpur and Sadar Hills and Kuki inhabited areas in Naga dominated districts of Ukhrul, Senapati and Tamenglong is viable because these are the ancestral lands of the ethnic Kuki people' (ibid.).

The large majority of Kuki organisations, civil society groups, and even militants have sought a peaceful solution for their fifty-year-old demand for an ethnic homeland within the Indian republic and not outside it. As Seilen Haokip pointed out, 'The absence of war does not necessarily imply peace' as violence is simmering beneath the surface (ibid.). The greatest challenge for the Indian democracy is to sustain peace, initiate meaningful political dialogue between the warring factions within the ethnic groups, and forge a common cause in order to find a solution to the ethnic homeland issue

180 *Vibha Arora and Ngamjahao Kipgen*

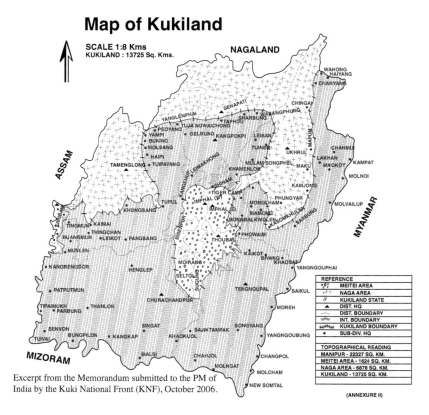

Figure 6.2 Map of Kukiland

Source: Redrawn map based on the memoranda submitted by the Kuki National Front (KNF) to the prime minister of India.

Disclaimer: Map not to scale. The international boundaries, coastlines, denominations, and other information shown in any map in this work do not necessarily imply any judgement concerning the legal status of any territory or the endorsement or acceptance of such information. For current boundaries, readers may refer to the Survey of India maps.

of the Kuki and the Naga groups in Northeast India. We conclude our critical examination by emphasising how the hills of Manipur will continue to witness violence and ethnic hatred while these political demands live in the imagination of the elites and percolated to the masses. A solution of these problems is a challenging task for any effective maturing of democracy here. So long as these ethnic demands engender violence, the meaning of democracy would be a contestable one.

Notes

1 We thank the Indian Institute of Technology, Delhi, for providing us with necessary funding for writing this chapter. The usual disclaimers apply.
2 This chapter is largely based on a review of relevant literature. However, some fieldwork insights and interviews conducted in 2009 by N. Kipgen are incorporated here.
3 According to the Scheduled Caste and Scheduled Tribes List (Modification) Order 1956, Part X, Manipur has twenty-nine tribes. This order modified the Constitution (Scheduled Tribes) Order, 1950. The 1950 order had simply categorised all the Naga and Kuki tribes in present-day Assam, Manipur, Meghalaya, Mizoram, Nagaland, and Tripura as 'Any Naga tribe', 'Any Kuki tribe', and 'Any Lushai tribe' without giving any specific 'tribe' names.
4 Arora and Kipgen (2012) have detailed how 'Nagaisation' is weakening Kuki ethnic identity and leading to its fragmentation.
5 This is against the all-India reservation of 7.5 per cent, based on proportionate composition of 'tribal' communities at the national level. According to the 1971 Census, tribal communities make up 31 per cent of Manipur's population (See Manipur SA # G-FA/12/54, R/18-5, 352, on this debate in the Parliament). Also see 'Memorandum' to the 'National Commission for Scheduled Castes and Scheduled Tribes, New Delhi by Scheduled Tribes Welfare Association of Manipur, on 25 April 2006'.
6 Anderson (1991: 15) has argued that nationalist and ethnic ideologies should be classified with religion and kinship rather than with fascism and liberalism.
7 A word in Thadou Kuki language. It refers to an auspicious ceremony wherein a *mithun* (bison) is ritually slaughtered and its heart and liver are collectively consumed mainly by the chiefs and elders to cement and affirm their political commitment to a cause.
8 J. C. Higgins's letter No. 1243 dated 7 November 1917 to the Chief Secretary of Assam, Foreign and Political Department (New Delhi: National Archives of India).
9 Minute Paper. Secret Political Department, Government of Burma, Rangoon, 23 December 1919, Foreign and Political Department (New Delhi: National Archives of India).
10 http://dipr.mizoram.gov.in/article/what-price-twenty-years-of-peace-in-mizoram-per cent281986–2006per cent29per cent3A-a-kuki-perspective/lang/en (accessed on 25 September 2010).
11 Interview with S. T. Thangboi, president (since 1993) of KNF in Ebenezer Camp, Sadar Hills, Senapati district, during March 2009.
12 A graduate from Manipur University, Pu Nehkholun Kipgen showed his zeal for Kukiland even during his studentship. An elderly man recounted how he used to venture out in the night and write 'Why not Kukiland for the Kukis?' in public places.
13 Pu Thangkholun Haokip, the founder and commander-in-chief of Kuki National Army, was killed in a clash on 24 June 1993.
14 He gave up his job in a bank and joined the Kuki National Organisation on 20 December 1994 to advance the Kuki cause.
15 Resolution of the Kuki Nampi Consultative Convention, Kuki Inn, Imphal, on 29 January 2005.

16 The 'Kuki Inpi', the apex organisation of the Kukis, was revived in 1993 during the peak of Kuki–Naga riots.
17 See Kuki Inpi Manipur, *Anniversary Souvenir*, 1994.
18 Memorandum submitted by All Manipur People's Convention to the Minister of Home Affairs, Government of India, Imphal, dated 17 September 1965.
19 Furthermore, the United People's Front (UPF), formed in 2006, which is another umbrella organisation comprising Kuki-Chin revolutionary groups, also signed the same 'Suspension of Operations' agreement on 22 August 2008. The objective of the KNO and UPF is identical ('Cabinet Nod to SoO Deal', *The Sangai Express,* Imphal, 23 August 2008; 'State Government Authorises Principal Secretary to Sign SoO Agreement with Kuki Militants', *The Imphal Free Press*, Imphal, 3 August 2008).

References

Anderson, B. 1991. *Imagined Communities: Reflections on the Origin and Spread of Nationalism*. London: Verso.

Arora, V. 2007. 'Assertive Identities, Indigeneity and the Politics of Recognition as a Tribe: The Bhutias, the Lepchas and the Limbus of Sikkim', *Sociological Bulletin*, 56 (2): 195–220.

———. 2009. '"They Are All Set to Dam(n) Our Future": Contested Development through Hydel Power in Democratic Sikkim', *Sociological Bulletin*, 58 (1): 94–114.

Arora, V. and N. Kipgen. 2012. 'The Politics of Identifying and Distancing from Kuki Identity', *Sociological Bulletin*, 61 (3): 401–22.

Barth, F. (ed.). 1969. *Ethnic Groups and Boundaries: The Social Organization of Cultural Difference*. Boston, MA: Little Brown and Company.

Baruah, S. 2003. 'Citizens and Denizens: Ethnicity, Homelands, and the Crises of Displacement in North-east India', *Journal of Refugee Studies*, 16 (1): 44–66.

Bhaumik, S. 2004. 'Ethnicity, Ideology and Religion: Separatist Movements in India's Northeast', in S. P. Limaye, M. Malik and R. G. Wirsing (eds.), *Religious Radicalism and Security in South Asia*, pp. 219–44. Hawaii: Asia-Pacific Center for Security Studies.

———. 2007. 'Insurgencies in India's Northeast: Conflict, Co-option and Change', *East West Center Washington Working Papers*, Number 10: 1–69.

———. 2009. *Troubled Periphery: The Crisis of India's North East*. New Delhi: Sage Publications.

Brass, P. 1991. *Ethnicity and Nationalism: Theory and Comparison*. New Delhi: Sage Publications.

Calhoun, C. 1993. 'Nationalism and Ethnicity', *Annual Review of Sociology*, 19: 211–39.

Chakravorty, B. C. 1964. *British Relations with the Hill Tribes Bordering on Assam since 1858*. Calcutta: Firma K. L. Mukhopadhyay.

Chaube, S. K. 1973. *Hill Politics in North-east India*. Calcutta: Orient Longman.

Chishti, S. M. 2004. *Kuki Uprising in Manipur 1919–1920*. Guwahati: Spectrum Publications.
Cohen, A. P. 1985. *The Symbolic Construction of Community*. London: Routledge.
Crawford, B. and R. D. Lipschutz. 1998. *The Myth of 'Ethnic Conflict': Politics, Economics, and 'Cultural' Violence*. Berkeley, CA: University of California Press.
Dalton, E. T. 1872. *Descriptive Ethnology of Bengal*. Calcutta: Firma K. L. Mukhopadhyay.
Dena, L. 2008. *In Search of Identity: Hmars of North-east India*. New Delhi: Akansha Publishing House.
de Vos, G. 1975. 'Ethnic Pluralism', in G. de Vos and L. Romanucci-Ross (eds.), *Ethnic Identity: Cultural Continuities and Change*, pp. 1–42. California: Mayfield Publishing Co.
Elly, E. B. 1978/1893. *Military Report on the Chin-Lushai Country*. Calcutta: Firma K. L. Mukhopadhyay.
Elwin, V. 1969. *The Nagas in the Nineteenth Century*. Bombay: Oxford University Press.
Encyclopaedia Britannica. 1962. Volume 13.
Friedman, J. 1994. *Cultural Identity and Global Process*. London: Sage Publications.
Gangte, P. 2002. 'Human Rights Violation in Hill Areas', in Threatened Indigenous-Peoples' Society (TIPS) (ed.), *Human Rights Review*, pp. 19–22. Imphal, Manipur: TIPS.
Gangte, T. S. 1993. *The Kukis of Manipur: A Historical Analysis*. New Delhi: Gyan Publishing House.
———. 2007. 'Struggle for Identity and Land among the Hill Peoples of Manipur', *Eastern Quarterly*, 4 (2): 91–100.
Gellner, E. 1964. *Thought and Change*. Chicago: The University of Chicago Press.
———. 1983. *Nations and Nationalism*. London: Basil Blackwell.
Glazer, N. and D. P. Moynihan (eds.). 1975. *Ethnicity: Theory and Experience*. Cambridge, MA: Harvard University Press.
Government of Manipur. 2003. *Statistical Tables: Human Development Series*. Imphal: Directorate of Economics and Statistics, Government of Manipur.
———. 2004. *Statistical Abstract of Manipur*. Imphal: Directorate of Economics and Statistics, Government of Manipur.
Grierson, G. A. (ed.). 1904. 'Tibeto-Burman Family: Specimens of the Kuki-Chin and Burma Groups', in G.A. Grierson (ed.), *Linguistic Survey of India* (Vol. III, Part III). Calcutta: Office of the Superintendent, Government Printing, India.
Guibernau, M. 1999. *Nations without States: Political Communities in a Global Age*. Cambridge: Polity Press.
Haokip, P. S. 2006. 'What Price, Twenty Years of Peace in Mizoram: A Kuki Perspective (1986–2006)', available in the official website, *Information and Public Relations*, Government of Mizoram, 8 September 2006, http://dipr.mizoram.gov.in/article/what-pricetwenty-years-of-peace-in-mizoram-

%281986–2006%29%3A-a-kukiperspective/lang/en (accessed on 25 September 2010) in references (accessed on 12 November 2014).
———. 2008/2003. *Zale' n-Gam The Kuki Nation*. Imphal: KNO Publication.
———. 2010. *Presidential Address on 23rd Kuki National Organisation Raising Day on 24 February*. Camp Salem, Mongbung: Manmasi.
Haokip, S. 2014. 'Gunshots Talk Louder Than Words: KNO', http://zalengam.org/kno-profile/gunshots-talk-louder-than-words-kno.html (accessed on 10 June 2014).
Hodson, T. C. 1901. 'The Native Tribes of Manipur', *The Journal of the Anthropological Institute of Great Britain and Ireland*, 31 (January–June): 300–9.
Horowitz, D. L. 1985. *Ethnic Groups in Conflict*. Berkeley, CA: University of California Press.
Kabui, G. 1995. 'Genesis of the Ethnoses of Manipur', in N. Sanajaoba (ed.), *Manipur Past and Present: The Ordeals and Heritage of a Civilisation* (Vol. III: Nagas and Kuki-Chins), pp. 21–47. New Delhi: Mittal Publications.
Kamei, G. 2006. *On History and Historiography of Manipur*. New Delhi: Akansha Publishing House.
Kipgen, N. 1993. 'Why Not Kukiland', *The Shillong Times*, Shillong, 1 October: 18–21.
Koireng, A. S. 2006. *Kuki–Naga Conflict in Manipur (1990–2000)*. PhD Thesis, Manipur University, Manipur.
McCulloch, W. 1859. *An Account of the Valley of Manipur and the Hill Tribes*. Calcutta: Selections from the Records of the Government of India, No. 27.
Nabakumar, W. 2004. 'The Inter Ethnic Relationship of the Different Communities of Manipur: A Critical Appraisal', *The Orient Vision*, 2: 29–32.
Palit, D. K. 1984. *Sentinels of the North-east: The Assam Rifles*. New Delhi: Palit and Palit.
Phanjoubam, T. 2007/2004. *Bleeding Manipur*. New Delhi: Har Anand Publication.
Phukon, G. 2003. *Ethnicisation of Politics in Northeast India*. New Delhi: South Asian Publishers.
Reid, R. 1997/1942. *History of the Frontier Areas Bordering on Assam, 1883–1941*. Aizawl: Tribal Research Institute.
Sahlins, M. 1992. *Anahulu: The Anthropology of History in the Kingdom of Hawaii*. Chicago: The University of Chicago Press.
Sanajaoba, N. 1995. 'The Roots', in N. Sanajaoba (ed.), *Manipur Past and Present: The Ordeals and Heritage of a Civilisation* (Vol. III: Nagas and Kuki-Chins), pp. 1–20. New Delhi: Mittal Publications.
Scheduled Tribes Welfare Association of Manipur. 2006. 'Memorandum to the National Commission for Scheduled Castes and Scheduled Tribes, New Delhi', Churachandpur, 25 April.
Shakespear, J. 1909. 'The Kuki-Lushai Clans', *The Journal of the Royal Anthropological Institute of Great Britain and Ireland*, 39 (July–December): 371–85.
———. 1912. *The LusheiKuki Clans, Part I and Part II*. London: Macmillan.
Shaw, W. 1929. *Note on the Thadou Kukis*. Calcutta: Government of Assam.

Sivaramakrishnan, K. and G. Cederlof. 2005. 'Introduction', in G. Cederlof and K. Sivaramakrishnan (eds.), *Ecological Nationalisms: Nature, Livelihoods, and Identities in South Asia*, pp. 1–40. New Delhi: Permanent Black.

Smith, A. D. 1991. *National Identity*. London: Penguin Books.

Stavenhagen, R. 1995. 'Ethnic Conflict and Human Rights: Their Interrelationship', *Bulletin of Peace Proposals*, 18 (2): 509–10.

Stewart, P. J. and A. Strathern. 2003. 'Introduction', in P. J. Stewart and A. Strathern (eds.), *Landscape, Memory and History: Anthropological Perspectives*, pp. 1–15. London: Pluto Press.

Strang, V. 1997. *Uncommon Ground: Cultural Landscapes and Environmental Values*. Oxford: Berg.

Thomson, T. 1971. *The Hill Patron*. Motbung: Manipur.

Weiner, M. 1975. *Sons of the Soil: Migration, Ethnicity, and Nativism in India*. Cambridge, MA: Center for International Studies, Cambridge.

7 Displacement from Kashmir[1]

Gendered responses

Charu Sawhney and Nilika Mehrotra

The escalation of political turmoil in the Kashmir Valley led to the displacement of minority communities, mainly the Kashmiri Hindus, from Kashmir. The weak democracy in Jammu and Kashmir and the majority–minority dynamics in the state led to the displacement of about three lakh persons (primarily Hindus) from the valley in 1989–90 (Mishra 1999). It is more than two decades since the displacement of minorities from Kashmir, and their prolonged living in the new locations has resulted in social and cultural changes post-displacement. The shift to a new location has significance in analysing how the traditional structures and practices are redefined in the new locations.

An atmosphere of fear and threat developed in Kashmir after the alleged rigging in the 1987 state assembly elections, and this heightened the frustration of a large number of Kashmiri youth due to malpractices of the government. Secessionist organisations called for a boycott of those opposing the sentiment of *azadi* (independence) in the state. Fear was instilled among the members of the minority communities and the Muslims who did not endorse the sentiment of *azadi*. The majority community (Muslims) saw the minorities as being opposed to the movement for secession of Kashmir from the republic of India (Verma 1994). There was targeting of prominent Hindu personalities by the militants, and the Kashmiri Hindus felt insecure in such an atmosphere (Duschinski 2008). In 1989, the minority communities started receiving notices through varying media like newspapers and loudspeakers in mosques to leave Kashmir (Verma 1994). Kashmiri Pandits, the non-Kashmiri Hindus, Kashmiri Sikhs, and other minorities who felt threatened were forced to migrate from Kashmir and resettle outside their homeland in camps or private rented accommodation.

Although identified as 'migrants' by the Government of India, the displaced people feel that the term, as applied to them, has a negative connotation, as they are not mere migrants who voluntarily left Kashmir; they were forcibly displaced because of armed conflict. The displaced Kashmiri people wish to be identified as 'internally displaced persons' (Mishra 2004). The Kashmiri Hindus, displaced from the valley, resettled in urban centres elsewhere in India. Large sections of them were educated, and a significant number of them were government employees. It was thus possible for a large section of them to manage to avoid the harsh conditions of living in the camps.

The resettlement of displaced Kashmiri people in urban centres has led to certain changes in the traditional gender equations and roles. This chapter looks into the redefinition of men's and women's roles and responsibilities as members of community and society. Women experience discrimination during displacement from homeland and consequent resettlement in the new territories. The comparative class experience of the displaced individuals in the resettlement phase implies differences in the negotiation of the displaced men and women belonging to varying classes within their context. Displacement from one's homeland implies a state of loss, but it may also lead to an expansion of one's horizon in the new territory through increased access to opportunities, as has been the case with Kashmiri women.

The experience of displacement of Kashmiri Hindus has proven that individuals use their acquired capital – social, economic, and material – to resettle in new areas. According to Pierre Bourdieu (1984), the concept of capital is to be extended to include cultural capital in addition to material and social capital in the conventional sense. Family plays a crucial role in the reproduction of inequality (Béteille 1993). In the case of displaced Kashmiri persons, social capital in the form of migration networks comprising friends or relatives facilitated access to resources or information in the new areas. The economic capital possessed by migrants in the form of movable property, bank deposits, or cash was utilised by the urban, educated, professional middle-class Kashmiri Pandit community displaced from Srinagar city. The cultural capital in the form of education and skills possessed by the professional class among them facilitated access to greater opportunities after displacement and relocation.

According to T. N. Madan (1965), salaried jobs were the main source of income for the urban Pandits, with trade and ownership of land in village (absentee landlordism) coming second and third. Literacy was more in Srinagar, and college education and technical training institutions were practically confined to the urban Pandits. In the countryside, female literacy was almost absent, whereas in the city, many female Pandits attended schools and colleges. An increasing number of villagers, mostly men, attended schools newly opened in small towns or the Srinagar colleges.

The Pandit community displaced from rural areas and settled in camps rated low with regard to the possession of education and exposure to bigger cities. Their basic possession of economic capital was land or property, which they could not transfer. It is because of the resulting differential access to resources that inequality is perpetuated after displacement. As Bourdieu (1984) puts it, 'class' is a generic term for social groups defined by their conditions of existence and their corresponding dispositions. Class divisions are not defined by differing relations to the means of production but by differing conditions of existence, differing systems of dispositions constructed by differential conditioning, and differing endowments of power or capital (Crompton 1988: 148). The dispositions shared by individuals which are products of different conditionings facilitated the movement of the people from rural areas of Kashmir to the camps in Jammu or that of the people from Srinagar city to the metropolitan region of Noida. This also had a bearing on how the men and women exercised their 'agency', whether they were settled in private rented accommodation in cities or confined to the camps in Jammu (Malhotra 2008).

There are significant differences of the experience and response to conflict by both men and women. According to N. C. Behera (2006), in earlier studies of gender and conflict, men were portrayed as perpetrators or agents, while women were portrayed as victims or passive. Studies in India have viewed the impact of violence, conflict, and migration on gender relations. The literature has focused on the specific experience of conflict by women in times of war (Butalia 2006; Kishwar 1998; Manchanda 2004). In the earlier literature, change in women's and men's roles and relationships within family and kinship after displacement to new areas is not discussed much. Dutta A. Bhardwaj (2006) has analysed how women in the post-partition period in Punjab redefined themselves despite the trauma that many women encountered.

According to B. R. Sorensen and M. Vincent (2001: 271), for women, displacement prompts a range of emotions from anguish as to how they would be able to provide for their family, to enthusiasm about their newly won freedom and new opportunities to disappointment about the new burdens they must shoulder and the continuing obstacles erected by the surrounding society. It is the context-specific female and male positioning that influences their agency in patriarchal gender systems.

This chapter is based on an ethnographic study of two locations in India – Jammu camps and Noida apartments – where a significant proportion of the displaced Kashmiri persons are resettled. The techniques of data collection were unstructured interviews using schedules. The narrative method was employed to study the specific experience of violence, displacement, and consequent resettlement of the displaced Kashmiri persons. Through individualised personal narratives linked to displacement, the meaning of violence suffered by the survivors and the redefinition of men's and women's roles was understood.[2]

Women used as scapegoats

At the height of militancy in Kashmir, the militants managed to create fear psychosis among the minority Hindu community, in general, and their womenfolk, in particular. The Hindu women were used as scapegoats by the militants. It is well known that, in times of conflict, women experience sexual assaults targeting their community identity. The informants described how the militants gave repeated warnings to the Kashmiri Hindu men to leave Kashmir and to leave their Hindu women behind, and the men became increasingly apprehensive about the safety of their womenfolk. The insurgents employed propaganda to displace the Hindu community by using women, who were unable to protect themselves, as the vulnerable targets and portrayed them as symbolic of the Kashmiri Hindu community in general.

Most of the informants reported that they were not harmed personally, but the fear psychosis that gripped the valley in 1990 caused the exodus from Kashmir, although some targeted killing did take place (Duschinski 2008). The interviews with the displaced Kashmiri Pandits in Jammu camps and Noida apartments revealed that it was the 'sense of threat' that developed in Kashmir in 1989 and which was directed at the minority community, the Kashmiri Hindus, which triggered their exodus. The major source of fear that was noticed among the Kashmiri Pandit community members was the threat to the security of their womenfolk.

The case of Aditi shows how an atmosphere of fear and insecurity was created to trigger the exodus of the Kashmiri Pandits. Aditi's family lived in Srinagar, and when the conflict started, they left their property and ran for their life to Jammu. Aditi narrated:

> *Ghar chorke Jammu aagaye. Kashmir mein militant awaz utha rahe the ki panditian ladkiyo aur aurato ke sath Pakistan banayege. Jo Kashmiri bhagh ke aaye aur baad mein vapis gaye thee unko militants ne maar diya.* [We left our house and came to Jammu. In Kashmir the militants were swearing slogans that they would establish Pakistan with the Kashmiri Pandit women. People who ran away from Kashmir but later returned to collect their belongings were killed by the militants.]
> (Interview with Aditi in her Noida apartment, March 2005)

According to Rita Manchanda (2004: 4181), institutional regimes of protection and care have recognised gender-based violence in conflict situations. This is evident in the International Criminal Court of Justice recognising rape as an instrument of war. Gender-based violence is significant in the group dynamics of community identity and nation-state formation.

In the context of South Asia there has been revisiting of gender-based violence during the 1947 and 1971 partitions and the construction of women as an allegorical and symbolical marker of community or nation. Apart from the partitions of 1947 and 1971 in the context of South Asia, a more recent instance of gender-based violence occurred in Gujarat during the 2002 Hindu–Muslim riots.

During the insurgency in Kashmir in 1989–90 and the consequent eviction of Kashmiri Pandits, the Hindu women were identified and teased by the militants. This throws light on how violence at times of conflict is sexualised. Fear of sexual assault existed at the time of the political conflict in Kashmir, but women's stories were rarely brought out into the open. Urvashi Butalia (1993) states how, because of the stigma it carried, it was difficult for survivors/families to speak of rape, abductions, or forcible marriages that took place during the partition of India in 1947. They speak of it but only in a general way. Families who had daughters were more apprehensive about their safety and were consequently the first to leave Kashmir. Stigma is attached to bringing to light events that show how women were misbehaved with during the conflict situation in Kashmir; it is regarded as a dishonour to the family to bring to the fore a woman's experience of sexual assault. Gita and her mother-in-law Rama's responses during the interview in the Jammu camp depict this:

> *Hum camp mein ek dusare se sunte hain ki iske sath Kashmir mein militants ne bura kiya. Par koi bhi aurat khudh nahi bataye gi ki hamare saath bura hua.* [We do hear stories in the camp area of how the militants abused particular women. But no woman who was misbehaved with will personally tell you.]
>
> (Interview with Gita in her Jammu camp, June 2005)

There is an attempt to repress the memory of threats experienced by the Hindu women, but the issue of threat invariably comes to the forefront during conversations with other women. Rama's narrative signals an instance of overt threat experienced by women prior to the eviction of minority community from Kashmir.

> *Meri behin gaun mein school teacher thi. Woh ek bar militancy ke samay kaam pe gayi aur wapis nahi aayi. Uska kya hua kisi ko bhi pata nahi. Abhi bhi bahut dukh hai.* [My sister was a school teacher in the village. During the phase of militancy once she went out to work and did not return. No one knows what happened to her. We grieve for her till now.]
>
> (Interview with Rama in her Jammu camp, October 2005)

Even after two decades of displacement, the threat of militancy is alive in the minds of the women who were targeted as 'Hindu women', especially when passing references were made about (not) wearing the marker of their community identity in Kashmir. Shobha, an old woman who spent a major part of her life in Kashmir, made some direct reference to threats at the time of conflict in Kashmir.

> *Kashmir jana toh bindi mat laga kar jana. Woh* [militants] *tumhe maar dale ge.* [Do not go to Kashmir wearing a *bindi*. They [militants] will kill you.]
> (Interview with Shoba in her Noida apartment, January 2006)

Home was recognised by the displaced Kashmiri women as one with which they shared a sense of belonging and derived an identity. Kashmir used interchangeably for home by the displaced women was also associated with a sense of danger to move about freely wearing one's markers of community identity. In an interview with Nidhi Razdan of NDTV, Radhika Kaul, a 17-year-old Kashmiri Pandit girl, narrates her visit to Kashmir, her homeland, with which she felt an urge to be connected. Her family visited Kashmir after fifteen years.

> When we boarded our flight from Delhi to Srinagar, I remember my mother taking off her sindhoor which is a symbol showing her to be a Kashmiri Pandit woman and that was ironic because it meant that we were afraid to be what we actually were in our own land.
> (YouTube Video 2010)

Both Kashmiri Hindu and Muslim women have been hit by the militancy in Kashmir and have suffered violence at the hands of militants and Indian security forces. Nyla Ali Khan (2010) refers to the violence experienced by women in Kashmir at the hands of the security forces and also the non-state actors as they are sexually violated, rendered widows or half-widows due to custodial killings or disappearances. Manchanda (2001) holds that gender relations got transformed in the process of conflict in Kashmir. The insurgency left Kashmiri Muslim women in Kashmir vulnerable to male predatory violence at the hands of security forces and the militants. The women who were victims of conflict as 'grieving mother', 'martyr's mother', and 'raped woman' exercised agency. Women were, however, agents in moving to the public sphere, seeking employment, and challenging their traditional roles.

The narrative of 40-year-old Zoya, an internally displaced Kashmiri Muslim woman from Kashmir to Jammu who experienced violence at the hands of the militants, is insightful. Zoya's husband was a government servant and he took to militancy. When she did not agree to her husband joining militancy, he divorced her. The militants time and again threatened her and looted her jewellery. In 1992, she escaped and resettled in Jammu city (interview with Rama in her Jammu camp, August 2005). The resistance by Zoya, a Muslim woman, to her husband joining militancy led to a situation where she was kidnapped, misbehaved with, and looted. As single women who were widowed or divorced with children, women played a significant role in providing for their family after displacement. With the onset of militancy in Kashmir and the consequent repression by the security forces in Kashmir, both Hindu and Muslim women were thus targeted.

Change in status identities

The shift to a new host community involves issues such as change in identity and change in the meanings and perceptions of ourselves and others' perceptions of us. The leaving of home is about regaining a sense of identity and a culture that is associated with the territory one leaves behind (Khattak 2006). Kashmiri poet Sunita Raina, who lives in Sahibabad near Delhi, provides poetic expression to the longing of displaced persons for their homeland in the following poem:

> *Yeti aasi shihul hum raaz panun*
> *Lay aasi panin tae saaz panun*
> *Yeti aasi lasaan andaaz nyerul*
> *Tati gyevzyen phulvain myen ghazal.*
> [Where the shade is ours, my friend
> Where the tune is ours and the song ours
> Where there is uniqueness of style
> Only there you should sing my ghazal.]
> (http://www.kunear.com/styled-35/)

The exposure to a new unfamiliar place may lead to fear of the 'unknown', but, on the other hand, migration to a metropolitan city with abundant educational and job opportunities may also lead to a greater self-confidence about one's prospects. Neither for women nor for men social life is built upon a single discourse. As social actors they face alternative ways of devising their aims, however restricted their resources. The strategies and cultural constructions they utilise are drawn from a stock of available discourses (verbal and non-verbal) that are shared by the members of society. Numerous contexts (place and location) in the construction of identities and differences also determine how agency (knowledge/capability) is differently constituted. Identities are situational, and contexts determine how individuals wish to be identified (Parpart and Marchand 1995).

In contrast to the freedom that the women enjoyed under the protective umbrella of the family in early Kashmiri society (Toshkhani 2004), there were certain irrational curbs imposed on women after the onset of militancy by certain fundamentalist groups. R. Punjabi (1999) holds that, after the onset of secessionist movement, the nationalistic component of Kashmiri identity came to be replaced by Islamic orientation. The focus was to bring about structural changes by impacting the syncretic culture of Kashmiri society. The educational institutions for girls became special targets of attack as some militant outfits were opposed to the education of girls. A. Ray holds that

> soon after issuing a diktat to Muslim women to wear the *burqa*, the Lashkar-e-Jabbar, asked non-Muslim women in Kashmir to wear *bindi* on their foreheads and the Sikh women to don saffron colored *duppattas* for identification and exempted them from wearing the *burqa*.
> (2009)

After the exodus of Kashmiri Pandit women in 1989–90 and resettlement in bigger cities and cosmopolitan centres, the women felt free, as the irrational curbs imposed by some fundamentalist groups did not exist and they were not labelled as 'Hindu women'. However, women reported feeling unsafe in the initial years of resettlement. Yogesh, residing in the Nilgiri apartments in Noida, mentioned that his mother never opened the door to strangers because she constantly feared thefts in Noida. In the evenings women feel inhibited to go to deserted places. According to K. Viswanath and S. T. Mehrotra (2007), the quality of a city is judged by what it offers to its residents – the right to live, to move around, and to work with safety and dignity. In Delhi, many of its residents, especially the marginalised populations, are vulnerable without these basic rights. Women's access to public space is restricted because it does not offer women safety to move around in it. The city, while offering freedom of movement to the women, also imposes restrictions on women's movement in public space.

Migration to big cities has, however, led to greater access to job and educational opportunities for women who migrated from both urban and rural areas of Kashmir. Notwithstanding this, after displacement, the unequal possession of cultural capital played a significant role in reproducing inequality among these women. The displaced women from the rural areas, resettled in the camp areas in Jammu, rated low with regard to educational achievement in comparison to their counterparts displaced from Srinagar city and resettled outside the camps, in bigger cities. The women in the camp areas in Jammu were not integrated into the professional sphere and were occupied with household tasks in their one-room tenements. In comparison, the women settled in Noida were employed as teachers, worked in private companies, or were retired government officials. Rural to urban migration led to increased job opportunities for women, but their educational background influenced their life chances after displacement. V. Sazawal observes that

> the displacement from the valley has particularly helped young KP's [Kashmiri Pandits] from remote villages of Kashmir (who had less than 40 per cent chance of ever completing their degree education) to find new vistas for education, jobs and social betterment.
>
> (2005)

Gender relations and boundaries

After resettlement in the new locations, the constraints experienced by men and women lead them to exercise choices within the structures of family and kinship. They exercised their agency by making use of the opportunities/possibilities in the new locations which may not have been possible back home in Kashmir. Women's agency refers to their ability to create a web of social relationships in an environment, which is both new and different from what they have known back home in Kashmir. This understanding of women in the post-displacement phase is akin to S. Jain's understanding about the Indian diasporic family living in a new milieu, 'Family is also an arena for debate and contest about marriage, sexuality, childcare and aging' (2006: 2313). Displacement and consequent resettlement may lead to the reversal of the power dynamics existing in the traditional home. It entails dispersal of families to different locations; it leads to a change in the roles and responsibilities performed in a traditional set-up back home (Malhotra 2008).

Resettlement in a new ecological setting implies changes in the patterns of visiting relatives by men and women. In the Jammu camps, the women informants noted that, back in Kashmir, where village exogamy was practised, and there was increased distance between the villages of natal and affinal homes, married women's visits to their natal homes were infrequent. After resettlement in the camps, however, the natal homes of married women were in the adjoining camps and their shopping trips sometimes got combined with short visits to their affinal homes. This is in contrast to the families that resettled in bigger cities, with relatives dispersed in different corners of the city or different locations of India.

The position of women within the family and kinship networks is subject to change, as within new living arrangements in the new host community, the relationship of women with the wider society is bound to change. In the past, it was believed that kinship was an objectively defined system (Palriwala and Risseeuw 1996: 18), complete in itself. Because of economic and political changes experienced by a community in the new location, response strategies employed by women lead to changes in position and roles within networks of family, marriage, and kinship. The distance or fear that was there between women and their in-laws earlier is reduced after displacement. This view was held by both the elderly generation and the middle generation of displaced persons.

Through the concept of negotiation one can understand how gender relations are altered in the new setting after displacement. The middle-aged men and women were involved in the work sphere. In contrast to Kashmir, in the new territories there may be changes in how 'boundaries' are to be maintained with relatives. For instance, in accordance with the tradition in Kashmir, during male guest visits, women would avoid the guest room. A distance was maintained between the in-laws and the daughters-in-law. Elderly displaced women covered their heads with a veil out of respect for elders. They lived in collateral joint families in the villages in Kashmir, and as daughters-in-law of the joint households, they undertook tremendous responsibility. Because of familial obligations, the women could not venture out freely. There has been a change in these customary practices, implying some kind of laxity in the attitude of and towards the married women. In the new locations, the second generation of Kashmiri Hindu women has greater choice in terms of participation in the work sphere and movement in the public sphere.

In the camps, there was a predominance of nuclear families, as each married couple had separate one-room tenements. These tenements were not big enough to accommodate joint families. While in Srinagar there was predominance of collateral joint families or nuclear families, after resettlement in Noida most of the informants lived in extended families in apartments. (Patri)virilocal residence was the norm both in the Jammu camps and in the Noida apartments. Although the joint family obligations existed after displacement, more so with those staying in joint households in the new locations, the obligations have decreased, as, after displacement, each family was more concerned about its own survival. The visits to relatives were confined to rituals and ceremonies and took place to a lesser degree than when they were in Kashmir. There has thus been a diminishing role of traditional basis of support as that of the kinship networks.

Changing conjugality in camp conditions

The state governments provided one-room tenements to the displaced families from Kashmir. However, due to lack of space in these tenements, the marital and sexual relationship between married couples is adversely affected. There is no privacy in the camps. As the whole family lived in a single room, married couples have difficulty in engaging in intimate physical contacts. Despite the 1991 Executive Committee Guidelines for the Protection of Refugee Women, the systems of protection and care in the camps aided by the United Nations High Commissioner for Refugees are also gender insensitive, especially in South Asia, where national laws reinforce gender discrimination (Manchanda 2004: 4182).

The entire family lives, dines, and sleeps in one room in which it is housed. The camp incumbents held that there is no *sharam* (inhibition) in the tenements. Gita elaborated on the concept of *sharam* in an uncomfortable manner:

> *Hame sharam aati hain, par hum kya kare. Hamare pati kabhi raat ko zabardasti karte hain. To kabhi hame unki baat maanani parti hai. Bare logon ko to ab aadat si ho gayi hai. Woh ab apni aankhe band kar lete hain. Par hame bachon ke liye bahut bura lagta hai. Woh jab yeh dekhega to preshan ho jaye ga aur apne camp mein dost se puchega. Hum jab pati ko mana karte hain to din bhar ladai hoti hai. Kabhi to hum pati patni yeh jo chota sa kitchen hamne ORT* [one-room tenement] *ke sath apne liye banaya hai, wahan so jate hain. Par kabhi jab ORT mein hote hain to bahut sharam aati hai.* [We feel shy here but we are helpless. Our husbands are forceful at times and we have to submit to their wishes. The elderly people cannot help also so they got accustomed to it. They just close their eyes and pretend that they are not seeing anything. But we feel bad for the mental development of children. When they will see this act, their mind will be bewildered and will enquire from their friends in the camp area. When we refuse our husbands the days go by fighting. Sometimes the husband and wife sleep in the kitchen adjoining our ORT. But when we sleep in the ORT it is embarrassing.]
>
> (Interview with Gita in her Jammu camp, June 2005)

The conjugal relationship between husband and wife is affected especially in the camp areas, as is evident through the case of Ashwin, a resident of Muthi camp. Ashwin's wife noted that, after resettling in Jammu, the sexual relationship between her husband and her got adversely affected. Ashwin, his wife and their children, and his brother lived together in a one-room tenement. His brother was about 35 years old and was not given a separate tenement by the government as he was unmarried. It was uncomfortable for Ashwin's wife to stay with her brother-in-law in the same tenement as she did not have any privacy (interview with Ashwin and his wife in their Jammu camp, September 2005). Ashwin's brother sold vegetables in the camp area and shared his earnings with Ashwin and his family. Family economics or the dire need to survive in the new locality necessitates readjustment of marital relations.

The resulting decline in the Kashmiri Pandit population can be partly attributed to the lack of privacy and altered living conditions in the one-room tenements in the camps. There has been a decline in the birth rate and an increase in the death rate among the Kashmiri Pandits in the post-displacement period (YouTube Video 2011). 'Kashmira Vahini', a Kashmiri Pandit women's organisation, is taking steps to address this decline by adopting three-children-per-family norm.

R. Dhingra and V. Arora (2005) state that, due to altered living conditions in the camp area, the roles and relationships of family members have changed. The male members of the displaced community are no longer satisfied with the kind of roles they play. There is a feeling of despondency and helplessness faced by the men with regard to the responsibility of running their homes. The challenge to their traditional role as the breadwinner leads to anger, uncertainty, frustration, and helplessness among male members and is expressed in the form of violence against women in the family. Men suffer more from losing their homes and employment because that loss has direct consequences on their sense of identity and dignity.

In March 2011, the displaced Kashmiri persons living in the camps in Jammu region were allotted two-bedroom flats in a satellite township, Jagti, 85 km from Jammu. But life in resettlement colonies of Jammu for over two decades has had significant implications for the lifestyle, gender relations, and sense of dignity of the Kashmir Pandits.

Displacing gerontocracy

There is a change in the intergenerational relations after displacement, and a feeling of loneliness is felt by the elderly generation. The resettlement of elderly in the metropolitan regions or the migration of the aged from the rural to the urban areas magnifies their problems. The elderly often have problems with mobility and may find it difficult to participate in the various subcultures that large cities have to offer. In small towns, however, where social networks are close in terms of distance, the elderly may find it easier to keep in touch (Amato 1993). In the new locations, the urban elderly have become increasingly isolated, as their friends and family members are dispersed to different regions of India after displacement.

The aged among the displaced persons experience mental tension, and it has taken many years for them to get used to displacement and relocation. The retired government officials among them held that they would have experienced a better retired life back in Kashmir. Retirement and accompanying reduction in income implies that the aged are unable to extend the kind of economic support they might have in the past. This reduces their social value and results in diminished social contacts and involvement with others (Unruh 1983: 24). The elderly are living with their children in the big cities where the younger generation is running the households. This results in a situation where the head of the family is old, but the economic sphere of the household is dominated by the son and the daughter-in-law. When the parents resettled in private accommodations in big cities, they move to their children's house, which the latter may have purchased on loan. There is a longing for the property (house or land) which they have left back in Kashmir. The elderly experience economic dependency, and the increased expenditure in the new locations adds to the sense of helplessness. The younger generation is constrained to make a living in the new setting and has no time to socialise with the aged. This scenario points to the changing power dynamics in the new context.

For the displaced elderly men and women living in the apartments in Noida and Jammu, there is loneliness, as they are confined to their apartments and their health does not permit them to interact with the people in the surrounding areas. In the camp areas in Jammu, it was observed that many aged men were whiling away their time playing cards. The aged women who are used to community living and working together with other women find it hard to cope with the camp life. They were observed sitting in a corner and brooding. Some of the elderly do not know the local language of the host territory and are not able to converse with the host population.

There is a constant longing among the elderly men and women to go back to their hometowns, and this is illustrated by Parvati's narrative. Parvati, an aged woman from Baramulla district in Kashmir, is now living at Muthi camp in Jammu. She feels alienated and misses everything Kashmiri. She did not like it in the host community. In Kashmir, all women sat together in an *angan* (sitting place in front of the house) and socialised. She could not go to the market to purchase vegetables as the shopkeepers would not understand her. She misses the community living back in Kashmir. The languages of the host community are beyond the comprehension of some of the aged Kashmiri women (interview with Parvati in a Jammu camp, October 2005).

Depreciation in health levels due to old age and displacement-related stress has resulted in an increase in the instance of diabetes and blood pressure for the aged. In Noida, there were two cases of senile dementia.

Displacement from Kashmir 199

Shobha, an old woman in the Noida apartments, had lost her senses in the host community. In a small room she was sitting on the floor. As she was physically immobile, the only sunlight that she saw was through the windows of her unkempt room. She conversed with her family members in incoherent Kashmiri. On seeing me, she warned in incoherent utterances that one should not visit Kashmir wearing a *bindi*, as it was unsafe for Hindu women. One of her neighbour's daughters was raped by the militants. The trauma of the incident was still alive in her memory (interview with Shobha in her Noida apartment, January 2006).

Siddharth Gigoo's novel *The Garden of Solitude* (2011) is a memoir and depicts the pain experienced by the displaced Kashmiri Hindu families in the Jammu camps. Gigoo holds that, after displacement, the elderly suffered from dementia and their memory was adversely impacted. To quote an excerpt from the novel:

> In an adjacent tent a family of five torture an old man, their foster-grandfather, who lost his mental balance upon seeing his house fade away in a hazy distance. The old man is a burden for his son and daughter-in-law. Another mouth to feed, they feel! He moans at night constantly, and intermittently wakes up to a cold shiver – a nightmare. His son and daughter-in-law taunt him for their amusement. They whisper in his ears that his mother was dead and that she was beaten mercilessly to death. The old man groans and pleads them not to utter the atrocities. Every evening, the torment continues. The maddening laughter of the men ricochets from the tattered canvas tent. Every night the old man cries. He gapes at his son and daughter-in-law and gives them his blessings.
>
> (Ibid.: 99)

This excerpt depicts that, for the aged, the loss of their home, livelihood, and all other things associated with the territory in which they were born were very hard to cope in the closing years of their life. Their social value has decreased due to their loss of economic assets and dependent status. Their resettlement in a new location makes them constantly long for the lost homeland, and this has adversely affected their health.

Displacement and consequent resettlement in the new territory impacts age groups differently. The middle-aged groups are constrained to sustain economically in the new terrain. For the younger generation, born and brought up in the host territory, the sense of longing for their homeland is not as strong as the elderly generation. The younger generation identifies more with the host territory, leading to constant intergenerational differences with the displaced elderly persons.

Conclusion

Displacement leads to certain changes in gender roles in the changed social and cultural context. Identities are redefined, and there is a change in how boundaries are maintained in the changed context. In the resettlement phase, faced with new constraints and opportunities, men and women utilise varied response strategies, leading to changes in their roles in the public and the private spheres.

The comparative class experience of the displaced women in the resettlement phase implies differences in the negotiation and agency of the women with their surroundings. The experience of displacement is different for individuals with social and cultural capital as compared to those who do not possess such capital and are confined to camps (Malhotra 2008).

The response of the state regarding the provision of the basic infrastructure in the camps for the displaced persons has minimally addressed the needs of women. Viewing the agency of the displaced women does not imply that their survival struggles can be ignored. Planning for human settlements implies that the social, cultural, and economic issues of the forced migrants should be taken into account. Special attention should be given to the vulnerable sections of the displaced populations, and the welfare provisions should be gender sensitive.

Notes

1 This chapter is a revised version of an article published in *Sociological Bulletin*, 62 (1), January–April 2013. The Indian Sociological Society's permission to reproduce it here is gratefully acknowledged.
2 This chapter is based on Charu Sawhney's MPhil (2004) and PhD (2009) dissertations submitted to the Centre for the Study of Social Systems, Jawaharlal Nehru University, New Delhi. In Jammu, the fieldwork was conducted in the quarters/camps – Muthi, Gol, and Purkhoo – where a significant number of persons displaced from the rural areas of Kashmir were staying. The informants belonged to the working class. In Noida, the fieldwork was conducted among the middle-class professionals resettled in the Nilgiri, Aravalli, Himgiri, and Dhawalgiri apartments Sector 34. The research has spanned almost a decade from 2002 to 2011.

References

Amato, P. R. 1993. 'Urban–Rural Differences in Helping Friends and Family Members', *Social Psychology Quarterly*, 56 (4): 249–62.
Behera, N. C. 2006. 'Introduction', in N. C. Behera (ed.), *Gender, Conflict and Migration*, pp. 21–71. New Delhi: Sage Publications.
Béteille, A. 1993. 'The Family and the Reproduction of Inequality', in P. Uberoi (ed.), *Family, Kinship and Marriage in India*, pp. 435–51. New Delhi: Oxford University Press.

Bhardwaj, D. A. 2006. 'Gendering Oral History of Partition: Interrogating Patriarchy', *Economic and Political Weekly*, 41 (22): 2229–35.
Bourdieu, P. 1984. *Distinction: A Social Critique of the Judgement of Taste*. Oxford: Oxford University Press.
Butalia, U. 1993. 'Community, State and Gender: On Women's Agency during Partition', *Economic and Political Weekly*, 28 (17): WS 12–21.
———. 2006. 'Migration/Displacement: A Gendered Perspective', in N. C. Behera (ed.), *Gender, Conflict and Migration*, pp. 137–52. New Delhi: Sage Publications.
Crompton, R. 1988. *Class and Stratification: An Introduction to Current Debates*. Cambridge: Polity Press.
Dhingra, R. and V. Arora. 2005. 'At the Crossroads: Families in Distress', *Journal of Human Ecology*, 17 (3): 217–22.
Duschinski, H. 2008. 'Survival Is Now Our Politics: Kashmiri Hindu Community Identity and the Politics of Homeland', *International Journal of Hindu Studies*, 12 (1): 41–64.
Gigoo, S. 2011. *The Garden of Solitude*. New Delhi: Rupa and Co.
Jain, S. 2006. 'Women's Agency in the Context of Family Networks in Indian Diaspora', *Economic and Political Weekly*, 41 (23): 2312–16.
Khan, N. A. 2010. *Islam, Women and Violence in Kashmir between India and Pakistan: Comparative Perspectives*. New York: Palgrave Macmillan.
Khattak, S. G. 2006. 'Violence and Home: Afghan Woman's Experience of Displacement', in N. C. Behera (ed.), *Gender, Conflict and Migration*, pp. 116–34. New Delhi: Sage Publications.
Kishwar, M. (ed.). 1998. *Religion at the Service of Nationalism and Other Essays*. New Delhi: Oxford University Press.
Madan, T. N. 1965. *Family and Kinship: A Study of the Pandits of Rural Kashmir*. New Delhi: Asia Publishing House.
Malhotra, C. 2008. *Internally Displaced Kashmiri People: A Sociological Study of Response Strategies and Change*. PhD Thesis, Jawaharlal Nehru University, New Delhi.
Manchanda, R. 2001. 'Guns and *Burqa*: Women in Kashmir Conflict', in R. Manchanda (ed.), *Women War and Peace in South Asia: Beyond Victimhood to Agency*, pp. 42–101. New Delhi: Sage Publications.
———. 2004. 'Gender Conflict and Displacement: Contesting Infantilisation of Forced Migrant Women', *Economic and Political Weekly*, 39 (37): 4179–86.
Mishra, O. 1999. 'Kashmiri Pandits: Aliens in Their Own Lands', in S. B. Roy (ed.), *New Approach: Kashmir, Violence in Paradise*, pp. 117–25. Calcutta: Deep Prakashan.
———. 2004. 'Introduction: Coerced Population Movement', in O. Mishra (ed.), *Forced Migration in South Asian Region: Displacement, Human Rights and Conflict Resolution*, pp. 15–21. New Delhi: Manak.
Palriwala, R. and C. Risseeuw. 1996. 'Introduction', in R. Palriwala and C. Risseeuw (eds.), *Shifting Circles of Support: Contextualizing Gender and Kinship in South Asia and Sub-Saharan Africa*, pp. 15–20. New Delhi: Sage Publications.
Parpart, J. L. and M. H. Marchand (eds.). 1995. *Feminism/Postmodernism/Development*. New York: Routledge.

Punjabi, R. 1999. 'Forced Migration in South Asia', *Journal of Peace Studies*, 6 (1): 20–24.

Ray, A. 2009. 'Kashmiri Women and the Politics of Identity', Paper presented at the SHUR Final Conference on Human Rights and Civil Society, Luiss University, Rome, Italy, 4–5 June 2009.

Sazawal, V. 2005. 'Towards a Self-Reliant Pandit Community', Presentation made at a meeting of the All India Kashmiri Samaj held at Chandigarh on 4 September 2005, *Naad*, http://www.kashmirforum.org/towards-a-self-reliant-pandit-community/ (accessed on 8 November 2012).

Sorensen, B. R. and M. Vincent. 2001. 'Conclusion', in B. R. Sorensen and M. Vincent (eds.), *Caught between Borders: Response Strategies of the Internally Displaced*, pp. 266–83. London: Pluto Press.

Toshkhani, S. S. 2004. 'Early Kashmiri Society: Status of Women', *Kashmir Sentinel*, http://ikashmir.net/sstoshkhani/women.html (accessed on 1 December 2012).

Unruh, D. R. 1983. *Invisible Lives: Social World of the Aged*. Beverly Hills, CA: Sage Publications.

Verma, P. S. 1994. *Jammu and Kashmir at the Political Crossroads*. New Delhi: Vikas Publishing House.

Viswanath, K. and S. T. Mehrotra. 2007. 'Shall We Go Out? Women's Safety in Public Spaces in Delhi', *Economic and Political Weekly*, 42 (17): 1542–48, http://www.kunear.com/styled-35/ (accessed on 5 November 2012).

YouTube. 2010. 'Kashmiri Pandits in Exile: Missing Home for 20 Years', Nidhi Razdan from NDTV interviews Radhika Kaul. YouTube video uploaded on 26 January 2010.

———. 2011. Report by Zafar Iqbal on NDTV. YouTube video uploaded by Sanjay Moza on 24 January 2011.

Index

A-chyuk, Gaeebo (King) 97–100
AFSPA *see* Armed Forces Special Powers Act
agriculture 29, 31, 48
All Assam Students Union 69
Allen, N. J. 29
All India Institute of Medical Sciences 46
All Nepal National Independent Student Union (ANNISU) 139–41
Anderson, Benedict 165
Angami 55, 59–60, 64, 66, 71
Angus, Ian 27, 44
Ao 60, 64–5, 71
Area Council Members 58
Armed Forces Special Powers Act (AFSPA) 6
Arora, V. 29, 56, 71, 75, 118, 197
Arunachal Pradesh 17, 19, 55, 118–23, 126–7
Assam 11–12, 14, 55–6, 67, 69, 72, 163, 170–1, 180

Backward Area Development Fund 60, 63
backward tribes 16, 54, 56, 60, 75
Badrinaryan (Lord Vishnu) 41
Barth, Fredrick 164
Baruah, S. 12
Basu, Sudeep 10
Beetham, D. 1
Behera, N. C. 188
Bhagori 28, 30–1, 39
Bhardwaj, Dutta A. 188
Bhasha Samman Award 92

Bhasin, Veena 84
Bhaumik, S. 178
Bhotiyas 28–31, 33, 42
Bhutan 2–3, 11–12, 20, 82, 85, 99–100, 118
Bhutias 29, 39, 82–4, 86, 91, 95, 97, 103–4, 108
Bisht, B. S. 28
bongthing 91–2, 95
Bourdieu, Pierre 187, 188
Brass, Paul 164, 165
Brown, C. W. 29–30
Buddhism 29–30, 43, 82, 87, 91, 105, 119–20, 123–4, 130–1
Butalia, Urvashi 190

CA elections 139, 144, 147
census: basic facts 67–9; debate 69–71; enumeration 7, 16, 54–6, 58, 61, 64–5, 67, 73–5; identity construction 69–71; operations 57, 59, 64; politics of 54–78; role of 64–7; statistics 57, 67–9
census enumeration 55–6, 64–5, 67, 74–5
central committee member 143, 148–9
Centre National de la Recherche Scientifique (Paris) 31
Chakhesang People's Organisation (CPO) 62, 65, 67, 74
Chakhesang tribe 65, 66, 72
Chakri 72
Chang 56, 60, 64–5
Chatterjee, Partha 79, 80
Chekasang 55–6, 60, 74

China–India border conflict (1962) 15, 30
Chir 72–3
Chokri 66
Chongsa Rong-pas (Rong-pa) 31
Christian missionaries 85–7
Churachandpur district 166–7, 171, 175
civil society 1–5, 7, 15, 43, 57, 62, 64, 67, 70, 73, 79, 106, 107, 108, 179
civil society groups 1–5, 43, 62, 64, 67, 70, 73, 79, 106–8, 179
civil society organisations 57
Cohn, Bernard 55
communities, minority 186, 189–90
conjugality 196–7
consensus, pure 18, 137, 147, 149
Constitution Delimitation Bill 2002 65, 74
consumerism 71
CPO *see* Chakhesang People's Organisation
culture 14, 38, 42, 81, 83–4, 86, 88, 90–2, 94–5, 100, 124, 163, 168, 170, 192

Dahl, R. 3
Dalton, E. T. 163
Damsang Fort 89, 98–100
Darjeeling Hills 11, 14, 17, 19, 70, 81–2, 84–6, 90, 91, 101, 105–8
Das, Veena 33
Davies, B. 138
Dawa Lepcha 106–7
deliberation 18, 137–40; genuine 140–2; real-world 140, 142
democracy 1–6, 10, 15–18, 20, 27–53, 80, 117–18, 126, 132, 135–7, 145, 150–1, 180; Bhotiya 29–30; development programmes, impact of 39–40; displacement 30–3; effects of elections 38–9; emerging identities 44–7; gender 36–8; The Jads 34–6; local *pahari* society 41–3; margins of 27, 29, 31, 33, 35, 37, 39, 41, 43, 45, 47, 49; overview 27, 47–9; participation in local politics 44–7; participatory 16–17, 80, 117; politics 36–8; process of nation-building 27; relocation 30–3; state power, presence of 39–40
Democratic Alliance of Nagaland (DAN) 59
democratic competition 149–50
democratic institutions 3, 8, 14, 16, 19, 79–80, 87, 108, 150, 166
democratic politics 2, 7, 16, 87, 91, 120, 124, 131–2, 147
democratic process 36, 38, 45–6, 48–9, 89, 136, 138, 141, 145, 151
democratisation 1–6, 12, 14–16, 20, 132; and politicisation of identity 6–15
development grants 61–3, 66, 73
Dhingra, R. 197
Dimapur 60–1, 64–5, 69–70
Dirang 17, 119, 121, 124–5, 127
disorder, 3, 13
Dunda 31–2, 34

Eastern Naga People's Organisation (ENPO) 66
eastern Nagas 56, 60, 65–6
ecology 15, 20, 84, 95, 100, 106, 162
elections 16–17, 19, 38–9, 56–9, 62, 117, 119, 121, 123–7, 129–33, 135, 137, 139, 141–5, 149–50; participation of monks in 117, 127
electoral democracy 55
electoral politics 8, 10, 16–17, 56, 58–9, 61, 67, 73, 75, 80, 117, 122, 124, 132, 137
enumeration, census 54
enumerators 58–9, 62
environment 5, 81, 106, 194
Escobar, Arturo 28
Essential Services Act 66
ethnic conflict 3, 15, 19, 164, 166, 175, 177
ethnic groups 27, 45
ethnic identity 75, 108, 161, 163–5, 171
ethnicity 2, 18, 162–3, 165–6, 168; historical context 71–5
ethnic nationalism 18, 161, 163–5, 167, 169–71, 173, 175, 179, 181

Index

ethnic violence 4, 18, 161–2, 174
ethno-nationalism 54–5
exodus 12, 99, 189, 193

factionalism 59
financial powers, decentralisation of 66
Foning, A. 83, 85–6, 90, 95, 97–8
Friedman, J. 164
FSU elections 150
Fung, A. 140
Fürer-Haimendorf, Christopher von 15, 29, 55–6, 70–2

Gaeebo A-chyuk 97–100
Galey, Jean Claude 41
Gangotri 40, 43–4
The Garden of Solitude (2011) 199
Garhwali Rajputs 33, 41, 44, 46–7
gender 16, 19, 36–7, 47, 188, 196, 200; relations and boundaries 194–5
Gender-Related Development Index 65
gerontocracy 197
Glazer, Nathan 166
Gorer, G. 82
Gorkhaland movement 70
Gorkha Territorial Administration (GTA) 108
governance 40, 47
Government of India 8, 13, 39, 56, 58, 104, 118, 171–2, 174–5, 178–9, 186
Government of Nagaland 58, 60, 175
Gramsci, Antonio 89
Grierson, G. A. 162–3
Guha, Sumit 33
Guwahati High Court 57, 65, 74

Habermas, Jürgen 138
Haokip, P. S. 169–70, 172–3, 175, 179
Harrison, P. 120
Harsil 30–1, 34–5, 45
Hazarika, Sanjoy 61
Hindu women 42, 189–91, 193, 199
Hodson, T. C. 55
horticulture 31, 65
Houtzager, Peter P. 5

Human Development Index 65
Human Poverty Index 65
Hutton, J. H. 55

identities 27–53; Bhotiya 29–30; community 189, 191; development programmes, impact of 39–40; displacement 30–3; effects of elections 38–9; gender 36–8; The Jads 34–6; local *pahari* society 41–3; participation in local politics and 44–7; politics 36–8; relocation 30–3; state power, presence of 39–40
ILTA *see* Indigenous Lepcha Tribal Association
Imphal 167, 174, 178–80
independence, political 170–1
Indian democracy 27, 30, 33, 86, 179
Indian Penal System 57
indigenous identities 54
Indigenous Lepcha Tribal Association (ILTA) 90, 92, 98, 100, 107
Indira Ahwas Yojana 65
Indo-Naga ceasefire 174
Indo-Tibet Border Police 34, 39
Intensive Wet Terrace Rice Cultivation Programme 63

Jad Bhotiyas 15–16, 28, 46, 49
Jads 28, 30–48; relationship with Indian state 34–6
Jad village 31–2
Jamir, S. C. 61, 65
janjati 33, 46, 48
Joshi, M. P. 29
Judeo-Christian theology 38
junglee 32–3, 40, 42–5

Kacha Nagas 71
Kahimungen 60
Kalimpong Lepchas 83, 88–91, 95, 101, 103–5, 108
Kalimpong stimulus 79, 81, 83, 85, 87, 89–107
Kalyo Kengyu Nagas 71
Kamei, G. 168
Kashmiri Hindus 19, 186–7, 189, 195

206 Index

Kashmiri Pandits 186, 189–91, 193–4, 197
Kathmandu 148
Kauffmann, H. E. 71
KNA *see* Kuki National Assembly
Khan, Nyla Ali 191
Khan, S. 138
Khezha 66, 72
Khiamungans 56
Kipgen, N. 18, 56, 71
KNF *see* Kuki National Front
KNO *see* Kuki National Organisation
Kohima 60, 64–5, 69, 72–4, 171
Koireng 171, 174
Konyak 55–6, 60–1
Konyak Nagas 60–1
Kothari, Rajani 3–4
Kshatriyas, Garhwali 42
Kuki-Chin groups 8–9, 11, 163
Kuki groups 163–5, 168
Kuki Inpi Manipur 174, 179
Kukiland 161, 163, 165, 167, 169, 171, 173, 175, 179–81
Kuki National Assembly (KNA) 171–2, 174
Kuki National Front (KNF) 172–3, 180
Kuki National Organisation (KNO) 173, 178
Kuki tribes 70–1
Kuki villagers 166, 170
Kuki villages 162, 169–70, 172, 177
Kumar, B. B. 72
Kumar, Dinesh 59

Ladakh 13–14
Lama, Dalai 10, 43
lamas 9, 33, 43, 102, 128–31
landscape 4, 17, 19, 20, 85, 88, 89, 100, 101, 167
lay-monastic interface 128–31
Lepcha, P. T. 92
Lepcha Development Board 106–8
Lepchas 15, 17, 79–87, 81–2, 90–102, 105–8; community 81, 90, 92, 97–100, 106; culture 84, 86–7, 89, 92, 97, 100; of Darjeeling Hills 81, 84, 91, 105–6; of Dzongu 84, 89, 102–3, 107; house 103–4; language 81, 85, 90, 94–5, 103, 107; leaders 89, 106, 108; museum 89, 91–2; pilgrims 102–3; regional differences among 84–9; of Sikkim 17, 82–3, 85–7, 91–2, 100; subaltern 16, 79–81, 105, 108; vanishing 82; of West Bengal 83, 85, 101, 104–7; youth 87–8, 96
liberal democracy 137–43
local *pahari* community 33, 41–3, 44
Lotha 60, 64, 71
Lyangsong Tamsang 90, 92, 95, 100–2, 107

Madan, T. N. 187
Mahatma Gandhi National Rural Employment Guarantee Scheme 62
Mainwaring, G. B. 82
Manchanda, Rita 189, 191
Manipur 6–7, 9, 13, 18–19, 55, 161–8, 170–5, 177–8, 180
Maoists 136, 139–41, 150–1
Mazumdar, L. 41
Mehrotra, S. T. 193
Meitei 162, 164, 166–7, 171–2, 178–9
Member of the Legislative Assembly (MLA) 59, 61, 64, 73
Me-Parang 32, 43
migrants 11–12, 69, 186–7
Mikori 72–3
militancy 6, 18, 162, 189–93
militants 6, 173, 179, 186, 189–91, 199
Mills, J. P. 55, 72
Ministry of Development of North Eastern Region 62
Mitra, Subrata K. 12
Mokokchung 60, 64–5
monkhood 17, 119, 129–31, 133
monks 17, 117, 119–25, 127–33
Monpas 17, 117–18, 124–5, 128
Monyul 117–24
Moynihan, Daniel P. 166
Mt. Tendong 92–3, 95–7
multi-party democracy 135–6, 141
Muslim women 191–3

Naga civil society 64, 70
Naga Hills 55, 57–8, 60, 67, 71–2

Naga identities 71–2
Naga insurgents 13, 175, 178–9
Nagaisation 164
Nagaland 7, 11, 13, 16, 55–65, 67, 69–70, 72–5, 173–5, 180
Nagaland Commoditisation of Institutions 66
Nagaland State Human Development Report 65
Nagaland State Legislative Assembly 60, 66
Nagalim 56, 70, 75
Nagamis 55
Naga People's Convention 56
Naga People's Front (NPF) 59
Nagas 7–10, 12, 15–16, 18–19, 55–7, 58, 59–60, 62–3, 64, 67, 70–1, 161–6, 168, 171–2, 174–5, 177–9; eastern 56, 60, 65–6
Naga society 54–78; competing claims 54–78; emergence of 'forward' and 'backward' 60–2; fear of numbers 54–78; village councils 62–4, 66; village development boards 62–4; village politics 64–7
Naga Student Federation 75
Naga sub-tribes 55–6, 59, 62, 74
Naga tribes 55, 57, 59–62, 65, 70–1
Naga villages 62–3, 66
national conventions 18, 136, 139, 143, 145–7, 150
nationalism 18, 162–3, 165, 169
Nationalist Socialist Council of Nagaland (NSCN) 56, 74, 173–5, 179
Nepali Congress (NC) 135–6, 144, 146–7
Nepali politics 135–7
Nepalis 11, 82–3, 85–6, 97, 107, 136–7, 142, 149, 151
Nepali student organisations 18, 136, 149
Nepal Student Union (NSU) 143, 145–7, 149
1991 Census of Nagaland 61, 74
North East Council 62
North-East Frontier Agency 56
Northeast India 3, 5–6, 8, 10, 12–13, 54, 58, 161–3, 167–70, 178, 180

North Sikkim 83, 86, 88, 99
NSCN *see* Nationalist Socialist Council of Nagaland
NSU *see* Nepal Student Union

O-Hanlon, Rosalind 80
organic intellectuals 17, 79, 81, 89–90, 97, 105

pahari society, local 41, 43–4
Pandey, Gyanendra 79–80
Pangerungba, Richard 74
pan-Naga identities 75
pan-Yimchunger identities 73, 75
Pellizzoni, I. 138
People's Movement 135–6, 144
Phizo, A. Z. 55
Phoms 55, 64, 67
Pichori 56, 60, 64, 67
pilgrimage 102–4, 106
plantation farming 65
politics: attitudes 18, 136; elite 7, 9, 12–13, 17–18, 75, 81, 106, 161; ethnic 11–12, 165, 168; history 81, 85, 99, 142, 170; identities 7, 45, 70, 165; power 19, 122, 132, 166; space 16–17, 80–1; unity 170–1
polyarchy 3
Poole, Deborah 33
process, electoral 17–18, 117, 137, 140, 142
pro-democratic fragmentation 5
Public Interest Litigation 65, 67, 70
Punjabi, R. 193
pure democracy 135, 137, 139, 141, 143, 145, 147, 149, 151

radical polycentrism 5
Raina, Sunita 192
Ramble, Charles 29
Regional Council Members 58
Rengma Nagas 64, 71–2
resettlement 19, 187, 193–5, 197, 199
Rinpoche, T. G. 118, 121–4, 130, 132
Rio, Neiphiu 59, 61
Routeing Democracy in the Himalayas 2, 4

sacred 17, 37, 38, 94, 95, 101, 102, 168
Sangtham 56, 60, 66–7, 72
Sax, William 41–2
scheduled tribes 7–9, 15, 27–8, 43, 70, 80, 82–3, 87, 118, 162, 165
Schneiderhan, E. 138
Scott, J. C. 58
Sema 60, 64, 71
Senapati district 167, 174, 177, 179
shamans 9, 87, 90–1, 95, 97, 101–2
Shamatur village 73
Sikkim 7–8, 11–12, 17, 19–20, 29–30, 39, 81–9, 91–2, 94–5, 97–103, 105–6, 108, 118, 120, 122
Sikkimese Lepchas 86, 88–9, 92, 96, 102, 105
Sikkim government 86, 95–6, 102, 104
Sikkim Lepcha Youth Association 89, 95
Silverstein, P. A. 27
Single Age Population Distribution 69
Smith, A. D. 168
Snellinger, Amanda 18
social identity 44
social work 17, 119–22
Sonam Tshering Lepcha 92–3
Sorensen, B. R. 188
Spencer, J. 137
State Legislative Assembly 54, 56, 59, 62–3, 65
Stavenhagen, Rodolfo 165
Strang, Veronica 167
student organisations 18–19, 136–7, 142–3, 147, 149–51
subaltern groups 79–80, 89, 94, 97, 99
subalternity 79–80, 84, 107–8
subaltern Lepcha citizen 105–8
sub-tribal identities 7, 55, 57, 64, 70
sub-tribes 7, 16, 55–7, 62, 64, 72, 74

Tamenglong district 163, 166, 172, 174, 177, 179–80
Tamsang, Azuk 89
Tamsang, K. P. 89, 92

Tamsang, Lyangsong 89, 95
Tawang monastery 118–19, 129–30
Thakur, R. N. 84
Thankgkul Nagas 71
Tibet 10, 15, 29–30, 32–4, 43, 99, 118
Tibetan Buddhist 10, 17, 117–18, 120, 123–4
Tibetans 10, 30, 33, 42–4, 82, 117, 119
Tikhirs 72–5
Tikhir Tribal Council 75
Tuensang district 56, 57, 62–6, 70, 72–3
Tuensang Government College 64
2011 Census of Nagaland 58–9, 73
2001 Census operation 54, 56–7, 59, 61, 64–7, 69

Ungma village 64–5
upper-caste identities 30, 33
Uttaranchal movement 45
Uttarkashi 15, 19, 27–8, 31–2

Village Council Act 1966 58
Village Council Act 1978 62
Village Council Act 1979 62
Village Council Model Rule 1980 62
village councils 16, 35, 59, 61–4, 66
Village Development Board (VDB) 16, 61–4, 66
village *devta* 41, 44
Vincent, M. 188
violence, gender-based 189–90
Viswanath, K. 193

West Bengal 81, 83, 85–7, 94, 103–7
West Kameng 17, 117–19, 121, 124–5
West Sikkim 87, 97
women 4–6, 8, 19, 31–3, 35–43, 46–8, 60, 102, 129–30, 144, 152, 187–95, 197–8, 200; charge of village affairs 47; desire to become

nuns 48; displaced 191, 193, 200; as scapegoats 189–92; works by 31, 36
Wright, E. O. 140

Yimchunger 56, 60, 62–3, 65, 69–70, 72–5
Yimchunger-Langa 72
Yimchunger Naga 62–3, 72
Yimchunger–Tikhir conflict 72, 75
Yimchunger Tribal Council 72–3
youth 10, 85, 88, 92, 94, 102, 105, 125
Yurchak, Alexei 141

Zeliangrong Nagas 71